Tales from the Pandemic: an anthology

Selected stories from Your Library's 2021–22 writing competition

Tales from the Pandemic: an anthology is published by
Eastern Regional Libraries Corporation
1350 Ferntree Gully Rd
Scoresby Victoria 3179
Australia
www.yourlibrary.com.au

Collection © Eastern Regional Libraries Corporation 2022
Individual contributions © individual authors 2022

ISBN 978-0-6455986-0-5 (print)
ISBN 978-0-6455986-1-2 (ebook)

All rights reserved.

Without limiting the rights under copyright above, no part of this publication shall be reproduced, stored in or introduced into a retrieval system or transmitted in any form or by any means (electronic, mechanical, photocopying, recording or otherwise), without the prior permission of both the copyright owner and publisher of this book.

Copyediting: Daniel Car and Benjamin Cumming
Design and layout: Lorna Hendry
Printing: IngramSpark

 A catalogue record for this book is available from the National Library of Australia

Tales from the Pandemic
an anthology

Selected stories from Your Library's
2021–22 writing competition

 IngramSpark

Contents

Introduction	1
COVID baby Jessica Pritchard	4
The monster Robinson	9
That's my job Olivia Sedgwick	16
'In a minute …' Paul Gallagher	20
A family divided Kathleen Klug	29
We are all adapting Nina Dykstra	40
Curfew Liam Connolly	46
The Zoom funeral Heaven-Leigh Porter	54
Ghosting Kirsty Lock	59

Contents

The daily walk   63
    Trina Bergmann

The numbers   67
    Mandy Mercuri

A cold comfort: tales from the fridge   70
    Kimberley Hanson

Health is more important than hair   78
    Amelia Rowe

An outsider's perspective   85
    Sally Fornaro

Rest, breathe, recover, heal   90
    Karen Hageman

Daddy in lockdown   100
    Michael Hansen

Cancelled   109
    Rachel Briscoe

To breathe or not to breathe   118
    Yvonne Fein

Moth drift   129
    Keren Heenan

Unmasked   136
    Kelly Simpson

The promise   140
    Zarin Nuzhat

Bearing up   150
    Frances Sensi

Anywhere but here   159
    Marisa Black

The deal 　Elaara Wylder	166
Surviving from home 　Alyce Caswell	176
Small things 　L. E. Morgan	185
Animal adaptation 　Kat Beaton	190
The animals will save us 　Catherine Edwards	193
The stranger 　Roanna McClelland	199
Week eighteen 　Marian Matta	203
The lockdown diaries 　Kristy Rhoades	213
The little C 　T. J. Rowntree	216
A tale of twin towns 　Christine E Betts	225
All the lovely eyes 　P. S. Cottier	234
Woman sits at home 　Katelin Farnsworth	236
Isolation 　Laura Jayne	244
COVID baby 　Annie Green	254

Contents

Lorikeets Jessica Kilkenny	257
Virtual competition Prateeti Sabhlok	264
2020–2021 Zoe Clark	274
Crossing the border Bruce Clark	283
Against all odds Olwyn Backhouse	288
The tides of life Sheila Knaggs	297
Finger lime Ashleigh Mounser	302
Sweet tooth Maria B. Joseph	306

Introduction

When three unsuspecting librarians from *Your Library* (Eastern Regional Library Services) visited Ingram Content Group in Melbourne's Dandenong South, an initial meet-and-greet quickly turned into an altogether different affair. We had heard of print-on-demand, but seeing the great whirring print machines in action, with books of different shapes and sizes forming before our eyes, was nothing short of mesmerising. The possibility of producing a book of our own became real and a writing competition in partnership with IngramSpark (Ingram's self-publishing platform) was born.

Now, writing competitions are not uncommon in public libraries, but formally publishing an anthology – a time capsule for posterity – had previously felt out of reach. Deciding on print runs and managing stock was all in the 'too hard' basket – but here we were, during a brief lull in the long Melbourne lockdown, thinking the veil had lifted and feeling full of optimism. We could publish our book, print just what was needed, when needed, *and* even make it available for global sale.

We coined the theme 'Tales from the pandemic' with a presumptive air of retrospection ... little did we know. We were barely halfway through when the lockdown resumed. Nevertheless, our spirits were not dampened, and the competition was launched. The brief was as follows:

> 'It was the best of times, it was the worst of times'
> Charles Dickens, *A Tale of Two Cities*, 1859.

> The past two years have seen most of our assumptions, habits and expectations thrown out the window. Eastern Regional Libraries (Your Library) would like to record the tempo of the time while it is still fresh and preserve it for the future. In collaboration with IngramSpark, Your Library is calling for short pieces of fiction or non-fiction writing up to 3000 words. A selection of entries will be professionally published, printed and distributed in an anthology by IngramSpark.

The entries poured in – sad, funny, wry, furious. There were many more than we expected and the standard was high. A lot of stories were written from a first-person perspective, reinforcing the sense that the pandemic was a time when we were forced back on our own resources and could take time to reflect on our place in the world.

The idea of 'story' was challenged in many cases where it was unclear whether the piece was fiction, non-fiction or autofiction. When it is difficult for the reader to tell the difference, the not-knowing adds an edge to the reading experience.

The winners are:
   First – *COVID baby* by Jessica Pritchard
   Second – *Sweet tooth* by Maria B. Joseph
   Third – *The promise* by Zarin Nuzhat
   Local prize – *2020–2021* by Zoe Clark

These stories were singled out as highly commended:
Isolation by Laura Jayne
The numbers by Mandy Mercuri

We have chosen a selection which we feel represents the many facets of the pandemic experience and showcases the writing talent within the library community and beyond. As librarians we know that keeping connected to books and stories kept many borrowers sane during the endless weeks of lockdowns. The libraries became busy packing-centres sending off hundreds of boxes to people stuck at home. It was nice to see these boxes of library books mentioned in some of the stories.

It is our hope that as the events of 2020 and 2021 fade into the distance, this anthology will become a reference for future readers to experience the craziness, the scariness and the mind-numbing boringness of the COVID-19 pandemic.

Joseph Cullen
CE, Your Library

Sarah Hopkins
Corporate Manager, Your Library

Debbie Lee
Senior Sales Manager, IngramSpark
Ingram Content Group Australia

COVID baby

JESSICA PRITCHARD

'I have a birth plan for you,' Bree said.

I wasn't surprised – Bree was already making jams and preserves in case the supermarkets ran out of food. Toilet paper was hard to find, but damn it, we would have kumquat marmalade on our toast.

'If you can't go to the hospital, then Jack will sterilise the bath. Tom will be your emotional support, and I can deliver the baby.' Bree is a lawyer, but seemed the most qualified of the three.

I was a third of the way pregnant, and the pandemic had just begun.

The home we bought wasn't ready, so we moved in with Tom's brother Jack and his mastermind wife, Bree. We had no idea what was going on, or how apocalyptic it might get. So, I was glad to have a kind-of joke-but-maybe-not emergency birth plan.

This was the first lockdown. The one where everyone was making sourdough, watching Tiger King, and 'in it together'. The four of us were lucky enough to keep our jobs and found our corners in the house to work from. I mostly sat outside and watched the golden leaves fall.

Living with our family felt like being at camp. (With a lot more news running in the background.)

When Easter came, Bree made an evening Easter egg hunt by candlelight through their house. Four grown-ups looking for chocolate in the dark while some kind of circus music played. She also made a Sunday Devonshire tea with her best china. She made things special.

I walked the same path every day with exposed roots and loose stones, talking to the baby and trying not to slip.

* * *

When the first lockdown lifted, Tom and I moved into our cottage by the creek. It felt like we were emerging from a fever dream.

As my maternity leave began, the second lockdown was announced that same day. We had one last meal out and the waitress had tears in her eyes – she had been so happy to be back.

In the absence of work, and a late-arrival baby, I found an abundance of alone time. I read novels, wrote poems and walked the same daily trail, gradually expanding.

Once, at the forty-week mark, I bumped into a stranger who asked me how I was – with a sincerity that caught me off-guard. I burst into tears. When was the last time I had spoken to a stranger? I never knew how much I would miss it.

I had recurring dreams of bustling markets.

* * *

In the end, we didn't need Bree's emergency birth plan. I was able to go to the hospital, but we were in the heart of our strictest restrictions to date.

Behind their masks, the midwives were telling me I was doing great; there was something wrong; they needed the doctor to come look.

I could only see Tom's eyes widen over his mask as he was asked to push the emergency button and my bed was flung backwards.

Our baby Ella was born, and behind the mask, the doctor was telling me I should get a C-section next time.

Tom and I ate Vegemite toast on white bread and it was somehow the best meal I had ever tasted. I got to see his smile.

After we visited our baby in special care, Tom had to leave. I was wheeled into my room without my baby or my husband, and asked to wear a mask when the nurses came in. I had not seen so many people in months, and I had never felt more alone.

Tom wasn't allowed back until 5 pm the next day. The hours stretched as I held my new baby, and wondered what world she was coming into. I tried to find the smiles in the nurses' eyes.

When 5 pm came, Tom was only allowed to stay for two hours, and it felt like twenty minutes. We were sent home the next night, even though the nurses said they would usually keep us in longer.

'COVID,' they explained. No further words needed.

* * *

Ella was one week old, with a full head of dark hair and grey-blue eyes. The winter storms had caused another power outage in our house.

We were huddled by the fireplace and changed her by candlelight. We still had no idea what we were doing, but thought it was important to keep the baby warm. When we got word that the water was contaminated, we had to laugh (and curse our electric stove). As we went out to get bottled water, we realised we couldn't – the 8 pm curfew.

Later, we realised our firewood was treated pine, which gave Tom high levels of arsenic in his blood from tending to it night after night.

Still, from that time, my journals are filled with tiny moments of wonder. The first burst of wattle, the books the library had sent me and the newborn baby cuddles. I was stubborn in my pursuit of joy.

When Ella first got to see the world out of lockdown, I took her to a market. I watched her take in all the different people, and listen to live music. I watched her little feet move. I wanted to hug everyone there, but I settled on jovial 'hellos'. I cried when I bought a secondhand book.

* * *

Ella was about ten months old and we were back in lockdown. After several short stints throughout the year, this one was longer. It took me by surprise.

I was bored, but in a way that felt nostalgic. I couldn't remember the last time I was bored like this. We threw tennis balls at the wall. We followed crows around in circles. We hunted down any green patch of land in our five-kilometre radius.

I left a fairy statue in an old tree stump behind our house, and every so often the fairy was moved by a stranger, or wild flowers were placed next to her. This invisible interaction made me believe in some kind of community that I could return to one day.

We had rituals. Every night, Ella and I walked across the road to inhale the jasmine flowers. We said hello to the birch tree on our daily walk and skipped over the little wooden bridge. I told her about waterfalls, cities, the ocean, and promised that I would take her to all those places one day.

* * *

When the last lockdown lifted, I took Ella to the city. We trailed our fingers through the water wall at the NGV, walked through the twisting alleyways, and watched Gog and Magog chime their bells. Ella gazed in wonder at the giant Christmas trees and shiny baubles, and the children jumping up and down the steps.

I talked to strangers with an unexpected ease, and I could see we were all hungry for it. Those small comments about the weather, about our children, about the holidays. I had never been a fan of small talk, but now I delighted in every bit of it. You could have talked to me about finding a car park, and I would have been enraptured.

I knew it wasn't as simple as being 'back to normal'. The last two years had only emphasised that the future is always uncertain. The joy came from the deep appreciation of things that can be taken away in an instant.

I don't know how long this magic spell of appreciation will last. I've learnt that we humans are quite an adaptable bunch. We can adapt to hard times, and we can adapt to the good too. I hope to stay in the wonder. So, I have decided to relish in each shared meal and every smile from a stranger. I hug my friends a little longer, I dance a little when I op shop, and in the summer, I showed my daughter how to splash in the sea.

JESS PRITCHARD is an art therapist and writer, and lives in the Dandenong ranges with her husband and tiny child. This is her story of having a baby during the pandemic, and the bright things she found along the way.

The monster

ROBINSON

The pandemic was a monster.
Its sandpaper scales gleamed a blue so dark they appeared black. Its talons were as sharp as knives, its eyes like a moonless night. Its jaws hung ajar in a menacing snarl, teeth bared and dripping poison. Frost flowed from its cold heart, with icicles clinging to its wings and wintry breath freezing all it touched.

The Monster lived in the shadows. It lived in the news stories of death and destruction, of tear-stained families huddled around hospital beds, if they were lucky enough to say goodbye. It lived in the numbers plastered over all our screens, the exponential growth of cases and panic. It lived in the broken lives and missing memories. The Monster lived in the darkness.

Initially at school, the virus was a joke. '1.5 metres, guys! Stay away from me,' people laughed, taking a comically large step away from their friends only to bounce back beside them a moment later. They rolled their eyes as they smothered their hands with sanitizer and organised bustling meetups with crowds of others. Two cases in Australia? Of course there was nothing to worry about. That's what we all thought, anyway. Perhaps the Monster didn't like being mocked.

Only a week later the dread set in. The Monster's claws slashed into my skin and latched on, breathing icy terror down my spine and setting my nerves on edge. Its poison made my heart race and my hands shake. The media was overwhelmed with horror and fright, and swamped with conflicting information and opposing advice. The words 'quarantine', 'lockdown' and 'self-isolation' were thrown around like a meaningless game of catch. Fear was frequent and stress was strong, but I pushed it down and set a smile on my face. Good thing that's fiction material, I thought. No one could live through that. Not in reality.

Too early and too real, the announcement boomed through the school loudspeakers. Lockdown. My jaw slackened and my breath caught at the back of my throat. Various shouts conveyed the range of emotions from my peers. The TV hummed steadily at the front of the classroom and the breeze continued rustling exercise books open on desks, constants in a world that had completely fallen apart.

At first the Monster was weak and few, but like the virus, it spread like wildfire. Obsidian talons tripled in size and muscles rippled beneath its hide. Powerful wings stretched from its body, carrying it from person to person like a flash of lightning. What was once an occasional visitor was now an intruder refusing to leave.

The Monster flew in repeated, uniform circles around me, and the pandemic routine soon formed, each day unfolding like clockwork. Wake up at 7:30, eat breakfast and open my laptop at 8:47 to start online learning at 8:50. A 20 minute Microsoft Teams call and half-an-hour of work, then a short break before the next subject. Rinse and repeat, rinse and repeat, day after day after day. Weeks whizzed by, unbearably slow but impossibly fast. I wrote the date in the corner of my notebook; Tuesday, or maybe Thursday. I didn't know anymore.

Soon, all hope was crushed. 2020 turned into 2021. New Year's midnight arrived to a dark sky, the vibrant fireworks cancelled and the weakly twinkling stars faint with distance. We were pelted with wave after wave, sending us into endless lockdowns. I fought to swim in a world that seemed determined to drown me.

I scrolled through the ABC News live blog, caught up on the daily press conference. I checked the day's numbers – always rapidly rising. Thousands of pixels mingled on my screen, but all I saw was the Monster staring cruelly back at me.

The Monster's ice swept the world, freezing our lives. Thorned weeds thrived in the cracks of once-busy footpaths, and dull shutters covered the dusty windows of abandoned businesses. With the ring of steel surrounding Melbourne, I could no longer see Dad, missing his fiftieth birthday. Restrictions increased and I couldn't see my grandparents, then my friends. My peers were circles on my laptop, cameras and microphones turned firmly off. My family was great, but I longed for outside contact. We began to truly understand the idea of isolation.

The Coles' automatic doors grumbled as they slid open, but I paused in the spitting rain until my phone registered the QR code, Mum beside me for my only outings. The shelves were stripped bare, peeling off-white paint visible where they used to be consistently covered. The shopping list was crumbled and shoved back into a handbag. We grabbed what we could. People zoomed through the aisles, eager to return to the safety of their own homes. Masks covered their faces, concealing their expressions – although I doubt there was a smile in the whole building. The Monster circled every one of them.

The Monster pressed an impossible weight on my back, becoming a burden too heavy to handle. Its ice numbed my emotions, a cold so deep that nothing could penetrate it. I shook uncontrollably. My head pounded in an incessant throb. Perhaps it was the excessive screen time, or the sleep deprivation, or the water I forgot to drink, or the never-ending stress. My muscles ached and my energy was low. Dark purple shaded my eyes – I was always exhausted, spending my nights staring unwillingly into the darkness. My concentration slipped and my motivation waned.

Things that used to be easy became impossible, even the enjoyable ones. My phone beeped cheerfully, a notification I was too tired to reply to. Ink blurred on the pages of an exciting book. I dragged myself out of bed to attend my favourite subjects, and took a little longer to write things than I used to. People gradually began disappearing from online classes, and the teachers cut down content to make it more achievable for those of us who still showed up. I wasn't the only victim the Monster caught, it seemed.

The Monster began to stretch its wings above me, a darkened storm cloud spanning incredibly far, blocking the light and drenching me with rain. Deafening booms of thunder and flashing strikes of lightning shook me with fear. Its icicles speared me, a frostbite inside poisoning me from within. Runaway trains of thought spiralled in my mind. An anguish no one could see, an agony I couldn't describe. All I wanted was for it to end.

But from the pandemic, another creature emerged.

The Creature's golden scales shined and shimmered, light glittering off their back. Ginormous eyes glimmered, both compassionately observant and openly honest. Their muscled tail swished from side to side with confidence and strength, and expansive wings arched from their back. Gentle warmth radiated from their scales, like a kiss of sunshine reaching through the clouds.

The Creature lived in the light. They lived in neighbours that smiled with their eyes as they walked past, and the children laughing loudly as they played merrily in their backyards. They lived the ninety-two-year-old who walked out of ICU with a smile on her face. They lived in the essential workers, the selfless doctors and the nurses that gave everything they had. The Creature lived in the everyday heroes.

The hearts of gold.

My family encompassed me with their ever-lasting love, their golden hearts warm and compassionate. Mum would make food for me when I struggled to do it myself, and play a card game with me to cheer me up. My step-mum made sure I always had clean clothes to wear, and watched a movie with me as I rested on the couch. My sister would help me with my schoolwork when I was confused, and we'd walk around the neighbourhood together when I lacked the motivation to exercise alone. They were listening ears when I wanted to talk, light-hearted chatter when I needed company and caring souls when I felt alone.

The Creature landed softly on my shoulder and healed the lacerations. They melted the ice surrounding me, embracing me with comforting warmth that eased my pain. The icicles trickled away and the dark cloud dispersed. Dread was replaced with content. As fast as the Monster, the Creature spread swiftly. They entered people's lives like a ray of sunlight, shining through open windows as Winter turned to Spring. The Monster was here to stay, but so was the Creature.

I began walking again, and suddenly the world was vivid with life. Birds soared across a sapphire sky and clung to spindly branches, ruffling their feathers and singing sweetly. Emerald leaves swirled in the treetops, and gravel crunched beneath my feet. I breathed in deeply, and the air was rich with the scent of earth and gum trees. A creek gurgled as I dipped my hand in the cool water and let the current rush through my fingers. The tension in my muscles slowly melted away, taken by the gentle breeze.

I picked up the hobbies that I had lost. Soft thread glided through my fingers and a thin needle slid through punctured fabric. The activity wove peace and calmness in my day, and the stress ebbed away. The joy of creation was intwined through my embroidery, rows of crosses forming a spectacular creation. A Japanese garden made up of a lake, a bridge, paths, bushes, flowers and cherry blossoms – so many parts making a whole.

The Creature's sparkling golden eyes appeared in the people around me. A friend would send me a picture of her dog, with fur like fluffy white fairy floss. I smiled as I sent back a photo of my own snoozing cat, a memory shared even when we were apart. My recent contacts list grew, the conversations insignificant but nonetheless meaningful. I downloaded WhatsApp and a group chat was made, with vibrantly coloured nametags accompanying pinging messages. Communication fostered connectedness and belonging. I heard their voices beyond the uniformed letters, and felt their presence through the loneliness.

My motivation returned and my concentration followed. I broke the awkward silence in class and unmuted myself to answer a question. Keyboard keys clicked and clattered as words flowed from my fingertips. A pencil tip brushed softly against paper as equations churned in my mind. I felt I was behind, so I tried harder to catch up.

My teachers helped me through, their faces smiling through the screen no matter what obstacles were thrown at them. My Japanese teacher, who practiced speaking with me through voice calls and corrected unfamiliar grammar. My Maths teacher, who taught me the skills I needed and encouraged me to problem solve complex questions. My English and homegroup teacher, who extended my essay writing and helped me adjust to the chaos of returning to the classroom. The Creature gazed from their hearts of gold. They were always enthusiastic to teach, and ready to put in the time and effort to help me achieve what I have now. They went the extra mile, and even when I doubted myself, they believed in me.

Finally, there came a time when it was my turn to roll up my sleeve. The slight ache of the jab was nothing compared to feeling part of the national solution. Cases declined and vaccinations rose. Freedom was on the horizon as hope began to flourish. People tentatively emerged from their houses like snails coming out of their shells. Eyes broke into smiles as loved ones were reunited.

The Creature smiled quietly, their shining scales reflecting golden light across the nation. A comforting heat streamed from their heart, a joyous warmth that filled me.

Now that the Monster has retracted its claws, I emerge from the pandemic a completely different person than when I entered. I hated the Monster's presence, but in a strange way, I'm grateful for it. It broke me, but without it, would I have seen the hearts of gold? Sometimes it takes hardship to see the blessings in life.

You can't have warmth without the cold.

You can't have light without the darkness.

You can't have the Creature without the Monster.

ROBINSON has a passion for writing and reading, and enjoys stories that are meaningful and emotive. She likes to spend time with her family and friends. She additionally has anxiety, hypersensitivity, and is on the autism spectrum. She loved to share this story with you and explore her own challenges with the COVID pandemic due to her neurodiversity.

That's my job

OLIVIA SEDGWICK

At 5:30 am, my phone pings with a message; 'You're working in COVID today'. That's the COVID ICU ward, where we care for critically ill COVID patients.
My heart starts to race. Not again.

I close my eyes and press my forehead. I was in there only yesterday. My face is still sore from my mask; the purple welt across the bridge of my nose is still throbbing. I don't want to spend another twelve hours in all that PPE.

I arrive at work and get changed into scrubs. I change my shoes just in case I bring sickness home to my two babies. I've decided to leave a pair at work to lower the risk for my family. Hand hygiene. Gown on. Hand hygiene. Mask on. I wince. Fuck, it's so tight. That bruise on my nose is killing me. Hair net on. Face shield on. Hand hygiene. Gloves on.

I breathe and the shield mists over; there's a leak in my mask. I can't see properly.

I already feel claustrophobic and it's only been a few minutes. How do I survive twelve hours in this again? It's okay, you can do this, I whisper to myself.

Okay, time for work. My God, it's hot in here. It's not long before I'm soaked with sweat under layers of PPE. At next break, I'll have to change my scrubs.

We need to intubate a patient. Damn. I guess the scrubs will have to wait.

We work on the patient for almost an hour. I'm so hot, so trapped in all my layers of plastic, that I think I'm going to pass out.

The doctor is trying to put in an arterial line. He's looking through a face shield that is so foggy that beads of condensation are dripping from the shield. He can barely see as he inserts a cannula into a main artery. Got it. Thank God. We rush off to change our sweat-soaked scrubs.

In one twelve-hour shift I could change in to and out of PPE ten times. Don on, work. Doff off, break. Don on, work. Ugh, I need to pee. Doff off. Don on, work. Doff off, break. Don on, work. Doff off, break. Don on, work. Doff off – shower and home time. I've got to be quick, there's only one shower. I need to shower before I get in the car. Then I'll shower once more at home before I kiss my babies. It's my family I worry about the most.

At home, I stare at my face in the bathroom mirror. There are red marks everywhere. My face is burning. Angry acne blooms across my chin, memories of being a teen. I touch the deep welt on my nose and tears prick my eyes.

I'm done, I can't do this again tomorrow. But I will. We're already short staffed. I can't call in sick, I'd be letting the team down.

The next morning, at 5:45 am, I wake up to my alarm instead of a text. That must mean no COVID ICU today. Sweet relief.

At 6:01 am, as I'm sipping my coffee in the kitchen, my phone lights up. 'Sorry for the late text, you're working in COVID today.'

My heart races. Here we go again.

I once held a woman's hand as she died because her family were too frightened to see her that way. I couldn't let her die alone. I promised them I'd sit by her side as long as it took. I wept as I watched her taking her last breath. Not because death was new to me, but because the thought of her dying alone was unbearable.

Alone.
    Let that word sink in.
    Alone, is what every one of our patients is facing now.
    In pain. Alone.
    A new cancer diagnosis. Alone.
    A major surgery. Alone.
    The news that there is nothing more the doctors can do for you.
Alone.

We FaceTime our patient's families these days. I apologise over the phone to yet another family member who cries because they can't see their loved one.
    I feel their frustration.
    I cry too.
    I get angry too.
    'I'm so sorry', I say.

Luckily, even in these times, there are some circumstances in which we can allow visitors. These circumstances include when someone is unlikely to recover and when someone is imminently dying. How lucky.
    You can come and visit your family member now, who you haven't seen in three weeks, because they are dying.
    Those three weeks that you didn't have with them because of a pandemic? You can't get it back.

Tomorrow you might have to say goodbye.

Again, I'm so sorry.

I love my job as an ICU nurse. Like, really, really love it. Nursing is what I was born to do. It's what I've always done.

It's a tough job, of course. You see people die, you see people at their most sick, their most scared. Despite that, or maybe because of that, I love it. It's a privilege.

But I liked it a lot more when we weren't in a pandemic.

These days I've been fit tested for a perfect mask (or three) and now my nose doesn't bruise or bleed. It's tight, it's uncomfortable and my skin hates it, but I'm safe. I've been vaccinated. I've got all that sweaty PPE to protect me. I'm thankful for these things.

And despite being bone tired, I'm ready for anything that this pandemic can throw at me, at us.

That's my job.

OLIVIA SEDGWICK is an intensive care nurse with over fifteen years' experience. Nursing is more than just a career for her, it's a passion. She is dedicated to her career, and passionate about making a difference to the wider community. She has recently moved into an education role within the ICU and thrives on being a role model to the staff, from the most experienced to new graduates. She is the mother of two boys, and hopes that one day they can appreciate hard work and kindness, and find a career in which they can practice both.

'In a minute ...'

PAUL GALLAGHER

Sunday 1 pm
Judah ran out the front door, sobbing.

Almost as quickly as he raced down the front steps, Karen flew after our three-year-old grandson, hoping she could catch him before he reached the end of the driveway and burst into traffic.

I could hear him as I stood watching, keeping my balance with a wooden walking stick as my wife gained on him.

All the time, we could hear him crying, calling out three words as he ran, repeating them to anyone, everyone: 'In a minute,' he said. 'In a minute—'

'It's okay darling,' Karen said as she intercepted Judah with a half-hug, half-embrace, bringing her face against his teary cheeks for reassurance. 'Your Oma is here. I'm not leaving you.'

Three words that broke our hearts
The dramatic escape said everything about the lockdown we had just endured in Melbourne.

It had been months since we had seen Judah in person, and this day, Sunday, was the first official childminding allowed. Rules were easing and we had counted down the days and hours to spending time with our grandson.

'In a minute ...'

The words, 'In a minute', had come up earlier, in the form of a cute request to keep watching a YouTube video of me reading him a story. I had made several of the short videos over the last year, hoping the granda/grandson connection would be sustained without loss.

I think we had laughed earlier in the morning when he had said those same three words, noticing they were one of the new phrases and behaviours that Judah had gained during lockdown. That was hard; seeing how much he had grown on his own, without us witnessing every milestone.

Judah lives just 800 metres away, with our daughter, Beth, and her husband, Luke. They were working that morning, hosting a video for the suburban church they run, the same congregation we are a part of. The rules from Chief Health Officer (CHO) Brett Sutton had said childminding was okay, as long as it was for reasons of work.

What Brett couldn't say (we feel that we are on first name basis with the CHO now), what Brett didn't know, was the effect on young children left without social interaction as long as Judah had been. There had been an effort to find out the effects. One study published in *The Lancet Psychiatry* had found a definite impact on young people, but that was from the UK in April. What would they know? Melbourne was beyond the wire, a place few cities had gone. Mandated masks, five-kilometre limits, armed forces nearby at a checkpoint to the regional centres, permits for work.

What we had in front of us was our little grandson, our sign that we'd achieved something in life, crying in our arms, mouthing three words that broke our hearts.

He wanted just one more minute, more time, with us.

Judah was every child in Melbourne that day.

We got it
It's not like we were anti-Dan people. Quite the contrary. We'd been supporters for months, the type who say in their living room comments that will never be heard nor published: 'Keep going Dan. Let's get this done. Don't give in to the minority with the loud voices.'

Nobody heard us, but that didn't matter.

What our Victorian government was doing was trying to stem the loss of elderly lives, a community already devastated by COVID running through local facilities. In truth, the government was saving my life, giving me the best chance of avoiding the coronavirus that would have tested my already weak body.

Thankfully, the government kept its nerve and we did eventually get to a low point in the spread of the virus. For now, at least.

Even when Judah came over that Sunday, we had kept our masks on, conscious he could be carrying the virus without us knowing. It was wisdom, on our part, and as a public health measure. (We'd love to thank Brett for that. Maybe one day when he can come over, seeing that we're on first-name basis.)

Still crying as Karen walked him back, we reassured him through our masks that he could stay a little longer.

'Can you come and get him?' I secretly told his dad on my phone. 'He's had a moment and doesn't want to leave us.'

Grandkids, grandparents share difficult days
The lockdown in Melbourne had been tough for otherwise healthy grandparents too, although I doubt there's a PhD thesis being edited on that front. Pure anecdote from the realm of my home is proof enough.

We missed Judah terribly, and probably would have mouthed the three words – 'In a minute' – ourselves, if Judah hadn't beaten us to them.

Regular video calls were the best way to stay in touch, along with the occasional glimpse of his room when Karen called by to pick up some lemons. It was only ever fleeting; not enough for our liking, or his. Those visits were usually rushed, legal ones as Karen hurried to work, managing a cafe closer to the city.

'I could hear him, Paul,' Karen would tell me when she got home after work. 'He was down the hallway when I picked up the bag from the front porch. Talking with his Mum I think.'

Our plight was nothing, though, compared to the grief and loss being experienced by too many families forced to farewell elderly loved ones in mostly Victorian facilities. *The Lancet* described Victoria's 682 deaths in aged care homes from COVID-19 as contributing to one of the highest global rates of deaths in the sector, compared with overall fatalities.

April 2016: The start of a personal lockdown
What made our isolation worse – and may have contributed to Judah's pain at the thought of leaving us again – was the need for me to isolate more than the average fifty-something Melbourne male.

I am one of the 'vulnerable' people; someone with the autoimmune disease multiple sclerosis, or 'MS'. The condition can be quite benign for some, though had deteriorated in me since diagnosis at the start of 2016.

A decade or so earlier, I would have been the one running after Judah. Those were the days before doctors found the telltale scarring of MS through an MRI scan. A chronic illness with no cure, MS had already put my career on pause, and my life into a personal lockdown in the years and months before Judah's race down the driveway.

The disease had, since diagnosis in 2016, limited my walking to slow motion bursts of twenty metres at a time. A wheelchair had become my most common mode of personal transport in public. And at home, I had started moving ever slower in 2020, held by two walking sticks as sunset neared, adding pain, fatigue and spasms to my limbs.

MS was one of the diseases that COVID had in its sights. Not content with plaguing the elderly, the pandemic took a shine to people like me, whose chronic illnesses or preconditions made our bodies less able to fight such a novel coronavirus.

January 2020: 'This looks serious'

I had been particularly careful as the year unfolded. We'd gone to a wedding in Sydney to see a niece wed her partner. I had hired a wheelchair in January to help me last the reception, but I'd gone pretty well and used the chair more for bags and coats for family members.

Behind the scenes, in toilet breaks (they are always many, and lengthy) and whenever I was staring at my phone, I watched for news from Wuhan in China. A journalist by training, and a writer (at least until MS slowed the word count), I was well aware of the looming threat that was giving jitters to health authorities.

'This looks serious,' I said to Karen as we were packing our bags to fly from Melbourne to Sydney. Or more specifically, as Karen packed our bags and I rested on the bed from another bout of fatigue.

'It's pretty bad in Wuhan right now, but I think it's inevitable that it will get out and travel on planes to everywhere.'

By the time we were back home from the wedding, the anxiety at the government level and in my head was rising to hourly attention.

What added to my concern was the presence of an expensive, time-releasing drug inside me, routinely given to many MS sufferers in Australia. Ocrelizumab, or Ocrevus, targets the body's immune system by further degrading it. A bit like chemotherapy, the infused drug sits in the body for six months at a time, slowly and regularly releasing its 'valium' to the immune system.

Even worse, I was due to have my next round of the treatment at Maroondah Hospital after we got back from the wedding. Specifically, late February! Of course, I got sick with a flu-like infection just before treatment. At the time, the protocols in place were to continue with treatment as long as I hadn't been overseas to any places affected by COVID-19. I hadn't, so they continued.

Within 24 hours after treatment, I was having trouble breathing and looked a lot like a COVID patient if the news reports were anything to go by.

'What seems to be the problem?' the paramedic asked as she came inside and stood at my door one morning.

We talked about the toll the infection was taking on my body, but the chances were still very low of an actual COVID infection. Box Hill Hospital Emergency confirmed that when we got there in the following hours. What they did find was a collapsed lung.

'I could barely breathe'
Every breath was painful, even lifting my arms was an effort. The lung had partly fallen in on itself, collapsing my world more than my chest.

'You need to stay home, away from as many people as possible,' the doctor had said.

If life wasn't hard enough, it became more introverted overnight. If COVID hit me, I may not have the capacity to fight it, much like an elderly resident of one of Melbourne's many vulnerable aged care facilities.

What I really wanted was another minute with my family, another hour playing with Judah, another day catching a train to the city to visit a library.

I needed just one minute more, the very gift I could not have.

March to September 2020: Lonely in isolation
Between COVID, MS, the immune suppressant medication, and

my lungs, 2020 was forcing me either back to bed or so close that I felt like COVID might even be an improvement.

Most of all, I was lonely.

Karen went to work each day, returning later in the afternoon when my daily fatigue decline was nearing its lowest ebb.

Sometimes, I would find a book to read Judah via video and send it through the family chat. I called them *Story time with Granda*, and his parents told me he couldn't get enough of them.

Karen felt it too; the pain of zero or minimal physical contact with other family members. 'Will he remember us?' she would ask, half serious. 'Or will he just have grown up and not see us as special anymore?' I would always reassure Karen that she had nothing to worry about, and then privately worry myself.

I didn't know what this year would do to Judah or to ourselves as we hoped, prayed, chewed our fingernails each day, fearing the lower active cases and deaths would be a mirage.

We had crazy thoughts too – that the restrictions of this year would harm our relationship with Judah for years to come, that it would harm all the kids in Melbourne in some way.

We knew the Premier was right. The state needed to be locked down to stem a horrid disease especially targeting people like me. But the cost was going to invoice every one of us before the year ended.

Sunday 8:30 am: Before 'in a minute' run

On the day Judah came over for his first return visit, he couldn't get enough of us. It was like he had stored up in his mind everything he wanted to do again.

There was the walk to the park, where he wanted me to count with him as he swung on the little kids swing. Plus, the ride back on my knee, holding onto the handle of my scooter as we made the five-minute slow motoring back to our adjacent garage.

He also had specific videos in mind to watch, mostly of me

reading *Story time with Granda*. I then had to read the same book again in person and try to remember the different annotations I had included in each embellished video version of the stories.

Now that I look back on it, he was worried that this might be his only chance to connect, that maybe Mum and Dad wouldn't allow him to see us ever again. He had to pack in everything! Every video. Every book. Every game of hide and seek. Every comforting behaviour we shared from his memories that made us who we are and our relationship what it is.

Every minute he was spending with us could be the last, he thought.

So, when it came time to bring up the topic of going home again, it had all come too soon. This was it; no more visits. Lockdown again. Loneliness. Grief. Loss.

Not now, he thought.

Not again.

Just one more minute.

Wednesday 10 am: Three new words, healing ones
There were, however, three other words Judah said that week, after the shock of 'In a minute'.

It happened a few days later. Judah was back again, over for some more childminding with me and a daughter who lives with us.

Karen was at work, busy making coffees in a Melbourne cafe while juggling QR code spreadsheets as part of the hospitality sector's return to trade.

I was pretty tired at the time. The usual. Settling down in front of the television, I was staring at myself reading Judah a story – another of the videos Judah loved of me reading a story.

He looked at me for a moment and then tried to get my attention: 'Hey, Granda?'

'Yes, Little Man,' I quickly replied, hoping he would say we could stop watching me for the tenth time on the screen nearby.

'What is it?'

'I love you.'

Three words. On his own. No prompting.

Not a reply. Not even a mimicked response to something in a book or on the TV screen.

There was a smile as he said it, but a knowing, an understanding of the true meaning of the words that made them so profound.

In three words, he had made me again.

I leaned over to the table in front and picked up the book that was currently being read by the video version of me on the TV. 'How about you come over here and we read this together?'

'Oh yes, Granda!'

Another three words. Healing.

PAUL GALLAGHER is a Melbourne writer, published biographer (*Faith and duty: the John Anderson story*, Random House, 2006), journalist, editor and poet. Besides dealing with the effects of multiple sclerosis, Paul is a husband, father and devoted 'Granda'. His website can be found at www.Paul-Gallagher.com.

A family divided

KATHLEEN KLUG

January 2020
A fleeting kiss on the cheek, soft lips on withered skin. When Ada kissed her *Ya-Ya* goodbye, she didn't realise it would be for the last time. The car engine idled as Ada grabbed her suitcase and headed for the departure terminal. A new year, brimming with opportunity. When her boss had mentioned the company was expanding their Queensland office, Ada had been the first to apply. A promotion and a fresh start in the sunshine, a chance to break-away from her overbearing family. She was thrilled to be offered the job. She could feel it in her bones, 2020 was going to be her year!

March 2020
Ada had never lived alone. Home was a too-crowded semi-detached in Melbourne's Northern suburbs. Three generations under one roof. The one-bedroom furnished apartment her company had organised felt like luxury. She walked from the bathroom to the kitchenette in her underwear and made herself an instant coffee with three sugars, no judgment here. She was looking forward to dinner that evening at a fancy river-side restaurant, celebrating one month in Brisbane, a chance to get to know the team outside of their office.

Ada had spent the afternoon getting ready. She curled her hair as she thought of facts about herself to share. There were sure to be silly games and get-to-know-you questions. But on arrival the mood was flat, the restaurant quiet. People sat uncomfortably and spoke in hushed whispers.

'Have you seen the footage from Wuhan? Bodies piled on the street like the plague.'

'I heard America has banned Chinese people from entering the country.'

'Did you see two international students were assaulted in the city last night, they weren't even Chinese, they were Indonesian!'

'This thing is spreading like mad, we're next.'

'They are telling Australians to come home, that the borders will shut soon.'

'The world has gone crazy!'

'I'm not even sure we should have come out tonight, they are recommending we stay home as much as possible.'

These people have gone crazy, Ada thought to herself. Her cousin in Italy had said it's spreading, but no worse than a cold, this thing will blow over in a month or so.

July 2020

Working from home has its perks. Ada has saved more money in four months than she had in the previous two years. No more coffees on the way to work, or café lunches. No more expensive Pilates classes and personal trainers; she had discovered YouTube workouts and has never been fitter. But Ada misses getting dressed up for work, she misses people watching at the gym. She craves social interaction.

Ada finds herself idling at the supermarket, making small talk with the check-out girl, no more than seventeen years old. They talk about toilet paper and flour shortages, people making sourdough. The check-out girl was spat on by a customer the day before because she told him he couldn't buy more than two packets of pasta. Ada exits the supermarket, then goes back in and buys a bunch of flowers and a packet of Tim-Tams for the girl.

'I'm sorry for what happened,' she says, handing over the gifts.

The girl flashes Ada a surprised, but joyful smile 'I'm just doing my job.'

'Well thank you for doing your job.' This small interaction was the highlight of Ada's week, perhaps even the happiest she had felt all month.

When she gets home, Ada FaceTimes her family. They crowd around an iPad to speak with her. She notices her mother's usual stylish hair is growing out, an inch of grey regrowth. Her brother Dom looks jittery, they have cancelled his soccer training. He lives for his local club, trains three days a week. Now his pent-up energy is visible, he moves restlessly from foot to foot. Her little sister is there too; Lucy is homeschooling for now, her final year of high school disrupted.

Ada's dad is angry at the Chinese. 'They did this on purpose, made the virus in a lab. It's population control, trying to kill the old ones, they have too many in China because of their one-child policy.'

Her siblings make side eyes at each other, and *Ya-Ya* sits to the side, silent, eyes clouded over in a daydream, weary with life.

November 2020
Things return to a new normal in Brisbane, the virus under control, locked out of the state with orange barricades and grounded airlines. Business is good, people are buying new homes, investing in renovations. Holidays cancelled, weddings postponed, external lives become internal, rent goes through the roof.

Ada moves out of her serviced apartment and into a sharehouse in the suburbs, her loneliness appeased. She hasn't really made friends in her new state, she doesn't know how to anymore. Socialising doesn't feel the same anymore, people are wary, they limit catch-ups to an intimate few. Numbers are restricted in venues and clubs, no dancing! The dinner party is revived, while restaurants and cafes close their doors for good. The city is quiet, offices abandoned for Zoom and Teams. Empty buses drive silently along city streets. Will life always be like this?

The situation overseas is dire, whole countries in lockdown. People shake their heads at Trump, at the situation in Brazil, China is lying! Facemasks are mandatory, will Christmas be cancelled? Still with the toilet paper shortages!

Ada wants to go home, but Victoria is suffering. Stage four restrictions, curfews and permit zones. Ada FaceTimes her family; they are in surprisingly good spirits, a shimmer of hope. The days are getting warmer, the numbers are dropping. Melbourne is winning the war. They are banding together, fighting a common enemy with puzzles, online scrabble, home-grown tomatoes and baked goods. They say goodbye with promises of weekly Skype chats that never happen. Ada is homesick. With optimism, she books a flight for 20 December, Christmas at home, what a crazy year!

December 2020

20 December comes and goes, flights cancelled, plans delayed. 22 December, Ada's sister is a close contact, her friend's whole family is sick, the grandpa is in intensive care. Plans on a tightrope, two weeks in quarantine.

'What difference does it make?' her mother asks, no different from everyday life for us.

Ada cancels her flight. Christmas is spent at home with her flatmate Bhakti, homemade dahl and roti followed by vodka shots and a headache. She FaceTimes her family. Their earlier cheerfulness has subsided. She notices her mother hasn't put up the Christmas tree, a family tradition. The same gaudy white pine that *Ya-Ya* kept under the house for thirty years.

'Where is the Christmas tree?' Ada asks.

'At the tip,' her mother replies. 'We had to clear room for your sister to study. These cramped quarters are getting to everyone.'

'What about my bedroom?' Ada asks 'Can't you turn that into an office?'

'Your father is sleeping in there at the moment.'

Ada wonders what is going on, but the look in her mother's eye tells her not to question further. When she gets off the phone, she sends her sister a text message.

'What's going on with mum and dad? And why am I the last to know?'

Her sister's reply is almost instantaneous, 'Because you're not here, you don't know what it's like.'

'So, what's it like, tell me?'

'Dad is angry, business is struggling. Stage four, they won't even let builders on site anymore. He's starting to rant about lockdowns, and border closures. Last week he refused to wear a mask in the shops, he even coughed at me when I told him he should put one on.' More texts quickly follow.

'Dad has been drinking too much. His first beer is getting earlier, and earlier.'

'Mum sometimes doesn't get out of bed at all, she has stopped cooking and cleaning. She survives on coffee and toast, watching crap TV in bed all day.'

'Dom keeps hooking up with random girls on Tinder and doesn't come home for days. He can have a one night stand but I can't go to school, or to the movies with a friend.'

'*Ya-Ya* has lost her spark, she is so quiet now.'

'I'm fucking sick of it, I'm waiting to find out if I got in to uni, but wondering what the point is. Even if I get in, I probably can't go to actual uni … online learning sucks!'

'I've been planning my eighteenth birthday for years, but there will be no parties, I can't even go to a nightclub, it's a shitty time to be eighteen!'

Ada feels helpless, there is so much her family has been keeping from her. She puts together a care package, soaps, candles, and a silly board game, knowing it won't make a difference.

January 2021
2021 starts with Delta on everybody's lips. Face masks, once an amusing flu-season accessory, are now the norm. Ada has been living in Queensland for a whole year, with not one trip home. She thinks she is lucky, to have got out, to be living in Queensland where life is relatively normal. But she wonders: if she had known that was part of the deal, that she couldn't go back, would she have moved to Queensland?

Ada's flatmate buys a puppy and names it Corona; after the beer or the virus, Ada isn't sure. COVID puppy-inflation means it is outrageously expensive and breaks the terms of their lease, but the girls don't care. The bundle of fluff brings unexpected joy to their days; walks to the park, puppies on every corner, people stopping to rub his ears. Ada realises how much she is missing human connection, simple conversations.

March 2021
Another Easter spent in lockdown, coronavirus a circling shark. The girls check-in with an app everywhere they go, big-brother is watching! The vaccine rollout has begun, but Ada isn't old enough yet; secretly she is pleased. The vaccine seems rushed, there is talk of people dying. Is the cure worse than the cause? Besides, is the vaccine really necessary in Queensland?

When the phone rings at 5 pm on a Friday, Ada feels tension build in her shoulders. She suspects something is wrong straight away, no work gets done past 3 pm on Fridays anymore, and her social circle has shrunk to the people living within the same four walls as herself.

Her mother is on the other end of the line. '*Ya-Ya* is in hospital.

She has been having heart palpitations, her blood pressure is through the roof. She collapsed in the driveway, collecting the mail. Lucky we were home to find her.'

Ada thinks 'Where else would you be?' but asks, 'Where is she now?'

'She's at St Vincent's, your father is there now, but I don't think they will let him in to see her.'

'Dad won't be happy about that.'

'Your father isn't happy about anything anymore.'

Ada phones her *Ya-Ya's* number, thinking maybe she would pick up or a nurse would answer, but it goes straight to voicemail. Her father isn't answering calls either.

A week passes, then two. Her condition deteriorates. Worried, Ada looks up flights to Melbourne. Brisbane is a hot spot after two girls bought COVID back from Melbourne. On arrival, Ada would need to quarantine in a hotel for two weeks, her holiday leave expired.

'It doesn't make sense,' she complains, 'Why do they need me to quarantine? It would be like going to the epicentre of the fire and leaping into the flames.'

'There is no point anyway,' her mother replies. 'I haven't been allowed in to see her.'

Ya-Ya slipped into the night without goodbye. Her heart had grown weak and stopped beating, an untallied casualty of COVID. Ada watched the funeral from her bed at home, crying silent tears into her keyboard, Zoom giving silent witness to life's poignant moments.

July 2021

The vaccination rollout is happening in earnest, too late for *Ya-Ya* to see the optimism and despair. People are marching in the street, protesting lockdowns and government-sanctioned poison, their anxiety turned to anger. Ada books in her first shot, common sense prevails. She is ready for this to be over; she wants to go home. Ada FaceTimes her family, to show off her bandaid with pride.

'Why did you do that?' her dad responds.

Surprised, Ada replies, 'I want life to go back to normal, to come and visit.'

'There is no proof the vaccination works, it's untested, too rushed. Why do we have to keep wearing masks, keep getting boosters if the vaccine works? I wouldn't trust our government for anything.'

Ada isn't sure what to say, hasn't her father lived through the worst of it? Why had he formed these views? Doesn't he want the lockdowns to end? Ada tells him, 'I did this for you, besides, we were vaccinated as children, the flu shot, the measles. What's wrong with this one?'

'It's outrageous what our supposed government is doing. The rest of the world is going back to normal and we are still locked down, we need border passes to visit our children. Soon we won't be able to leave the house unless we line up to be branded like pigs.'

Ada changes the subject, 'Where's Mum, can you put her on?'

'She's having a lie down, hold on.'

The iPad shakily changes scenes from carpet, to wall, to hallway, to her parents' bedroom before Ada views a close-up of her mother's face, sideways on the pillow, hair long and unruly, tangled over the pillows.

'What's going on, Mum?' Ada asks. 'It's the middle of the day!'

'Not much,' her mum replies, not much more than a whisper.

'Why don't you get up and have a shower? Go for a walk, get a takeaway coffee?'

'There is nowhere to go,' her mum replies.

She is right, but Ada needs her to get up, she needs to believe that when she gets home to Melbourne, life will be normal. 'Where are Dom and Lucy?' Ada asks.

'Lucy is out walking and Dom has moved out, moved in with his girlfriend.'

Ada is surprised again, how has she missed this? 'Who? I didn't even know he had a girlfriend!'

'Some girl he met online. We haven't met her yet; things move quickly with a deadly virus on the loose and nowhere to go.'

'What's going on with Dad?' Ada realises how much she has missed; how disconnected she feels from her family.

'The guys at his work are stirring up trouble, some of them don't want to get vaccinated, but they won't be allowed on building sites if they don't.'

'Why not?' Ada asks.

'I don't know,' her mum replies. 'So much anger, the city is seething, we were winning for so long and now it's out of control, 200 days of lockdown wasted. I'm starting to think it would be better to have the virus, to get it over with. It's inevitable anyway.'

'Don't think like that Mum, I heard about COVID parties overseas, apparently governments are banning them, people are dying after getting it on purpose. I can't believe they are that stupid!'

'Well, maybe you would if you lived here. If you were living it too.'

Ada doesn't want to get into an argument; she has no response that won't upset her mum further. 'Stay safe, Mum, I love you.' It's the best she could do before hanging up.

September 2021

Melbourne lockdown is extended. Ada's hometown makes the telly in America, Fox News.

'The city of Melbourne, Australia has had the longest and the strictest lockdown in the world.'

'Personal freedoms are being stripped.'

'A breach of human rights.'

Tradies must be vaccinated by the 23rd or they can't work. Her dad compares the lockdowns to Nazi Germany, a fascist state. He's getting ready to go to another protest. 'They can't make us get vaccinated, take away our jobs, they have already taken so much. What will it be next?' The protests are getting bigger, more frequent, rowdier.

Ada can feel the tension in the house when she talks with her mum on the phone, she can hear her dad in the background but doesn't know who he is talking to. 'You will be on the wrong side of history!'

Ada wonders if he is right, but it seems crazy, after sacrificing so much time to lockdowns, to fight the cure. She can't understand his thinking, she doesn't want to talk to her father on the phone anymore, she avoids his messages. Once again, she thinks she is lucky to be living in Queensland, to have escaped Melbourne.

October 2021

Ada's father is taken into police custody for resisting arrest and assaulting a police officer. He refused to offer his name when an officer asked, a sovereign citizen he claimed. When the officer pepper sprayed him, he fought back, outnumbered by the men in blue. Released on bail, he waits for his court appearance, his first ever. Ada wonders, how did it come to this?

But Melbournians are getting vaccinated, the uptake in droves. The young are leading the charge, taking B-grade vaccines; a slight risk of blood clot, but youth, health and optimism on their side. Her dad is released after a night in a cell, no charges laid. Luck and poor mental health on his side, his fight defeated.

December 2021

Christmas 2021, double vaccinated. Ada doesn't want to risk cancelled flights and Omicron air. She buys a crappy secondhand car and packs her belongings into the boot. So little to show for two years of her life. She has three weeks of leave but doesn't know if she will come back; she doesn't know what she will find when she gets home.

Ada leans in to kiss her flatmate goodbye, thinks better of it, and offers her elbow for tapping. Bhakti knocks her arm aside and pulls her in for a hug. Ada reconsiders, realising she does have something to show for her time in Queensland, something more important than a car stuffed full of belongings.

KATHLEEN KRUG grew up in the outer eastern suburbs of Melbourne and went to school in Lilydale, but moved to Queensland fifteen years ago. Like her character, she watched from afar as Melbourne suffered through lockdowns, feeling homesick for her friends and family. That, however, is where the similarities end. Kathleen is a happily married mother of two who is juggling parenting with studying a law degree and writing short stories in her spare time.

We are all adapting

NINA DYKSTRA

'We are all adapting,' I tell myself for the tenth time today.

I'm watching the Premier's face flicker on the TV as he addresses the daily COVID numbers, 794 new cases and eleven deaths. No one seems fazed at these new numbers as they are presented matter-of-factly to the waiting media. The Auslan interpreter, just behind the Premier, is the only face of compassion emanating out of the screen. How many times have I heard the words 'unprecedented times'? It comes with every press conference.

I wonder about those deaths, those eleven families grieving, their relatives and friends. Did those eleven die alone in a hospital ICU surrounded by strangers in PPE equipment? Did family members get to say goodbye, get to hold their beloved? The Chief Health Officer can dismiss these people with a three-day growth and kind eyes, but what is the aftermath? I know he cares; I know he wants the best for all Victorians but still, it seems so callous. 'We are all adapting.' It is the excuse I use when faced with the unknown, the unforeseen, the unbelievable.

I switch off the telly and contemplate my one hour of exercise today. I have WebEx meetings, phone calls and video lessons to make, and I sit for a moment and work my head around the day.

We are all adapting

At first, lockdown was a little exciting, the new experiences of picking and choosing how my day would run. I could sleep in late and wear pyjama pants all day if I wanted. My cat Grimsby became my plus-one in creating fun and fuzzy lessons for my class each day. 'Grimsby is under the blanket,' 'Grimsby is on top of the bookshelf,'; great lead-ins to discussions on location language and how grade one students could also use their pets or toys to show different locations. Now I look for reasons to go out. Do I need to get bread? What were my chances of getting toilet paper at IGA today? Maybe I would support local business and get a takeaway coffee and one of those delicious scrolls?

I message Mum to meet at the Warby Trail for a walk at noon. She gives me a thumbs up. At least I will get to talk to a real person today. I look at the exercise bike I moved into the lounge room to entice me to use it. Dust is evident on the seat and display screen. It may have been used all of three times. I had grand plans to help boost my Fitbit steps and weekly exercise. My Fitbit reminded me daily of how little I moved and how far away my daily goal of 10,000 steps was. Maybe I should lower the expectations and give myself a chance to achieve success. What is reasonable for a person who now spends most of the day in front of a desk? Can I get away with 4,000 steps?

This week I am calling all the parents of my students. It's a check in on their wellbeing and also an opportunity to get the parents' point of view. I want to know how I can better support both parents and students. I only see so much of a child through a computer screen. It might be the best ten minutes students can show me. I know all about their pets, the toys they like to play with and what they do at home when they are not doing school. I know for those video meetings I have to rise up and be the most upbeat I can be. I've played dancing competitions and dress-up mornings to try and keep the energy levels alive. Yesterday showed me that, for some parents, I was the only other adult they would talk to that day. There needed to be time to vent, to be heard, to be acknowledged. Today I was more prepared.

'I'm sure he's not doing the work right, and I can't get him motivated to finish anything.'

'We are all adapting, just try your best,' I say.

'I feel useless. I need to work from home and can't help her when she needs it.'

'You're doing what you can, we are all adapting,' I reassure.

'There's too much work.'

'You can only do what you can only do, we are all adapting,' I acknowledge.

'There is not enough work.'

'I'll see what I can do, we are all adapting.' I am on repeat and at the end of the hour I am frazzled. I allocated ten minutes per phone call but most have taken twenty. I've learned so much in the last year working at home but I am still adapting. Everything is always changing.

My lunchtime walk with Mum brings a brisk breeze and new scenery. I move my head side to side enjoying the ghost gums and the ivy. We are both in masks, which is the new normal but feels uncomfortable. My ears hurt trying to make room for the elastic alongside my glasses. When no one else is around we lower them to under our chin and consume large gulps of air. Mum has contemplated walking with an empty takeaway cup so she can keep the mask lowered while she supposedly is drinking. I understand her angst. Masks don't feel comfortable but I worry that this is just the beginning. Soon it will be as ritualistic as putting on underwear. Today we are on the lookout for early freesias that grow in the wild. We walk off the path when we see a patch and start picking.

I've never seen the trail as busy as it is in lockdown. Everyone is taking their one hour of exercise seriously and the need to get children out and about for a run. One person with a hoard of children stops.

'Hey, I know you,' she says. I don't recognise her. 'I see you on our computer screen,' she continues.

Then I see one of the little people surrounding her is a student from a grade one class. All the grade one teachers share the teaching video load so they get a range of faces daily.

I smile, 'Yes, I even have my own YouTube channel now.'

We both laugh.

Mum and I walk past the skate park. There is no noise, no laughter, no squeak of the swing. Leaves have blown over the cement quarter pipe. With numbers like today I do not think playgrounds will be opening any time soon.

I arrive home in time for a meeting with some teachers. We are planning out lessons for the following week. As we meet over WebEx, I eat my lunch; rice crackers with peanut butter and my third coffee. Another joy of working from home is the lack of forethought that goes into my food consumption. Previously I would plan my school lunches, pre-make my mini omelette muffins and freeze them in groups of two. Now I look for what is left in the fridge or for what I feel like. I lack the motivation to make healthy options. Each day gets harder as I look for the easiest options. My body is noticing the change.

I look at the other faces on the screen. All look weary. We spend at least some time on our own personal wellbeing before we get into lessons. We need it just as much as the parents. We share screens and troll through YouTube clips to find premade videos that might help with our lessons. We spend copious amounts of time looking at new websites and programs that give us fresh ideas on how to make our own lesson videos more interactive. These days I know how to do so much more via a computer screen.

The doorbell rings and I get excited: who could possibly need me? I don my mask to answer the door. The delivery driver is reversing out of my driveway. At my feet is a parcel. I've been ordering a lot lately. My phone, computer and iPad have all my passwords on autofill. I'm not sure what I will open today. The post is inconsistent. What I ordered four weeks ago still hasn't come and my two new tops that I ordered last week arrived today. Even Amazon can not promise overnight delivery anymore. I try on my two new tops immediately. Noise from outside distracts me. A family with a dog is walking past my house. Their chatter causes excitement on the now quiet roads.

Later I record myself reading a chapter of *The Lion, the Witch and the Wardrobe*, the book I was reading to my class daily before lockdown. If I don't start reading it to them this way, I am worried we won't finish the novel altogether. I stare at myself on screen and try and muster up excitement. How many children will even watch this? My YouTube channel tells me how many watches I get on my videos. It's obvious not all the students are, but for the five views I regularly get, I keep going.

I check my work emails and before I know it, it is 6 pm. I need to switch off, think of other things, but even what to have for dinner does not excite me. I log off my computer but my brain fails to do so. As I prepare my food I am still thinking about my students, how best to help them and the parents, and what advice to give tomorrow. I'm not sure if I'm adapting or winging it from the seat of my pants. What will be the fallout? I worry I am not doing enough. How do I convince them that they are trying their best and are doing a good job? How do I help them adjust when I am clawing my way through each day? I think further into the future, when we hopefully adapt back into 'normal' school days. Will I still be using the phrase, 'We are all adapting to the new school normal'?

My body feels like it has participated in a marathon, I am so drained. My evening consists of sitting in front of the TV to reruns of *Friends* and *The Big Bang Theory*. My brain has no room to concentrate on new mysteries or drama. It is done. I troll through Instagram photos of people in other states, eating out, going shopping, enjoying the theatre. Curfew here is at 8 pm but there is no place to visit anyway. We are locked in our own bubble of isolation.

As I prepare for bed, I am reminded that tomorrow it will all happen again. I am still adapting.

NINA DYKSTRA loves stories of everyday people living their lives. She grew up in Mount Evelyn and, along with being a local primary school teacher for over twenty years, she has pursued her desire to be a published author. Nina loves to write poetry and short stories which she has entered into competitions and read aloud at writers' events.

Curfew

LIAM CONNOLLY

Curbing
Us
Rigidly
From
Entertaining
Widely

I was going to say 'Entertaining Wildly' but those days are behind us, I think. When I first thought it up, I wrote 'Wildly', and a rebellious side of me wanted go with it but it's not us, not really. I'm not sure we've done anything wild for some time. The only time in recent memory we've made it to midnight on New Year's Eve was when we were both lost in our books that we'd got for Christmas and didn't realise the time.

I still consider that an entertaining sort of evening. It's only the 'wildly' part that I'm willing to reconsider.

> Wildly, hmmm, adverb - in a wild manner, from wild - (2) not civilised, barbarous; (4) unrestrained, disorderly, uncontrolled; (5) tempestuous, violent; (6a) intensely eager, excited, frantic; (10 colloq.) exciting, delightful.

One of the consequences of lockdown is having the time to look things up in the dictionary.

Later, I am amused by a run-on entry: wild turkey = plain turkey. If it was a maths equation as the equals sign suggests that it may be, then it would be possible to subtract 'turkey' from both sides of the equation and end up with 'wild = plain'.

We like *Letters and Numbers* in this household and, in particular, the delightful Lily Serna, which may explain the attempts to do equations with words.

We are law-abiding (I've never had a speeding, nor a parking ticket), we wear masks as required, we get vaccinated as required, we stick within our travel limits and we avoid unnecessary trips to the shops, but there is something about a curfew that rubs me the wrong way. It's not going to affect me, I'm not going to be out anywhere, but I see it as an unnecessary use of authority and it suggests a lack of trust my government has in me.

I want to call it out.

I wrote the above acrostic as my small act of rebellion.

Plain turkey, if you're curious, can also be plains turkey – the large, nomadic, often solitary game bird *Ardeotis kori* of mainland Australia.

Another consequence of having time available to me (what with not going out and entertaining myself, wildly or otherwise) is that I get to tackle my list of things I've been meaning to do. It's not an actual list. If it existed in physical form, I'm sure my wife would have gained access to it via some matrimonial *Freedom of Information* process and held me to account for its contents many years earlier.

I'm thinking of the outdoor chairs.

I had oiled the back deck last year, or stained it, or applied some sort of treatment to it that comes in what looks like a paint tin. Anyway, it had looked good after that and so I had also sanded back and treated the outdoor wooden table (with a different sort of treatment but that also came in what looked like a smaller paint tin). And so I want to do the chairs as well.

There is a note on my phone. It is dated 16 April 2014; it just says 'finishing oil'. It's not very descriptive as a note but I know what it means. I wrote the note the day I bought the outside table and chairs because the bloke there recommended I treat them with the noted finishing oil. The table and chairs were destined to spend the next couple of years in my storage shed before we moved out of the unit and into a house where an outside table and chairs could be useful. They had been a good special at the time and I liked the look of them, but I should have checked the boxes, because they were probably a good special because one of the arms was missing. I didn't spot that until well after the warranty period had slid on by. But that's not an issue for now.

So, after the success of applying the finishing oil to the table, it had been lingering in the back of my mind to do the chairs. Also, the two chairs at the edge of the deck, most exposed to the weather, are starting to look, well, weathered. I suspect it will end up being a finicky job.

My first step is to have a good look at one of them. I'm going to have to pull it apart, sand it back, then apply the finishing oil and reassemble. The sanding bit is going to be the biggest pain. I have hand sanded some other chairs before painting them and they were definitely fiddly and I ended up trashing the cheap sanding block I'd bought.

Perhaps I should buy a new sander?

> Well they've got that wrong. *Ardeotis kori* is the kori bustard, the heaviest flying bird in Africa. It is not a bird of mainland Australia (large, nomadic, often solitary or not).

The sander I go for is a detail sander, sometimes called a mouse sander – possibly a trademark of Black and Decker after they likened it to a computer mouse. I don't get the Black and Decker version so I probably should just call it a detail sander. The computer mouse got its name in the early sixties when it was being developed at Stanford Research Institute. The precursor to the mouse, a trackball, was developed as early as the 1940s. Early versions of the mouse were called a bug, but two characteristics (possibly) led to it being better known as a mouse. Firstly, the cord attached to the mouses in those days (or mice, both are acceptable) had the appearance of a tail and made them look more like a rodent. Secondly, apparently the cursor on the screen was sometimes called a CAT.

Another consequence of lockdown is that I also have the time to look up the internet and Wikipedia, for those occasions where I don't think my dictionary has the level of detail I'm curious about.

Back to the sander.

I order my detail sander online where I had the opportunity to peruse a range of sanders at a range of stores, but the five-kilometre restrictions currently imposed on me limit me to the local Bunnings, as no smaller hardware store has been able to survive locally within its mighty corporate shadow.

Since I was ordering the sander, I also make use of the opportunity to order some more paint brushes, a ball of string and a piece of steel, which I will cut down and cover for my wife to use as a backing board for the various magnets she's collected on our travels. I don't have anything that will suitably cut it at the moment, but that will be the focus of a future online shopping expedition, or I may ask my brother or some other form of friend for some help with it. I also get some epoxy glue because, you know, that stuff always comes in useful.

With my order made I wait for a confirmation email and then another email advising me that my order has been prepared and is awaiting collection. And so I drive in to a designated click and collect bay. I chose the one where, in happier days, the community barbecue used to take place. A laminated A4 page on the wall directs me to dial a particular number and follow the prompts.

Eventually a young man comes out with a trolley containing my purchases. I pop the boot of my hatchback and the bloke loads the piece of metal and a box which I assume contains everything else. I try to get a sense of the smell from the ghost of sausage sizzles past but I'm wearing a face mask and the smell probably doesn't exist anyway.

He closes the boot and I drive off.

> The plains turkey in Australia is also called the Australian Bustard (*Ardeotis australis*) and is one of the four species in the large-bodied genus *Ardeotis*. Large bodied because it stands around a metre tall and has a wingspan of about twice that.
>
> It does appear to tick the boxes about being large, nomadic and often solitary.
>
> Indigenous names for the Australian Bustard include kere artewe (Arrente), kipara (Luritja), danimila (Larrakia) and bebilya (Noongar).
>
> The locality of Turkey Flat (and subsequently the vineyard) near Tanunda in the Barossa valley of South Australia was named after the plains turkey (Turkey Flat website) – the wines look ... not in my usual price range.

I pull apart the first chair.

I take it apart piece by piece and stack all the wooden components together. For each of the fixtures I spray them with WD-40 and place them inside a resealable lunch bag. Residual WD-40 builds up in there so I am hoping they will be suitably coated when it comes to rebuilding the chair.

Initially I use clamps to hold the wood to the saw horse while I sand; after a couple I realise that the orbital nature isn't going to fling the wood in any direction with any notable force.

It takes a little while and it makes some noise. Underneath the original dark stain is a light-coloured wood. I'd probably guess pine but what do I know about wood. It had been the same with the table but I only took a small bit of the stain off that, so I try to do something similar with the chairs while still managing to get them reasonably smooth.

The noise I make won't irritate the neighbours – neither are there. Steve and Janice on one side went to Queensland when it was still possible to help their children with the grandchildren. Peter, who's in his nineties on the other side of us, is in the process of selling up. He's lived there for over sixty years and is moving to an over-fifties village where his daughter already lives. Peter was the rock on which this neighbourhood was built, but the current neighbourhood wouldn't know him.

The back and seat sections have fixed slats so I still have to do some hand sanding to get into the fiddlier places, but the detail sander has done most of the work and done it well. I then give each piece of wood a wash down and then leave them to dry.

> The bush turkey is not to be confused with the brush turkey (*Alectura lathami*) although it is also called a bush turkey or sometimes a scrub turkey. It is far more common in the eastern parts of the continent and doesn't mind trying to steal food from campers and picnickers. The brush turkey generally looks more like an American turkey than the bustard, despite not being closely related to the American turkey (or the bustard).

The restrictions on us are that we cannot leave our Local Government Area (LGA) and we cannot travel more than five kilometres from our home. We actually live on the edge of our LGA and there are three others within five kilometres of our house, so we can't reach the full five-kilometre radius. If you look at it as a pizza, it is a very wide slice but less than half the pizza.

One day we get ourselves some food – lollies, chips, chocolates – road snacks. We've decided to go on a road trip. We get into some comfortable road trip clothes and make sure to bring the 'Road Trip Platypus' from the lounge room – a plush platypus my wife bought at a rural tourist information centre while I was watching a local game of cricket. We take it on all our road trips and call it the 'Road Trip Platypus'.

Today we travel the roads that represent the border of our wide pizza slice. It doesn't take long.

When we reach the north-eastern corner of our legal range we stare wistfully as only about one more kilometre north east lies our roasted chicken of preference.

It's open. We know it's open because we've checked online.

We are law-abiding, we don't go there.

We continue on a road trip and go past the Bunnings where I'm yet to make any further purchases that require collection.

We don't leave our car while we were driving. We considered the risks and we don't think we created any unnecessary ones. It is probably an unnecessary trip (if you purely look at material acquisitions) but it makes us feel good to have gone for the drive. So we're okay with it. The car's engine also got to run for more than five minutes at a time which I feel is also potentially a good thing. The car's name is Flosso.

We come home and return the 'Road Trip Platypus' to the lounge room.

> I don't write a letter about the plains turkey being *Ardeotis Australis* rather than *Ardeotis kori*. I would probably write an email rather than a letter anyway. The dictionary gives me far too much pleasure to nitpick little mistakes. We all make mistakes.

With the wood prepared, it is time to apply the finishing oil.

I make use of the ball of string to hang each piece from the Hills Hoist and then apply two coats two hours apart of a natural colour of finishing oil. It looks good. I left enough of the original dark stain that it gives the chair a rustic look.

The fittings come out of their plastic lunch bag probably more doused in WD-40 than what is strictly necessary. I put the chair back together, occasionally referring to one of the others to make sure everything is in the right spot. I make sure everything is done up tight and it feels sturdy. I leave it in the weather for a couple of days so the oil can cure fully and people don't get that sticky sensation when they try to get up from the chair.

I get a small amount of pride from achieving something via manual work (I'm a pencil-pusher in real life).

I still have another four chairs to go. Five if I'm willing to try to make a new arm for the one that was missing.

Just like the deck and the table beforehand, it feels good.

> 'Curfew' for your information is derived from the old French 'cuevrefeu' a combination of 'couvrir' (cover) and 'feu' (fire). It was a medieval regulation requiring people to extinguish their fires at a fixed hour in the evening. Poor bastards had to sleep in the cold.

I hope after reading this you don't think me too plain, but remember from earlier that I mathematically showed that wild = plain, which means that plain can also equal wild.

9 pm on a Tuesday. The curfew starts and we must stay home. Ha. I think you know where this is going – not for me.

Time to take out the garbage bins.

I leave my property and get to the curb. I look up the street, I look down the street. There is no movement in my neighbourhood. The fires are all out as required.

I spend longer out on the street with my bins than I did prior to the curfew. Am I unrestrained, disorderly, uncontrolled? Am I wild?

I come back inside and smile.

I can still stick it to the man.

LIAM CONNOLLY is a middle-aged HR professional. He has an understanding wife, a tuxedo cat, a 2001 model laptop with floppy disk drive that he writes his stories on, and a road trip platypus. He may or may not be exactly as exciting as the character in his story, 'Curfew'.

The Zoom funeral

HEAVEN-LEIGH PORTER

'Just play the bloody music properly.'
A cousin, who didn't realise she had her video on, rolled her eyes.
There were awkward side-glances and pursed lips from the rest of the screens.
Normally, we would all be laughing at that. Catching someone's unbridled words when they thought they were protected by a mute button is one of the only joys we've known during the pandemic.
But it felt wrong to laugh now.
After all, it was a funeral.
And laughing during the ceremony was high on the list of no-noes. It was right up there with discussing the will and drinking in the church.
I hated this.
All of it.
My pop was a ninety-three-year-old gem. He deserved better.
As if it weren't bad enough that he died alone in the hospital in lockdown. As if it weren't frustrating enough that when the borders finally opened, and we thought we might actually be able to attend the funeral in person, the biggest flood in decades hit. And the bridges closed. And we were restricted once more.

The Zoom funeral

Who'd have thought there'd be a time when you couldn't just get in your car and drive to anywhere in Australia? State lines used to be a photo opportunity on a road trip. A picture of you with your thumbs up in front of the sign that told you which state you were entering. Not anymore.

Now here we are, zoomed in to Pop's funeral run by my cousin who is doing a half-assed job of it.

He works in tech and bragged non-stop about how proficient he is with Zoom because he uses it every week for his business. And here he is, playing the slideshow of Pop's life; first with the pictures without sound, then with sound and without the pictures.

I was past the point of crying. I wanted to laugh hysterically.

Scornfully, but hysterically.

Eighty-nine years old and this is what you get.

Your dumb nephew's sweaty face on the screen, panicked eyes darting around because he somehow managed to turn on the reverse camera during the slideshow.

Pop endured so many awful hardships in life. It was a different world back then. He taught me so much, about resilience, about family, and about what it means to be a decent human being who—

Oh great! They've minimized the pictures of Nan and Pop's wedding and we can see my cousin's desktop. It's some pervy-looking anime art.

What a knob.

My husband squeezed my knee reassuringly when I tipped my head back to let out an exhaustive sigh.

The worst part was there was nothing I could do but sit and watch this circus.

Pop would roll over in his grave.

Not that he was even in his grave yet.

The screen went black and little grey boxes with tiny writing popped up all over the screen.

My cousin's flustered voice crackled through the computer speakers.

'Uh, everyone? We're just gonna skip ahead to the eulogy.'

I punched my own thigh, no longer caring that people could see me. I had to punch something. I couldn't punch my husband. He'd done nothing wrong. Though he'd probably take that hit if it would make me feel better.

Sure, let's skip ahead. Eighty-nine years old, that doesn't deserve a slideshow of photos. We should just skip all his memories and accomplishments.

Aunt Lizzie poured herself a glass of red right in front of the camera.

I couldn't say I blamed her at this point.

An image of a man in Pop's congregation filled the screen. He'd known Pop for years and had performed the ceremony at several family weddings. He was a fitting choice to do the eulogy.

He adjusted his tie, and his thin lips began moving.

No sound came out.

'HOLY MOTHER—' My husband squeezed my hand like he was comforting me through labour.

The man's lips kept moving but the words to my pop's life were trickling away into nothing, lost to the ether.

Sure, I could ask for a copy and read it later. But that wasn't the point. We were supposed to be honouring him. It's 2022! Technology is not new. Why can't we just do this simple thing for him with dignity?

An image of Uncle Steve's face went full screen, his camera pointing up at him from the worst possible angle. We got a good look at his chins.

He bore an uncanny resemblance to Jabba the Hutt.

Patience wearing thin, voices began speaking all at once and piling on top of one another as more people unmuted themselves. It became like a test for your brain to try and piece together half-sentences that were cutting in and out, and to figure out who was speaking and to whom.

'We can't hear anything!'

'Joe? Joe! It's me!'

'Can they see me?'

'Goddam' thing.'

'Just hit un-mute! UN-MUTE!'

'Geez, Barry's gained weight again.'

Faces bounced around the screen, noise ricocheting out of every square.

My speakers began to vibrate with the volume. Loud feedback blared over the top of the cacophony, and it all began to echo because some idiot had two devices on in the same room.

I lunged for the computer, determined to rip the speakers apart and flip the table over.

My husband grabbed me around the waist and tried to calm me down.

'It's okay, they'll fix it. Let's just sit and wait.'

I threw my hands up to halt his infuriating patience.

'I'd rather crap in my hands and clap than have to sit here any longer!'

There was silence from the computer speakers. They were probably rebooting it. Then I watched my husband's eyes grow wide, and I followed his gaze to see myself highlighted on the screen and the little red bar missing from the microphone icon.

And finally, finally, after all the stress of not only Pop's dying weeks and the anguish of not being there for him when I wanted to be, and a global pandemic that changed society irrevocably, finally, I laughed.

I laughed manically, and hysterically, hard enough to bring on hot tears.

If I had to sum up this whole affair, it would be in that one moment.

It was a sound of panic, dread, endurance, and some inexplicable desire to keep going.

HEAVEN-LEIGH PORTER is the author of the children's book, *The Adventures of Henry Porter*. She works as a copywriter and loves working with other creative people. When she's not writing, you'll find her painting, restoring antique furniture, or chasing her dogs.

Ghosting

KIRSTY LOCK

> **Hey, check out this cute video**
> Dec 17
> [message unread]
>
> **Merry Christmas!** 🎄
> Dec 25
> [message unread]
>
> **You okay out there?**
> Jan 4
> [message unread]

It's January before I remember the global pandemic. January, when the weather is hot and sticky and wearing a mask feels like breathing through a wet sheet even in my supposedly climate-controlled office. I think about sending you a message about the weather then, asking you if it is snowing across the pond. An excuse to say hello without saying hello.

Then I see the previous unread messages in our chat.

Scrolling back, my heart sinks as I add up the days then weeks since our last conversation faded to silence. Almost a month of unseen photos and unacknowledged greetings. I don't think we've ever gone this long without talking.

The radio announces new public health measures while I stare at the cursor blinking in the chat box. They're warning about an overburdened health system, and I remember the death toll numbers coming out of the United States in those early months, multiplying until they lost all meaning beyond frustrated sadness.

That's the moment I start to worry.

You could be taking a social media break. It wouldn't be the first time. This feels different though, and I can't quiet the tiny fear that there's an announcement I haven't seen; that you've become part of a statistic I've never wanted to put a familiar face to.

We're not even two weeks into the new year and I click your profile only to find it deleted. Wiped away. If not for our archived conversations you might never have existed.

It's January, and something is wrong.

> To: a.clark@noa.com.us
>
> From: me
>
> Subject: Hello from the land of sunburn
>
> Hi,
>
> Just checking in since I haven't heard from you in a while. Hope all is well.
>
> Much love,
>
> Jess
>
> Sent: 2 Feb

February arrives with a flurry of pink hearts in every shop window.

My inbox is empty, empty, empty, and I mourn for hours at a time; convinced you're dead or dying. I can't even Google-stalk you because your brother has locked down all of his privacy settings and after ten years of friendship, I still can't remember your father's name.

Other times, I'm sure you're just avoiding your arsehole ex, and that our friendship has temporarily been caught in the crossfire. Sure that tomorrow you might pop up with an apology and some wild story to explain your absence. Then I check my inbox and start the whole cycle over again.

It's a Wednesday when I decide I can't just sit and wait.

I ring the US embassy and am put on hold for two hours before being transferred to a different queue. I fold my laundry to the tinny soundtrack of a low-quality Rachmaninoff concerto. Every time the track pauses my heart leaps into my throat as I prepare to talk, but it's only another recorded message.

When the bored sounding voice of some young customer service person finally comes on the line, I almost drop the phone in my fumbled haste to answer.

I give them your name and address. I give them the day and month you were born.

It's not enough.

They're very sorry, they'd love to help, they just can't release that personal information at this stage.

I only want to know that you're still alive.

AUSPOST RECEIPT
Airmail $3.40
Posted 25.02.22

I don't wait by the mailbox in March.

Already you're starting to fade from my everyday thoughts.

It's easier than it should be, both of us having drifted from the group which brought us together all those years ago. The only strings that tie us together now are ones of our own making and since they've been severed I have nowhere to throw a lifeline, no-one to ask if there's any news.

When I do think about you, it's often early in the morning or late at night, my brain seemingly hardwired to expect your name to pop up on my screen as our lives intersect at opposite ends of the day. Time zones forever at odds.

If I wake up one morning to a 'hello' in my inbox, I don't know whether I'll be more relieved or upset. I like to imagine you're happy though, wherever you are. It makes it easier to live around the gap you've left.

Easier, to get used to the silence.

Somewhere deep down, I'm almost prepared to never hear from you again. Prepared that the letter I posted might contain the last thing I will ever say to you. There were a million things I could have written but what it boiled down to was I miss you.

I don't know if you'll ever read it.

Am I mourning the death of a friend or the death of a friendship?

I'm grieving, all the same.

KIRSTY LOCK lives in Melbourne's western suburbs. When she isn't curled up with a cup of tea and a good book, Kirsty tells herself she should be writing. Occasionally, she's successful.

The daily walk

TRINA BERGMANN

I grab my keys. They fit nicely in the pocket of my jacket. I zip it up and think once again how great pockets are with zips. My black runners have a little hole starting near the big toe. They will do for a while yet. I lace them firmly and turn on my headphones. A lady's voice announces 'Connected' and now I can use my phone to select my listening piece for my walk. Hmm. The walk is just over thirty minutes, so that is the main criteria. I like to complete the whole thing on my walk. I skim through the podcast options. It's got to be good. I don't want to waste my walk listening to something pointless. Once again, I select the next episode of my usual podcast. Perfect length of time. I know it will be good content. It will take time to find something new that fits the time criteria. And I can't be sure that I'll enjoy it, so this is the safe option. I'll tackle the search for something new once I've made my way through all of these ones.

Mask on. Then headphones on. Press 'play' and out the door I go. Intro music starts and I'm down the driveway.

Deep breath in. This is good. This was worth the effort. I could have made my coffee and popped on the TV, but no, this is better. I will have my coffee later. I congratulate myself for doing this. A real break from my work.

At the end of the street, I turn left. I think about all the dogs who are loving life right now. They will be very sad when their owners return to the office. Look at them. I can see them smiling as they trot along. If they play their cards right, they might even get walked twice today.

The hill I climb next is always tough and my mask gets sucked in and out as I breathe heavily. I think about how great it will feel when this restriction is lifted. To be able to breathe deeply, unrestricted, without fogging up my sunglasses (which I will not wear right now due to this exact predicament).

I pass the school. There are a handful of teachers and students outside. The ones who have to be there. The others are all at home, doing their maths, reading their books, arguing with their parents. Wearing their slippers.

I continue on, past the coffee shop. This place is buzzing. A crowd of people are busy on their phones as they wait for their coffees to be brought out. Their dogs are waiting too. I marvel at how this ritual has become an event in people's day. How wonderful it would be if these strangers would chat and encourage one another. But no. They just want coffee. Then they go. Back home to their comfy chairs and their computers.

Around the corner and down the hill I go. A couple are coming towards me. Their dog looks like the girl. Same hair. It's funny how that happens. The guy has his mask down around his chin. He sees me, then pulls it up properly. We do awkward tiny waves in greeting. This is something that is evolving. The polite physical gesture as we pass each other. It used to be a little friendly smile or a quick 'Hi', but the masks have changed all that.

I get to the point where I can take a shortcut home if I need to. No work calls so far. Still twelve minutes left on my podcast. I keep going. Despite being such a cold day, I have warmed up nicely. My hands feel like they can creep out from my jumper sleeves now. They are free.

I love walking down this road. I start to imagine what the people are doing right this minute in these old houses. They might be just turning on the kettle, taking out the compost, phoning their sister, pulling up a couple of weeds in the garden, grabbing the dog lead for their own walk. They might be lifting a batch of cookies out of the oven, flicking through the junk mail or perhaps they are hard at work and in a virtual meeting. Whatever it is, they will not have had a haircut in a while.

I pass the paddock with the horses. They know I am not bringing food, so they don't look up as I stroll by. It feels peaceful here. They are happy to stand around here all day. I always feel like taking photos at this spot, looking out into their paddock. Sometimes I do, but a photo is just not the same as being here. Breathing in the fresh morning air, tinged with the smell of horse. There's something good about it.

At the end of the road is the little locked box that is the neighbourhood library. I take the key hanging on the nail in the fence and unlock its metal door. I stand close to catch any books that want to fall out. It is always very full. I scan the books in there. Some of them used to be mine. Read and donated so that others can enjoy them. Others I have read and returned to the collection. There are a couple that have me curious. Maybe I should take them and see if they are any good. Not today though. I tell myself to finish the book I have already started first, then come back and check this little library again. Obediently, I return all the books the way that I found them, lock the door, return the key and resume my walk. I'm on the home straight now. The podcast is starting to wind up. Nearly finished.

I play a game with myself next. If I walk faster in this last bit, I might beat the podcast and get home before it finishes. I pick up the pace. The idea of a coffee when I get home spurs me on even more. My street seems longer than it did at the beginning of my walk.

By the time I reach the steps to my front door, the podcast is finished and I remove the headphones. And my mask. Ahh, that feels better. I feel like my head has been all squashed up and is now released.

Shoes off. Slippers on. The mask gets thrown in with the growing collection waiting to be washed on the laundry bench.

That's my walk for today. Back to work now. I'll do it all again tomorrow. And probably for many days, even months to come. But I am thankful for this time. This strange and unpredictable time. My quiet, daily walk is predictable in these days, and is something I will miss when the busy days of normal life return.

TRINA BERGMANN is a local mum with a husband and two young adult daughters. She loves living and working in this area and tries to live a life full of gratitude and joy.

The numbers

MANDY MERCURI

The sticky sweetness of the donut quickly turned sour. She tasted bile as she forced herself to swallow. Jane couldn't quite share the joy of her colleagues. Laughing, one of them shouts 'Oh yeah, double donuts.'

But, for Jane, numbers had been no game. They'd haunted her these past few months.

5. The number of minutes notice she was given. The rough tap on Jane's shoulder had broken her rhythm. Knife. Fork. Knife. Fork. She had been summoned. At Rydges, if kitchen staff were called into the Sapphire Room for an emergency meeting, they were in trouble. Probably another hygiene complaint.

12. The number of bulleted new rules on the hotel letterhead. Her manager had flicked his eyes up and down. Name badge, clipboard.

'Jane. Meal prep and delivery on floor Q14, please.' He held out a blue and white face mask between thumb and forefinger, lips pursed in disgust.

19.48. Her hourly rate. With her husband out of work, the responsibility had weighed heavily.

13. The bland foil covered lunch trays on her trolley. Distribute the meals, collect the menus. Definitely no entering rooms under any circumstances.

720. The thickness of the plywood separating her from the guests. They were not told which ones had it and which didn't. A polite knock and move on. Everything had to happen with that door firmly closed.

1432. The room number with the family who passed her the photograph. They had been mostly silent for the first few days. Then the coughing and moaning began. Once, she heard a muttered 'thank you' between sobs but with the next meal she paused, strained. Seconds passed, a minute. Nothing.

2. Quick raps of her knuckles. 'Hello, is everything alright in there?'
   A bump, something being knocked over. A child crying. Tension knotted Jane's stomach as the door handle lowered.
   'Please, we are not allowed contact,' she called, stepping backwards, fear trumping her curiosity.
   'My family. We are not well. Please, we must see our relatives.'
   Jane had not known how to respond. They had been given no details.

247. The hotline she had tried to call for information, support.

16. The minutes she waited before hanging up and returning to her deliveries.

4. The number of hacking coughs she had heard before a tattered piece of film peeked under the door. 'Please,' is all he said. The corner enlarged to a small photograph slid under the door.

879. The house number scribbled in wonky letters. A name. In the gloomy hallway, Jane stared, then touched the photograph. Nodding with determination, she pushed it back.

17. Suitcases lined along the wall. People everywhere, multiple languages overheard, police and additional security guards. But no-one bothered Jane. Her grey starched uniform afforded her invisibility they would never understand. She had tugged at her collar, already sweating.

99. Eventually, the percentage of infections that would be linked to the choice Jane had made next.

MANDY MERCURI lives in the foothills of the Dandenongs with her family. She loves to share her experiences about self-managing chronic pain (Take Hold of Pain blog) and being mindful (Just Be – the mindfulness in daily life blog). Writing has played a big part in her professional (PhD, academia, report writing) and personal life (blogging, public speaking). Mandy is currently writing her first novel.

A cold comfort: tales from the fridge

KIMBERLEY HANSON

Do they know how hard it is to keep my cool air in when they open the door every couple of minutes? The last time it was this bad, She was on a diet again. Those cravings had her opening the door every half an hour, looking for the right food that would fill the ache inside her.

Preparations always begin the day before and this time was no different. She began pulling ingredients out and then putting in what She calls 'culinary delights' for me to chill. They were mainly sweet dishes to be enjoyed last. They looked very impressive. Chocolate mousse and cream swirled around in individual cups like a tornado with meringue and berry debris caught up in the whirl. There were mini custard tarts. I am quite proud of the effort I put in to set those; custard takes effort. With mousses and creams, it's only about keeping them from spoiling. Then She placed the heavy cake stand with her famous cheesecake on my lowest shelf. I know it is famous because I have stored it so many times. Every time She opens my door to serve it, I hear the comments.

'I was hoping for a slice of your cheesecake tonight.'

'That looks impressive.'

Little do they know that before it is put on the cake stand, a

A cold comfort: tales from the fridge

green cardboard box marked with the shop's logo has been waiting on my shelf.

She started early again on the actual day, taking out the milk for her breakfast earlier than usual and pulling out ingredients before the rest of the family had started with their juice, bacon and eggs. Every time She opened the door to put in a new dish, I could hear Vacuum working away, or the mini humans complaining about their chores. She must have set them all to cleaning.

Throughout that day, mains and entrees joined desserts. A charcuterie board took up my entire top shelf. As She lowered two platters of zucchini slice onto my shelf, I caught a glimpse of the salad bowls on the bench and started getting worried about fitting them somewhere.

There was a pause in activity later in the day, which was a relief. I was stuffed full of dishes by now and working hard to keep cool air circulating around all my new contents. Then the pressure was really on, as strangers began to open my door. I didn't mind at first, but then they began to get *creative*, piling dishes on top of others, saying:

'I'll just keep this in the fridge until we're ready to eat.'

Most of the containers they were stacking had lids so it wasn't too bad. I didn't have to worry about balancing, just make sure to keep pumping that cool air. Then It came.

The Over-caterer. There is always one. This one had cornered the salad market. It had made coleslaw, potato salad, pasta salad and some kind of vegan-quinoa-tofu-bean salad platter. Other guests had already deposited each of these, except the vegan platter, on my shelves. None of Its offerings had any kind of covering other than flimsy cling wrap. It swung open my door and spent the next ten minutes shoving its head around every shelf, moving every dish and even taking some out, so that It's salads could have priority.

In the background, I could hear the dinner party music that He puts on Stereo every time they entertain. Beyond my open door, guests clinked their glasses, and I glimpsed minis chasing each other around the kitchen with squeals of delight.

Finally, the door closed and I put all my efforts into replenishing the cool air It had let escape. I felt little shifts and heard little squeaks as the plates and bowls adjusted around each other. One of the platters jolted and clinked off the rim of a glass salad bowl. The flimsy cling wrap covering was the only thing holding it up, and that was warping under the weight. The seconds crawled by and I grew tenser, hoping the inevitable wouldn't happen.

The door was jerked open again and the shake caused a chain reaction. The cling wrap that had held on for so long finally gave way and the platter became a seesaw, pushing another container over and off my shelves onto the floor. That unbalanced other plates that then slipped and slid and spilled their contents on the floor. Crashes and bangs brought the party over. Everyone stared at me. On the floor in front of me was a giant mess. The tomato sauce had burst open and mixed with the chocolate mousse. Vol-au-vent polka dots complimented the sausages to make the puddle look like a twisted game of noughts and crosses on the floor. As they closed my door, I heard someone say, 'Has anyone got a number for the pizza place?'

Shortly after that infamous dinner party, we noticed some changes. Firstly, He and She were around a lot more. I could tell because they opened my door at strange times. Not strange like the middle of the night – I am very used to providing midnight snacks for a sneaky human – but lunchtime. Usually, the mini ones were at school and He and She were at work. The Laptops gave us the second clue. Usually they had a few different views when opened up; work, home and sometime even a cafe. But now, they were only being opened at home, and only seeing a view of home when they were expecting work.

TV solved the mystery for us. At first, he didn't pay attention to what he was broadcasting, but eventually, it was impossible not to realise what was happening. An insidious fog was creeping through the human world. Fear whirled around the edges of the cloud as it slowly crept and spread into every nook. They became afraid of touching each other or even breathing the same air. They called it coronavirus. At first, none of us were sure what that was but we figured out what it meant. They weren't allowed to leave home. TV was on at strange hours and often without much planning. He admitted to us that it gave him a headache when they frantically channel surfed looking for the latest press conference. While the channel surfing was bad, the press conferences, or Pressers, did provide TV and us with a lot of information.

Coronavirus, often called COVID, was like the Y2K bug that some of us older appliances remember. To the Laptops, Y2K was a ghost story, but, as the coffee machine continues to remind me, I am old and I remember it well. The humans were worried that we would all shut down on New Year's Day of the year 2000. They stocked up on canned goods and I was filled with extra bottles of water. I don't think they realised that we were also filled with fear. We thought we were counting down to our deactivations. It turned out to be nothing, but I won't forget that dread for a long time.

Coronavirus was making the humans act strangely. Corded Drill let us know what he noticed. The DIY equipment don't communicate with us house equipment often because they aren't plugged into the electrical socket unless they're in use. To be honest, they're a little rough, so we're not that disappointed if we don't hear from them. But this time they proved useful.

'He's had me working non-stop all blo ... all week. Then as soon as He puts me down, She picks me up. It's one job after another. First He had me fixing the garage shelving to the wall. Then She used me to put hooks in the walls. They even let the minis have a go screwing together planks of wood to make a veg garden. I tell ya, I need a break.'

Lamp, who sits on top of the piano, told us that Mini He was playing a lot more. Mini He had opened up the music cupboard, pulled out the haphazard stacks of music and dropped them on the table with a thump. He then spent the next few days rearranging them before putting them back in the music cupboard. It seemed pointless to me. Maybe he was getting rid of the music that was past its used-by-date as She and I do each month?

Then there was the online shopping. When my door was opened, I could see the minis at the kitchen table with Laptops. After a few weeks, the view changed. According to the Laptops' reports, the minis got new desk chairs and moved back into their bedrooms. They were keeping a running tally of all online purchases. New hobbies began appearing on that kitchen table. It was hard for me to work out what they were in the few second glimpses that I got when my door was open, especially when someone was blocking my line of sight. Occasionally, She would need to grab a forgotten ingredient for the last stages of cooking, and I got a glimpse of the fluster of activity that was the table being cleared and set before dinner. There were paint-by-number and diamanté kits. I also saw a train of fabric trailing behind Her; someone was trying their hand at sewing. Once I even saw a tool kit and piles of wood.

The cooking phase came next. This I quite enjoyed. Oven and I compared notes. Some days it was cakes and biscuits that Oven had to nurture, then the next day it would be slices for me to chill. They went through a phase where they made their own jams and sauces. I did not enjoy that: jars are heavy once they are full and they were hard on my shelves. Then there was the sourdough phase. They entrusted me with their starter, which they named, fed and watered. It still didn't look very impressive, just a container of muck. After a week, they took some starter out, mixed it up to create a loaf and then Oven had their turn. Oven was quite impressed with the outcome and admitted that it would be good to try it again. Unfortunately, this cooking phase passed like all the others. Pity; it was nice to have to put some specific effort into temperature maintenance again.

Then things got worrying. It took a while for the news to spread. The Bedside Lamps realised it first, and they passed a message through the electrical wiring:

'They got up late today.'

After a few days of this, we started tracking when they got up in the morning. I was able to provide the time they came to me for the milk, and Electric Toothbrush let us know when He was brushing his teeth. A pattern emerged; the Alarm Clocks were snoozed once, twice, three times; they were getting up later and later. We can't get information from Fitbits very often, but when we caught up, they confirmed our fears: the family was exercising less. They were giving up.

Signs of spring crept in. Heater's hours were cut. Lights were being turned on later in the evening. The soups and stews I had been storing were being replaced by salads and dishes that were eaten chilled, thanks to my hard work, rather than being reheated by microwave. This made them agitated. Light switches were toggled repeatedly so much so that bulbs began to blow. TV overheard squabbles over the remote. Stereo was turned up loud for half a song and then abruptly switched off. Our family was in need of help.

We weren't sure what we were going to do. We called an overnight conference and brainstormed. How could we help? We needed things to get back to normal, the bulbs were enough evidence of that. But no one had any workable ideas. Everyone in the house, human and appliance, was stuck.

After what seemed like a lifetime, things began to change but they did so slowly. Washing Machine reported that there were less masks to be washed. One day I noticed sausages, a premade potato salad and homemade zucchini bake were placed on my shelves then removed for a few hours before leftovers were returned in Tupperware containers. This meant only one thing: picnics. iPhone and Bluetooth Speaker filled in the gaps telling us that restrictions were easing and lockdown was ending. The minis went back to school and She to work. He was still working from home but we still got some of our privacy back.

Signs looked good. Christmas was coming. The DIY tools speculated on what new tool might join them, Stereo was excited about playing the good old Christmas CDs and we caught up with Christmas Lights again. The Christmas pudding took pride of place on my shelves which began to groan with all the food being prepared.

Summer came and went with a sense of joy and freedom and then, like the surprise inconvenience of a power loss, another lockdown was called. They were closing my door when the announcement came and I was able to hear one of the minis say:

'Only one week? We got this.'

And they did. They had this. It was almost like a mini holiday where they could go back to lazier habits while continuing with everyday life and then things opened up again.

But then another lockdown was called. In fact, the pattern continued off and on for the first half of the year. Sometimes they were buying new clothes but at other times, Washing Machine was busy making sure they didn't run out of leggings and tracksuits. The soups and roast vegetables began to appear on my shelves and once again TV told us that COVID cases were rising. We entered another snap lockdown. Seven days became ten. Ten days became fourteen, and then there was no end date set. We were in lockdown again, right back where we were the year before.

They slipped pretty easily back into the COVID habits. Getting up later, laptops on after breakfast, check in with TV for a presser around 11am. Take the dogs out for a walk around lunch, then back home to laptops, dinner, sleep, rinse and repeat. But this time, there were no home improvement projects to be done, no new hobbies to try. Things hadn't changed for us either; we still didn't know what we could do to help.

One day they all gathered around me without opening my doors. I felt the clunk of a big magnet bonding to my door, holding something in pride of place. Something intrigued me about this ceremony so I put the word out asking others who might have a better view. Between the Lights, Microwave, Kettle and Toaster, we deciphered what it was. It was a vaccine card stating the date of His first vaccine and the due date for a second dose. A card for Her soon joined this one and it seemed like an end was in sight. They began to leave the house more frequently.

Shortly after, it was Christmas again. Her cake was placed on my shelves again, safely inside its box and then on its platter. The Christmas pudding took pride of place inside me and chicken, turkey and ham all shared a shelf. My shelves began to groan with all the food I had to balance and my time was taken up with getting the perfect circulation of air.

After the last two years, the humans are a bit more cautious. Coronavirus is still around. People still need to be careful and the minis even got it. After a week in their bedrooms, they are back to what counts as normal in this COVID world. They aren't leaving the house all day, every day like they used to, but they seem to be appreciating what they used to take for granted. They take more time to enjoy things. And you know what? It's rubbed off on me. If the Over-caterer returns, I will even be glad to see its busy-body head poking around my shelves again.

KIMBERLEY HANSON is a regular contributor to *Boronia and The Basin Community News* and is currently studying a Bachelor of Arts in Creative Writing through Open Universities.

Health is more important than hair

AMELIA ROWE

'You've had a haircut.' The uncomfortable comment comes from the face of Jessie on the screen. The comment reminds me how long it's been since I was on a call with Jessie. It must have been the before-times, before COVID, when she last saw me. Before the era of video calls where large meetings mean leaving the video camera off. Today you rarely 'see' people, and even more rarely have these moments to chat casually. Where once I might have walked into Jessie in the corridor, getting a coffee, or in the lunchroom, now it's a rare meeting that might bring us together.

I hesitate before I respond. Do I say 'Actually, my hair is growing back'? That's always my first instinct when people compliment the now year-old short hairstyle. Do I mention that my new hairstyle was not some empowering COVID lockdown rebellion to go short, but a by-product of cancer treatment? Do I mention that it's short now because it all fell out during chemotherapy over a year ago?

I look at the faces on the screen, trying to judge their reactions to the question. I can't remember if I've told any of them about the cancer treatment. 'Oh, I last got it cut in December.' I opt for a safe reply with a forced smile. It's true, I did get a trim in

December. My hair was finally of a length to get the new short style I had decided to go for, an Eton crop. 'It's due for trim at the back.' I keep the conversation going a little. I don't mention the cancer. I don't mention why I went short in the first place.

I imagine how those faces on the screen would have reacted if I'd mentioned the 'C' word. Not the four-letter swear word, and not COVID. Cancer. I feel uncomfortable thinking of mentioning it to work colleagues. Jessie is not the first person at work to compliment my new short hair style.

Telling people about cancer was the hardest part of having cancer; I didn't get around to telling everyone. Telling your family, your friends, your parents. There are so many people in our lives, how do you deal with telling them all? I remember my mum was at the chemist picking up a script when I called her. I wasn't really sure what to say. 'Have you got a minute? I can call you back later if you need,' I offered when she mentioned having just left the chemist. I felt 'I have cancer' wasn't the kind of thing to tell her while she was walking between shops in the afternoon. It's the sort of thing movies suggest you should be sitting down for. I would have liked to visit my parents, to tell them in person. But Melbourne was in lockdown, so a phone call was as personal as it was going to get. My mum insisted that she could talk now. Between the unusual call – I don't call my mum very often – and the tone of my voice, she must have known it was important.

'Why didn't you tell us?' was her first response. I hadn't mentioned the lump or the tests to my family. It all happened so fast. In the span of one week, I'd gone from mentioning a lump to my doctor to a cancer diagnosis. I hadn't spoken to my mum in that short week; it hadn't seemed serious enough to call about. It wasn't serious enough to call about until I got the diagnosis. When I did, she was the first person I called.

Telling work colleagues was another thing. You don't have the same emotional connection with work colleagues so it's harder to know what to say. It doesn't feel right to talk health on a group video call. Often the reaction to the news of my cancer diagnosis was shock, a moment of stunned silence. Video calls make silence very noticeable. I remember my own awkward silence a couple of years earlier. I complimented a friend's mum on her new short haircut. It looked really good on her. She'd been the shoulder-length-with-a-blow-wave kind of lady last time I'd seen her. Very glamorous. Now she had a short pixie-esque style going on. Her response to my compliment was to tell me that she'd had breast cancer. Ooo boy, did I feel bad for having complimented what I thought was a haircut of choice. I didn't know how to respond and a silence ensued. Two years later, in the background of the pandemic, I was on the other end of those silences.

Video calls make it harder to remember who you've seen. Who you've spoken to. During the pandemic I lost track of who knew about my cancer and who didn't. I would be on a call trying to remember if I'd told this person. Trying to sus out if maybe someone else might have mentioned the cancer treatment to them. If they already knew then a throwaway comment about cancer or treatment was fine. Treatment was the focus of my life at the time, I didn't have much else to talk about. If they didn't know about my cancer, then a comment about it would be like throwing a spanner in the works. There was that pause, the shock, before they'd apologise, then most would say 'Let me know if there's anything I can do to help.' I don't think I ever had anything I could ask them to do to help.

By the time 2020 was ending, I had finished treatment and was more comfortable with sharing the news. Like coming to the end of the treatment made talking about cancer easier. Or maybe it takes months to come to terms with cancer, to be comfortable talking about it. There was a time, right after I'd finished treatment, when my hair had started to grow back. I was sporting a cute buzz cut look. When I was sporting that buzz cut, I was quite comfortable telling people about my cancer treatment. 'No, it wasn't a haircut,' I would say. It wasn't a COVID shave. It was chemotherapy and this is the regrowth. I guess I was so excited to have my hair coming back. An early sign of the healthy days to come. I was excited to share the news.

Today though, I feel guilty for thinking about it. For thinking about mentioning it. Like too much time has passed to mentioned cancer to anyone that doesn't already know. Guilt, I'm sure people would tell me, is something I don't need to feel. I don't need to feel guilty about having had cancer. But I do. Not guilty for having had cancer as such. Guilty for mentioning it. It's so awkward. I feel like I'm attention seeking. In the new era of video calls for meetings, everyone's listening; there are no side conversations before the meeting gets going. What you share, you share with everyone.

Perhaps it would have been easier to tell people if I'd gone through cancer before the era of video calls. If I'd physically been around people, they would have noticed the changes. It's amazing what you can hide on a video call. Plenty of people joked about wearing pyjama pants or trackie-dacks to work. I wore headscarves and make-up. The headscarf to hide the baldness. The eyeliner to hide the lost eyelashes. The mix of eyebrow pencil and smudged eyeshadow to hide the missing eyebrows. Few people noticed the paleness, the bags under the eyes, the low energy, the lost concentration. You can't see these things on a video call.

The pandemic brought benefits for me. Everyone worked from home, so I was no exception. My absences for medical appointments or treatment were less noticeable. Nobody can see you napping when you work from home. I became a regular napper. Twenty-minute naps two or three times a day. Set twenty minutes aside, lay down on the couch, pull up the blanket, snooze. When I got back to my desk to work no one would know I'd been gone. My absence went unnoticed. COVID and lockdown made hiding that I was going through cancer treatment easy. I didn't have to try to hide it. Working from home nobody would notice something was off unless you told them. It required a deliberate effort to tell people, an effort I felt uncomfortable making. It felt awkward drawing attention to the fact that I was a cancer patient.

COVID wasn't all bad. Is it wrong that I didn't mind the lockdowns of 2020? There's a phrase I came to repeat throughout the pandemic. What I would have missed because of cancer had already been cancelled by the pandemic. Trips away, work conferences, sporting competitions; they all got cancelled by COVID a week or two before the cancer diagnosis, which meant I couldn't participate. I didn't have to worry about missing out or not being a part of things. Everyone was stuck in the same little boat as me. It was a five-kilometre boat.

People suffering the effects of lockdown focused on growing indoor plants or learning new skills to cope. When the world is going crazy around you, focus on what you can control. I'm sure someone, somewhere said that. So many people learnt new things they could control. I was going through chemotherapy; I didn't have the energy for plants or new skills, so I focused on what I could control. Keeping fit was what I could control. Or more precisely, doing exercise. Every day I set myself the goal to do something. Be active in some small way. This is what I can control, I told myself. It felt good to have something I could control. I couldn't control getting slower, more tired, or weaker. I could control swapping from doing 'proper' push-ups when I got weaker to doing push-ups on my knees. You know the old saying. If you can't run, walk. And I added if you can't walk, stretch. Every day I focused on what I could control, on what I could do. Exercise. Move.

Health is more important than hair

The world was very small for a time. My world was a two-bedroom apartment, the park down the street, the 5km of streets I could walk most days, the café I could go to for a take away coffee and a pastry, and the hospital. My days were about having breakfast, taking my tablets, going for a walk, work, naps, exercise, and bed.

In a small world, some things get lost. Like my partner. Ever there beside me. Holding my hand during the two-hour long treatment, driving me around, cooking dinner, bringing me blankets to keep me warm. When restrictions tightened and visitors weren't allowed at the hospital, I was due to start radiotherapy. I realize now how much it hurt him to see me go alone. He wanted to stay beside me. To be there, to at least be present if he could do nothing else. But he wasn't allowed. Visitors were not permitted at the hospital. The hand holder was left out.

I failed at the time to pay attention to his emotions, his pain. I was so focused on my small world. On my little everyday goals. I should have known better. My eavesdropping at the hospital had taught me better. A man, maybe in his sixties, had been getting treatment diagonally across from me. He was telling the nurse, 'When you get home, tell your sister that you love her.' This man was so sure that telling people that you love them is the most important thing that you can do. He was terminal. This terminal man was telling the doctor how awkward his friends had been when he told them that he loves them. I sat with the needle in my arm and cytotoxins entering my body listening to this terminal man's story. He had visited his friends to tell them that he loved them. I got the impression they had not felt comfortable being told they were loved by a friend, nor do I think they were comfortable saying 'I love you' back. And that story has stuck with me. I do not know this man's name. I do not know if he's still alive. I do know that I learned how important it is to tell people how you feel from him. I have tried to share my emotions with my partner more since then. To tell him how thankful I am that he looked after me.

As I practice being more comfortable expressing my emotions, like the terminal man encouraged, I've become more aware of how I feel. I'm not sure if it's the terminal man's words, the cancer, or the pandemic, but I'm happier with little things. Like being able to breathe deeply when I run. The tightness, the cancer, in my chest is gone. I find myself more thankful of the people around me. I enjoy a coffee seated at a coffee shop sipped out of a cup. The novelty of the coffee shop hasn't worn off yet. I'm telling myself to appreciate these things, not to take them for granted.

Two years on, it seems like the pandemic is sliding away, or people are trying to pretend like it has. I am in remission. Jessie is seeing me in a meeting for the first time in two years and complimenting my short hair. I don't mention the cancer treatment of 2020. People are starting to talk like the pandemic is over. I'm not talking about the cancer treatment that is over. Let's not draw attention to the problems of the past. Let's focus on the things we can enjoy right now. Let's appreciate the pubs that are open and drink to our health.

AMELIA (MILLY) ROWE is a Melbourne-based librarian for whom writing is a hobby. As a hobbyist writer, Milly has rarely taken a story from draft to final version. After experiencing the pandemic and cancer, Milly decided to see a story through to completion, setting herself the goal to submit at least one short story to a competition. The story chosen for publication here is that completed work.

An outsider's perspective

SALLY FORNARO

People often look at me, but I am rarely seen. It is both a blessing and a curse. A blessing because it allows me the perspective of an outside observer. The opportunity to see and not be seen. A curse because I am regarded as other, separate, less than. To most, I am not someone, I am something. I choose not to dwell on this. Instead, I live in the moment. I funnel all my energy, each moment of each day, into pursuits that bring me joy. I am the epitome of their sought-after mindfulness.

From my outside perspective, I have watched them; the people that surround me. I have watched how they have changed over the last two years. I am rarely included in their conversations, but I am a natural empath, and I have seen the extremes of their emotion unfold like a great kaleidoscope. The colours shifting not just each day, but each hour, each minute and sometimes by the second.

I've watched how they have struggled to make sense of the changing world. I've heard the endless narratives, their attempts to find reason and purpose behind it all. To make the pandemic count. But you can't step back and see the grand design when you are part of the unfolding masterpiece. To gain perspective, you must be outside the framed canvas, like me.

When experiencing an earthquake, your every thought is consumed by the shaking. It is not until it is over that you can consider the changes that have taken place, the results of the shaking. From my outside perspective, the pandemic has been like the earthquake. It has reminded me of a great deck of cards being shuffled again and again. Attempts to ascertain your hand mid-shuffle are futile, but they continue to try. They are impatient. Not content to wait until the cards rest in their hands. They want certainty, clarity, normalcy. For them, the shuffling is deeply uncomfortable. They are not outside observers; they are the players.

My distance offers me perspective. My world is not shaking. From my place outside the canvas, I can catch a glimpse of the grand design. I see it in the choices they are making. Decisions that are at once painful yet priceless. As chaos reigns, they live more instinctively. They are no longer acting according to prescribed societal norms, for the world is no longer normal. Instead, they channel intuitive values they still don't even know they hold. They are living more authentically, honouring priorities they don't yet consciously recognise.

To them, it is just more change. More uncertainty, opacity; shaking. They grope for feelings of stability; trying to frame their reality with falsehoods like 'the new normal'. They are trying to build houses from the cards while the deck continues to shuffle. The constant motion is exhausting for them. They've lost all sense of time, but I never measured it in the first place.

They are becoming more like me; but they don't know it. Before the pandemic, they would sometimes pause amidst their societal driven obligations; their endless to-do lists, their clocks and their calendars, and they would see me. They envied me. They saw my capacity to exist in the moment, to be so full of joy, I couldn't help but dance and they wished for a moment to be me. But they would never actually choose my life. For I am less than. I am not a part of their society. I do not conform to their normal. I am other. I am me.

The *chaos* is making them choose. They don't yet know it. To them, there is just the shaking. But I see the masterpiece. I see it as the exhaustion, confusion, uncertainty and fear drives them to places they would never otherwise have arrived. The pandemic is making them real. They can't yet step back and see who they are becoming, but I can.

I see it as they choose to sever ties with long term employers. I see it as they pursue dreams that only existed in the dusty recesses of childhood memories. I see it as they finally walk away from broken relationships, as expectations give way to honesty. I see it in the brightly coloured hair, unconventional attire, and evolution of new family interactions. I see it as they relinquish sought after real-estate and quietly slip away. They no longer use terms like 'sea-change' or 'tree-change'. They no longer need society to endorse their choice to go. I see it as the pursuit of more working hours, more money, and more things, is transformed into a recognition that they are content with less. That the time they so coveted has been there all along.

I see it as they glimpse behind the once closed doors to each other's homes and lives. As efforts to hide the reality of being human are let go, and they embrace a sense of unity in the chaos. They grumble about being asked to wear masks, when in truth, for the first time, they are starting to take theirs off.

It will be some time before they know it, but the quickly forgotten mantras that once echoed the halls of their wellness retreats are slowly, quietly, and painfully becoming their reality. Before the pandemic they paid life coaches to help them tap into their inner selves. Now their inner self is all they have left. With all the trappings of their lives stripped away, with their calendars empty and their to-do lists gathering dust, they are indeed finding themselves. They are becoming the individuals they always were, but rarely acknowledged. Pretence has become futile. The pressure-cooker of life in lockdown has forced them to be real. Real enough that, even amidst constant, endless, bone-rattling shaking, they are making huge life changes.

It is a deeply personal, yet opaquely shared experience. Amidst their isolation, they seek a sense of unity, vainly, if subconsciously, hoping that when the shaking finally ends, they will not find themselves apart. They will not have become like me; other, separate, less than. To fortify that hope, they highlight efforts made by community to buoy spirits and extend care. Paradoxical slogans speak of 'staying apart to keep us together'.

Do not misunderstand me. I am not suggesting that they have lost a sense of community. Far from it. I have observed the genuine love and care so many of them have shown to others; even those who were once strangers. Community has indeed *arisen* amidst their isolation. Their kindness and generosity have become more real; less born of obligation or extended for commendation. But despite their efforts to remain, or become connected, each of their journeys is as unique as they are. Their masks are falling away, and they find themselves singular.

Early in the pandemic, some who sought meaning recorded lessons it had taught them that they hoped never to forget. But that was when they still thought it would end soon enough for them to be at risk of forgetting. Back when they believed that a new year would make everything return to normal. Back before they knew the pandemic would last long enough that, by its end, it would be their former selves and lives that they would struggle to recall.

I have watched them slowly surrender their expectations of a return to normal. They have not lost hope, but their hopes have changed. Their fatigue has stripped away not just their efforts, but their very desire to predict the future. They are learning to live in the here and now. They are seeking joy in the little things. The shaking may have brought them to their knees, but the landing woke them up and they are slowly struggling to their feet, remade.

By the time the shaking stops, the change in each individual will be complete. They will have finally become themselves.

Metamorphosis is an agonising process. Their emotions, once raw, are now numb from exhaustion. They wonder how much longer the shaking can continue. But there is nowhere to go to find stillness, and so they simply hang on.

I feel their fear, their pain, and their fatigue. It washes over me like a great tsunami, but I do not drown in it. My empathy drives me to reach out, to offer solace, comfort; to share their unshareable burden. I sit close to them, offering them my warmth, my presence, my mute understanding. I am other, but I am welcome in their sorrow.

I lean into their suffering, willing my eyes to communicate what I cannot say; my faith in their strength and their resilience; my knowledge of their incalculable value. My unconditional acceptance not just of who they were, but of who they are, and most of all, of who they are becoming, of their true self. There is no need for a mask of any kind with me. They reach out and stroke my soft fur, smiling as I wag my tail in response. I know it brings them comfort, and I am glad.

SALLY FORNARO decided to step away from the grey and white pages of academia and towards the colourful pages of life in a public library after two years in lockdown. One of the most profound lessons she learned from that decision is that there is very little in life that is more adorable than a story time full of giggling babies!

Rest, breathe, recover, heal

KAREN HAGEMAN

My name is Karen. I was born in Melbourne, Australia to my dad who is from India and my mum who's from Pakistan. I have one sister and her name is Samantha. We were brought up in a Catholic environment. Church most Sundays. We lived a pretty normal life, receiving a catholic education, and I went onto university where I acquired a degree in computing. I was always quite a high achiever, but for my family it was mostly about money and earning a living. I think I was the black horse. I did believe in this but I also had the desire to travel.

After I landed my first professional role at NAB as an IT programmer and had enough money, I thought it was time. I moved to London with my best mate. My memory of London is very hazy; it included drinking copious amounts of alcohol and enjoying the puff of marijuana very much. I think life there was the life a typical Aussie lived, but I was a little different.

Fortunately for me I was able to work in my field of IT and earn a very good amount of money which was more than enough to keep me going. We were also different because we didn't end up living in Clapham which is where most Aussies ended up, we lived in Hammersmith, Kensington and then Shoreditch. All places were amazing.

But that's how I felt about London in general. Every place had its own sense of amazing. The days were filled with work and then social drinks, weekends were filled with more social drinks, exploring or travelling around Europe.

One of my birthday presents from my flat mates after birthday drinks was, 'Pack your bags, we're going to Amsterdam, leaving in three hours!' That was how we rolled. To be honest it all seemed like one big blur.

Living in London during the London bombings was quite the scare. We were smack bang in the middle of the three stations which were bombed. Being so young and naive I think we all felt quite bulletproof. It still felt so far away from any of us being seriously injured or killed. There were a lot of phone calls from back home in Australia when it made world news. The streets were deserted … it was like a ghost town … never did I think I would relive ghost town again …

Coming back home was a shock to the system. I felt my freedom was stripped away from me. It was back to reality, I was twenty-seven still living at home with my parents in my old bedroom with my old toys, and my dreams of having a family by this age were out the window. Depression set in. Life back in Melbourne wasn't very exciting, certainly not as exciting as London. I just worked, moved out for a short period of time, went out a bit. My biggest nights were probably Friday nights. I worked as a business analyst and then moved into a project manager role at Accenture. At thirty, I finally found Andy, my knight in shining armour. He was my colleague, a friend.

Andy was also living at home. I think we both felt we wanted more adventure so we decided to move back to London. Yippppeeeeee … and gosh a lot of adventure we had. Thankfully we found a rental in the magical town called Greenwich. There were bars galore, food galore, entertainment galore, we even stood three metres from the Queen when the *Cutty Sark* reopened.

We bought a car, one of the best purchases, which enabled us to do so much effortless travel. We would just drive onto the train which would take us through the Eurotunnel from London right through to France. Our window to Europe. We lived and worked in London for two years before hitting the road with our blow-up tent and fold-up bikes. We drove for three months and visited sixteen countries. All sorts of amazing!!

The holiday feeling disappeared as soon as we stepped back on Melbourne soil. Andy and I were engaged so it was time to get real, find a house and settle down. We still liked to have our drinks but that soon changed when I fell pregnant, which is when our board game adventures began. It started with Magic: The Gathering, to Codenames, to Pandemic, a game where you cooperatively try to save the world from four diseases. There are infections, outbreaks and epidemics and, depending on the role you chose to play – medic, scientist, virologist, just to name a few – you can help cure the disease. It was a great strategic game and I thought the creator Matt Leacock was an absolute genius. It was a game we looked forward to playing almost every night.

The game got real
'Kaz, have you heard what's going on in China?'

Of course I hadn't. I barely watched the news or read up on anything.

'There's a virus which they're saying is deadly and it's spreading'.

'Seriously I think we've been playing one too many games of Pandemic'.

This would have been back in December 2019 before anything really hit the mainstream news. Andy started bringing extra tins of food home, which I would roll my eyes at, thinking he was being absolutely ridiculous, paranoid, and maybe even losing the plot. Weeks went by and Andy would keep updating me on what was happening. He told me it would take about one to two years to find a cure. WHAT!? Our neighbours had insider knowledge as their parents lived in China, Wuhan. They were getting locked up like prisoners.

Although I was hearing this, I still couldn't quite comprehend it. I started hearing about it on the news and I think my 'oh shit' moment happened when I decided to do a shop at Costco. The line was the longest I had ever seen and everyone's trolleys were packed with supplies, especially with the very precious toilet paper.

We didn't alter our lives that much at the beginning but probably about three weeks into COVID being a thing in our country, my cardiologist called me. She broke the news to me that I was at high risk from COVID and that in the next three to six months, I would need to undergo heart surgery to fix my congenital heart disease. What!? My mind exploded. I thought I was ten years away from this.

Andy and I sat down to digest the news. It was all very overwhelming. Firstly, that I was a 'high risk', and secondly, that I would need major heart surgery. We had to make some very quick decisions, and Andy suggested we would go into self-isolation. What would this mean!? We had to basically stay at home and limit external contact as much as possible, from people and products. We looked at what our commodities were and brainstormed what we would need for possibly the next few months.

Winter was also coming so we also needed to consider what we needed in terms of clothes for the growing kids. Toilet paper, bread, milk, vegies, alcohol, medicine for both us and the kids. We turned our fridge into a freezer and tried to freeze as much meat as we could, I also stored as many veggies and home-cooked meals. We bought as many tins and packets of foods, baked beans, pasta, pasta sauce, rice, flour, a bread maker and long-life milk. I did buy some frozen fruits to make smoothies and we planted a few veggies. I purchased lots of arts and crafts too.

What it meant for us physically was that Andy would only work from home. The kids, Harvey and Livvy (one- and three-years-old, respectively), would not attend childcare or kinder. It also meant we would only go to the shops on the rare occasion. This also meant we would physically cut off from family and friends.

Groundhog day
When I think back to that time, I have no idea how we coped with Andy working from home and me home every single hour of the day, especially with our one-year-old and three-year-old. We had all we needed to keep ourselves going for a few weeks, but on the rare occasion, Andy would do the shopping. Him coming home was like getting a glimpse of freedom. I would question him and ask him all about the amazing shopping trip, how many people there were, what it was like, and seeing what he had bought would feel like Christmas.

Melbourne was forced into a lockdown in March 2020. How was this possible? The ghost town I had experienced in London was nothing compared to what we were living through. Schools shut down, shops closed down, some businesses closed down for good, playgrounds ended up closing down, we couldn't meet up with anyone (not that we wanted to, but it was just crazy to think this could be enforced). We were only able to leave the home for essential services. Curfews were introduced, too, where we couldn't leave the home after 8 pm, and then we had to stay within a five-kilometre radius of our home if we did leave.

Our new life on the other hand, locked up with nowhere to go, felt so easy! We were one of the very fortunate families to feel this way. No pressures of having to go to the shops, making plans, social obligations, didn't have to rush off anywhere, didn't need to get ready for anything, could just wear sloppies all day, every day. My hardest decision was deciding what hoodie to wear today. Every day did feel like groundhog day, and I know I was so lucky to be stuck with the three people I love most on this earth; my husband and my two kids. We closed our front gates and it felt amazing. We were safe in our sanctuary and as prepared as we could be.

I really felt that as long as I had my family, I didn't need anything else. We made lots of food together, mostly involving flour. We played together. We did lots of arts and crafts and our board game collection continued to grow. We ate together, we danced together, we laughed together, we had lots of bonfires together, I did lots of DIY and Andy got into the art of brewing beer and distilling. We were sorted!

The shit storm

It was May 2020. I hadn't left the house since 13 March when I got my flu shot. We needed to book in a surgeon. Do I go for a mechanical valve or go through this less known Ross procedure? Higher risk as they replace the aortic valve with one of your healthy valves, the pulmonary, and I would receive a donor valve in place of my old pulmonary. This meant I wouldn't need to be on warfarin and I could live a more normal active life. It did also mean a longer surgery time of six hours.

We booked in Dr Skillington for the Ross procedure on 9 August 2020. It was the same day we left London to commence our road trip around Europe. Was this going to be my next trip, but a one-way ticket to heaven this time? Heart surgery was no longer a discussion point; it was booked in and it was really happening.

It was also so hard not being by my best friend's side when she decided to separate from her husband. It was the third time they had separated, but this time felt real. All I could do was be on the phone to her. I did leave the house to drop off care packages, but not being able to hug her or even help her was hard. The number of relationships that I started to hear were in turmoil was concerning. It was like COVID exposed those small fractures in relationships and really tested all types of relationships.

At the same time, Andy's cousin's cancer had come back. This time it was terminal. In her final days we broke the rules and spent a few minutes with her. Precious time that we will be forever grateful for. To see our family members mourning the loss of their daughter, sister, mum, aunty at the funeral on TV in the lounge room just felt so wrong and so surreal.

The heart ache and recovery
I lived every day of COVID like it was my last. Every single day with my family was a blessing and I was so grateful I had that time with them. The COVID numbers were at their peak, we still didn't have a vaccination and I was going in for heart surgery when I would be at my most vulnerable. A heavy cloud sat over me and I felt like I was suffocating with fear. Fear that I would never see my family again. I got out of my self-pity and became real about it. There was a chance I may not make it, but I've lived an amazing life and thankfully, the kids are young enough to not remember me too much, and I know Andy's a great catch so he'll find someone to mother our children!

I wrote out my will and even my funeral service, and I started making lots of family videos that one day I would hope Andy would share with the kids. I also made lots of video messages to them making sure they knew how much I loved them.

Leaving my family to go into hospital was the hardest thing I've had to do. First leaving the kids and then Andy dropping me off at the hospital. Unfortunately, again due to COVID, he wasn't able to stay. Although Andy wasn't with me physically, we spoke on the phone, and he helped calm me while I took the sleeping tablet. The tablet which would send me off to sleep until show time!

In the morning I had to scrub down and wear a hospital gown. I had nothing but my bare body, the hospital gown and my ID bands. I was just another body. Down the gas went and my anaesthetic kicked in. Six hours later, plus a few more for me to wake up, I was on the ventilator. But I was alive, and I heard my angel Andy's voice on the phone.

The next couple of days in ICU were hard. I was in a lot of pain, and I had a collapsed lung which made it very hard to breath. It felt like a big fat elephant was sitting on my face. Although Andy would have loved to be holding my hand, I felt that this was a battle I had to fight alone. I went into my own ward. I had the photo frame of my family and the cast of my Mum's hand holding mine and the cross she had held onto through her battle and until she took her last breath. How I had missed my Mum, her warmth, her hugs, her voice to tell me it was going to be okay. Mum passed away from cancer one year prior. My heart ached for her. Busy as I was at the time, with an eight-month-old and two-year-old, now my time to really grieve. To see the incision down my chest also reminded me of the car accident Mum was in. I felt like I was looking at her in the mirror. I cried and I cried. It was ten days by myself; solitude and recovery, physical and emotional.

The clouds parted

The morning I was due to leave, I had a whole team of nurses and doctors in my room. It wasn't allowed at that time due to COVID but they all wanted to be involved in sharing the news that I would be going home! There was lots of high-fiving and it honestly felt like I had just run a marathon and reached the finish line. There was so much happiness in that room; I will never forget the feeling. Coming home to my sanctuary was like I had been to war and back. The very similar feeling I felt when I had moved into my parents' place to nurse Mum through her final weeks. Coming home just felt safe and secure, and to reunite with Andy, Livvy and Harvey made me feel so complete. I continued walking every day and would often think about Mum. She was so brave, and although she didn't make it through her battle, I felt her spirit lived on and certainly helped inspire me.

We continued our healing as a family in solitude. Every day we recovered and became stronger and stronger. Today, two years since we went into our first isolation, we reflect on the time we had: being still, being present, being each other's only comfort, and we smile. Today we also test positive with COVID. Two years on, after 263 official days of lockdown, plus six additional total weeks of self-isolation and three vaccinations later, it's now a matter of living our lives with the virus.

I loved this poem Jacinda Ardern shared:

Rest now, e Papatūānuku
Breathe easy and settle
Right here where you are
We'll not move upon you
For awhile.
We'll stop, we'll cease
We'll slow down and stay home.
Draw each other close and be kind
Kinder than we've ever been.
Time to return
Time to remember
Time to listen and forgive
Time to withhold judgment
Time to cry
Time to think
About others
Remove our shoes
Press hands to soil
Sift grains between fingers.
Embrace it
This sacrifice of solitude we have carved out for you.
So be still now
Wrap your hills around our absence

Loosen the concrete belt cinched tight at your waist
Rest.
Breathe.
Recover.
Heal
– And we will do the same.

KAREN HAGEMAN always wanted to write a story but, as English was always her worst subject at school, she never had the confidence. Writing this story has been like therapy for her and she thought it would be good to write for her kids. Thanks for taking the time to read about her COVID tales.

Daddy in lockdown

MICHAEL HANSEN

'Bix!' shouts Amy, excited that it's Weet-Bix time. I place a bowl of Weet-Bix in front of her and give Katie her usual breakfast; Weet-Bix, Corn Flakes and Rice Bubbles all mixed together. 'Wave Bye-bye to Mummy, she's off to the train,' I tell them.

'Bye-bye,' waves Amy.

'Bye, have a good day with Daddy!' my wife says. She wraps a scarf around her neck and pulls on a mask before stepping outside.

'Is it still lockdown?' Katie asks. Katie is three.

'Yes, it is,' I reply. 'Still a lockdown; Mummy has to go to work because she's essential. But you can have a day at home with Daddy!' They seem happy enough with that. They are much more accepting than you'd expect sometimes.

'Train!' Amy says, pointing to the door.

'Yes, she's gone to the train,' I acknowledge. Amy's a COVID baby; she's a one-year-old, born in March 2020 just before Melbourne's first big lockdown. Her whole life has been in and out of lockdowns. None of our family were able to meet her as an infant, and most people met her wearing a mask over her face. This is normal for her. To be honest, as the pandemic goes on, it starts to become more normal for me too.

After breakfast I get the girls dressed and ready for the day. Katie's not happy with the pants I chose for her.

'What pants do you want?' I ask.

'The pink ones, these ones are too short now, I'm growing,' Katie replies. I look but don't see them.

'Mummy had them,' Katie says.

I don't know where they are. I will have to try to convince her to wear another pair; a tricky feat when your child has a strong sense of 'fashion'.

My phone buzzes. It's the first message of the day from work, asking a question about something 'urgent'. I told them I was away today; I've been away every Wednesday and Thursday for weeks. I briefly start to read the message.

'Daddy! Where are my pants!?' Katie asks, getting impatient. I put my phone in my pocket. I'll try to ignore work for a bit. 'These ones?' I ask, holding a pair of perfectly good blue pants.

'No, not those ...' says Katie. My phone buzzes again. I check it hoping it's not work again, but no, it's a video message from my mother. My parents both live in regional Victoria and due to lockdown restrictions, we haven't visited them in months.

'Nanny Marg's sent a video!' I tell them. They immediately sit down on my lap to watch it on my phone. Nanny Marg is saying 'Hi' and wishes she could come and visit.

Katie starts trying to talk to her. 'Nanny Marg, one day can we go and visit your house?'

'It's just a video Katie, she can't hear you,' I try to explain.

'Oh,' Katie says, looking glum.

'I guess it is hard to tell sometimes,' I sympathise. 'That's OK, shall we send a reply?'

They both seem eager, so we start recording a video. Katie rambles a long exciting story that no one can understand. Amy waves and says 'Bye bye.' I send it to Nanny Marg; she won't understand a word of it, but will be happy to see and hear from them both. We continue the search for the perfect pair of pants, while Amy puts her baby to bed over and over.

'Baby!' she says, patting her baby doll to sleep.

'This dress!' Katie shouts, excited at finding what she wants to wear; a summer dress, hardly appropriate for this time of year. I convince her she can wear it, but only over the top of a warmer top and wearing pants as well.

'And this jacket, and these shorts!' Katie says, arranging her eclectic outfit.

'Perfect!' I reply.

It's time to get out of the house and go for a walk. It looks like a nice enough day, but it's still a bit cold and wet from last night's rain.

'It's a gumboot day! Maybe we'll find some puddles,' I say.

'Boots!' Amy says, excited about wearing her dinosaur gumboots. I get some jackets to keep us warm. Then I get some beanies to keep our ears warm. 'Head,' Amy says proudly, putting both hands on her head as I help her put on her beanie. I bend down to help put on Amy's boots, and my longer-than-normal hair gets in my eyes; I haven't had a haircut in several months now. I tie it back with one of Katie's hair ties.

Leaving the house can take a long time nowadays. But we're finally ready!

'Pepper!' Amy says, pointing to our dog, sitting by the front door.

'Ah, of course,' I reply as I fetch the dog lead to the excitement of Pepper.

We walk outside and I lock and close the front door. We take two steps. 'Oh!' I exclaim, turning around. I forgot my mask! I fumble with the keys to open the door. Amy is sad now; she wants to hop on her pusher bike, not go back inside already.

'Bike,' she says, pointing to the garage.

'In a second, I just need a mask!' I say hurriedly as I try to untangle the dog lead and reach in to get a mask. I grab the mask left for me by the door; it's a blue denim style one today. I pull the loops over my ears and put my glasses over the top of the mask to prevent them from fogging up.

I place Amy in her pusher and we start the walk to the park. It's a brief walk but it seems somewhat unwieldy at first, trying to manage two girls, a dog and a pusher without getting tangled up. Although we are allowed to roam within a full five-kilometre radius from home, we rarely wander further than our block, and find ourselves following the same routine walk around our housing estate.

We arrive at the park. Katie runs over to the playground near the slide to look at the white sign cable tied to it.

'What does it say today?' Katie asks full of hope.

'Still closed,' I say to the sombre acceptance of the girls. Katie looks at the swings and Amy looks at the slide. 'Let's keep walking,' I say. We continue walking to pick flowers that are just starting to bloom; it's almost spring.

We stop at a group of flowers and Katie starts selecting favourites to pick for her and Amy. I briefly pull out my phone, realising I haven't checked the daily numbers. Ninety-one; they're going up. What's the seven-day moving average though? What's the Reff? ('Reff' refers to, on average, how many people are being infected by each positive case of COVID-19.) What time is the presser? I scroll through COVID stats when Katie tugs at my jacket.

'Here's your flower Daddy!' she says, prodding my leg and snapping me out of my daze.

'Thanks Katie-Pie!' I say. I put my phone away for now after taking a cute snap of them holding a small pink flower each.

We walk through the produce garden, one of the three communal gardens in our housing estate. I glance down the length of it to make sure no one else is here before we walk down the path towards the fruit trees.

'Min!' cries Amy as she sees the mandarin tree. I indulge her and pick a single small orange mandarin for her to hold and carry. Katie picks herself one and puts it in her pocket, along with the several flowers she has picked.

As we reach the top of the garden, Katie runs towards something exciting that has caught her eye. Amy reaches out to be let out of her pusher. They both run over to an empty bike rack, all shiny and smooth, looping metal, something so ordinary to me but fun and exciting for them. I silently watch them climb in and out of it for five minutes or so. Pepper sits and watches them with me in amazement at how much fun they are having as they make excited squeals at each other.

Our next stop is the puddle. The puddle, at the top carpark area of the third communal garden. Of all the places puddles show up, this one is the best; and I should know a thing or two about what makes a good splashing puddle. The puddle is big and wide, but also shallow and clean. The girls immediately, and without hesitation, run into and jump in the puddle creating splashes high enough to get them wet. I accept that they'll get a bit wet, letting them enjoy the moment regardless.

While they splash, I look around. It's a nice day; it's quiet and calm. The air is … I take a deep breath in … stuffy and mask-y! I look around to see if we're alone so I can slip my mask down and take a sneaky breath of fresh air. It's brisk on my now unmasked face, fresh and soothing. I savour the moment. My glasses were slightly fogged up, and now they start to clear. Some sun breaks through the clouds and things appear bright and colourful. The girls are splashing away in their bright coloured raincoats and boots without a care in the world; a world they have little knowledge of, of how it is and how it used to be, so accepting as to the rules and protocol we now follow.

After the puddle, we take a detour to look at the giant spike flower (as I call it to the girls) to see if it's bloomed. It's a gymea lily which has been growing steadily upwards for over six months now, through all the lockdowns and the gloomy winter months. It must be four metres tall by now. Amy points up high to the top of the spike; to her it must be unimaginably high. Katie marvels at it briefly before being distracted by a wiggling worm on the path. Looking closely, much to my amazement, the flower has just started to bloom! A small red petal of the lily is emerging as if to signal the start of spring and the start of better times. Perhaps it is indeed; playgrounds will open again next week, so that's something. Katie excitedly shows me a four-leaf clover she found. I smile at her.

'Wow, another one!' She must be the best in the business for finding these; once, she found four four-leaf clovers and one five-leaf clover during a single walk. Maybe there's something in the soil in this area, or maybe they're not as rare as we're led to believe.

I hear footsteps in the gravel path nearby and look over my shoulder to see a couple out for a walk, their masked faces making it difficult to make out who they are, or if they are smiling hello. I nod to them, then hurry the girls up for us to move on.

We head home in time for a scheduled video meeting with a local children's performer who, through day care, has been able to keep entertaining kids during the lockdown remotely. As we enter the front door, I pull out some hand sanitiser.

'Rub rub rub!' I say to Amy as I squirt a small drop into her hands. 'Wub wub wub!' she replies as she rubs her hands together.

Katie goes to wash her hands. I can hear her counting. 'Sixteen, seventeen, eighteen …' Katie sings, the process of counting to twenty before rinsing thoroughly ingrained in her mind.

My phone buzzes again, another message from work. 'I just have a quick question' is a common yet frustrating message. A quick question usually requires a complex answer and something usually needs to be looked up on a PC, not something I can do easily with the girls needing looking after. I answer briefly, hoping it will suffice for now.

'Time for Rhythm and moves!' I exclaim to the delight of the girls. They sit on their small purple couches in front of the tablet waiting for me to join the meeting. I unlock my phone to find the email which has the room codes and passwords. I awkwardly type in the room number and the password. It fails to connect. Damn.

'Ergh, the internet is broken again …' I tell the girls, frustrated. 'Don't worry, I'll fix it.' For reasons unknown, the internet has been having connectivity problems recently, an issue I seem to be able to circumvent by connecting to a VPN; a Virtual Private Network that uses a proxy server to … never mind it gets technical. Regardless, it solves the issue. The VPN connects, and I open the Zoom app again before it finally says 'Waiting for host'. Katie and Amy are chomping on bananas patiently while they wait.

Cam, the host, joins. 'Good morning!' he says. The digital greeting is awkward as always, Katie not knowing quite what to say and Amy watching on, not sure if it's a TV show or a real engagement. I encourage them to wave 'hello', but Amy still looks confused. Some participants are a little late, so Cam asks if there are any requests for favourite songs he can perform while we wait. Amy loves the 'rainbow song', so I suggest that one, but Katie has other ideas.

'Maybe … *Shake it off.*' she asks. *Shake it off* is a song by the pop artist Taylor Swift which Katie had heard on the radio the other day. I wince, and start to whisper that 'He probably won't know that one, he only plays children's songs' but before I begin to speak Cam says, 'My girls love that one too!' and starts to sing a simple rendition of it, much to Katie's delight. I grin widely, watching

Daddy in lockdown

from the side. Before long, the show has started. We've worked out the correct mute settings so we don't interrupt the performance, and the girls are spinning and dancing in front of the tablet, giving me time to sort out lunch.

After lunch, Amy has her nap and I get some one-on-one time with Katie. She likes to draw, so we spend a couple of hours drawing; Katie has some wild ideas of drawing and writing her very own picture book. 'What a great idea!' I say. She spends the afternoon drawing page after page for her book, which seems to me to be an interpretation of the characters from Frozen.

We draw until Amy wakes up, and have some quiet time with some snacks and TV while Katie adorns my hair with a selection of colourful bows.

'Very pretty!' she exclaims.

'Look, it's starting to rain!' I say, pointing outside the front window. 'Shall we play with our umbrellas?' I ask.

'Yes!' screams Katie. I put their raincoats back on, and send them out with the pink umbrellas. We walk out to the front yard in the light drizzle.

'Mail!' says Amy, or an approximation at least. We go to check the mailbox.

'No mail today,' I say as we both peer into the mailbox together.

'Oh, I like your hair,' I hear a voice say. I look up to see our neighbour checking her mail too. I realise I still have pretty bows adorning my hair.

'Oh thanks! Katie did my hair today ...' I explain sheepishly.

'It's LOTS of pretty bows!' Katie says excitedly, spinning her umbrella.

'Good job!' she says to Katie, as she heads in out of the rain.

I watch the girls enjoy the umbrellas and the rain until I notice someone walking down the road.

'Look who it is!' I exclaim, pointing.

'Mummy!' yells Katie.

'Mumma!' says Amy, dropping her umbrella completely. My wife waves as she gets closer, Katie running over to see her.

My day with the girls winds down. Some would say it's stressful times of late. It's hard and lonely. Sometimes we wish there never was a pandemic. Soon enough the lockdowns will end. Vaccines will become available. And with the bad there has been good; it has given me extra days to spend with my daughters, something I wouldn't change for the world.

'Okay, what should we have for dinner girls?' I ask.

'Bix!' shouts Amy.

MICHAEL HANSEN is a husband of a hard-working wife, and a father of two young girls. He works in IT, and during the COVID lockdowns was lucky enough to transition to working from home full-time, as well as caring for his daughters a few days a week while his wife worked in the city. He is passionate about his family and their upbringing, and was amazed at the resilience that his daughters would show during abnormal times of isolation.

Cancelled

RACHEL BRISCOE

So that's it then. My Year 12 formal is postponed. Maybe not just postponed, maybe even cancelled.

Sure. Why not? Why not just go ahead and cancel it like everything else? The musical is cancelled. Sports day is cancelled. All excursions, parades and parties are cancelled. So why not just go ahead and cancel the formal?

I should just stay here and never go out again. Ever.

Mum's in my room. I heard her tiptoeing across the carpet. I can't actually see her because I'm lying on my bed with my face buried – yeah, that's right – my face is literally buried in my pillow, like I'm a corpse or something.

She's patting my back now, trying to comfort me because I'm sobbing my heart out.

I don't want comfort. I don't want to hear her say, 'Sorry.'

I've heard that word so many times already this year and we're not even halfway through the year! Sorry, there won't be a musical this year. Sorry, you can't hang out with your friends. Sorry, that career choice isn't valid anymore. Sorry, you can't go anywhere unless you're exercising. Sorry, you can't go to your cousin's wedding because they can only invite, literally, ten people now.

Well, sorry, but I've sacrificed enough this year. I want my formal!

And I really, really hate that word cancelled. It keeps popping up like a red, angry pimple on the tip of my nose. Every email they send me from school, every text message, every announcement on the news includes that horrible, mean word on the subject line: 'Due to COVID-19 this event has been cancelled.' You know what? I want to cancel the word 'cancelled' from the dictionary. Yeah, it should be totally erased. Deleted. It should be illegal to even use it, like a swear word, but a really bad, really offensive, disgusting swear word.

It's not fair. Not fair! I've spent most of my life (in fact, the last twelve years of my life) at school – diligently learning and studying so I can get really good grades – knowing that one day I'll finally graduate and have a big, beautiful celebration.

That's right, I'm supposed to celebrate the end of my school life! I'm meant to have a wonderful evening to look back on with fondness, when I'm too old to celebrate anything; when I've got grey hair and wrinkles, but I can still remember the good old days.

Also – and this is the really tragic part – I've spent months and months searching for my dress for our 'Roaring Twenties' formal. Everything's been carefully chosen and paid for. Every detail planned. I've got my dress, my shoes, my earrings, my makeup sorted and even how I'm going to wear my hair. Plus, my friends and I have already booked the vintage car that was going to take us to the formal.

And it's not like I haven't already been very patient and understanding about all the stuff surrounding this pandemic. Like, I know we're in lockdown and studying from home and everything, so we don't get the virus or spread the virus. And I know us teenagers aren't likely to get that sick, but we might pass it on to older people like my grandparents and they might get really sick and die. Yeah, I've watched the news, I know all about those poor old people in Italy. So yeah, I've been really obedient and stayed at home, and I haven't seen Grandma, or Nan and Grandy for ages.

Also, I really do appreciate the fact that Queensland has been protected by closing the borders, so I haven't complained one little bit about not being able to go travelling anywhere.

And while I think of it, I didn't even get that upset (okay, maybe a little, but it was just a brief cry) when I lost my traineeship placement at that cute little travel agency because the place literally closed down – I mean, obviously it closed, seeing how no one can, you know, travel anywhere! And I haven't made any kind of fuss about the fact that I've wasted the last couple of years studying Travel and tourism for my QCE. What a joke!

Plus, I haven't whinged about not being able to do normal things like going to watch a movie, or shopping for non-essential stuff, or hanging out with my friends. And when I am allowed to go out, I've worn a mask without any complaints, even though it makes my face break out something shocking. I always use hand sanitizer too, despite the fact that the skin between my fingers is so dry it's practically raw flesh.

So yeah, I think I've been pretty good so far. I've shown a lot of maturity and understanding during this whole pandemic.

But now this. This is too much. They're postponing the formal and everyone's saying they might even canc— no, I can't even bring myself to say that horrible word.

I hate this year already. 2020 should be cancelled!

* * *

It's stupid, I know, having a big cry like this – okay, a total meltdown. If my brothers hear me, they'll call me a Karen, like those middle-aged women we keep seeing on the news who refuse to wear a mask and have meltdowns in the middle of shopping centres.

But what would my brothers know anyway? They don't care. Nothing about this stupid pandemic bothers them. When we finished our Easter holidays and we just didn't go back to school, they thought it was great. Woo-hoo!

And yeah, I have to admit, it was kind of fun. At first.

Ewan and I already use laptops at high school, so it's been pretty easy for us to log on at home and access all the work our teachers send us. Some days though, we have to join online meetings and that's not too bad – except for when our teachers have trouble using the technology and can't seem to log themselves on, or unmute themselves, or end up muting everyone else so we can't make a comment. So yeah, that's been a little bit frustrating.

James thinks the whole experience has been epic. I think he literally loves lockdown. Although, because he's in primary school it has been a bit more of a challenge for him – or I should say, Mum. She had to set up her laptop for him to use and I think she's been getting a bit flustered with everything. I know she gets loads of emails from his school and she has to print out all these worksheets for him to complete, then scan them and send them back to his teacher. Plus, she has to help James get logged on to the school's video conferencing app which apparently is a real nightmare for her.

But really, James only does a couple of hours of online learning, then he just plays his stupid computer games the rest of the day.

And Ewan, well, even though he plays drums in the school band, and all live performances have been cancelled for most of the year, it doesn't seem to faze him. He's still got another two years of high school left, so he just shrugs and says, 'Oh, well, I'll just keep practicing for next year.'

But that's the thing – I don't have a next year! School's finished for me this year.

So yeah, even though online learning was okay at first, now that everything is getting cancelled it's just not fun for me anymore.

But no one else understands.

Even Mum and Dad don't seem too bothered about lockdowns or all the restrictions. Dad works at the hospital and he says everyone's nervous about what's going to happen, but at least he still has a job and gets to leave the house to go to work as normal. And Mum, well, she works from home anyway, so nothing's really changed for her.

I'm the only one who's actually suffering in this family.

And yet, I don't complain.

I remember right at the beginning of lockdown, when I got a little bit upset because I couldn't go out and see my friends, Mum said to me, 'Think about Grandma. She's all by herself. At least you've got your family for company.'

And I did think about Grandma locked up in her retirement village all by herself. So that made me shut up and stop complaining. I even decided to suck it up and try to make the best of it, like Ewan and James.

For example: Ewan FaceTimes Grandy all the time, and both of them have set up their own chess boards and play virtual chess against each other; James has started growing herbs in all these little pots around the backyard and when he's not playing games, he's looking up how to grow plants organically. So I tried something new and looked up some Jamie Oliver recipes to give cooking a go.

But then, one day when Ewan was practising his drums in his bedroom and James had the TV turned up really loud so he could hear the Xbox over the noise, and I spilt caster sugar all over the kitchen while I was trying to bake a Scrumptious Sticky Toffee Pudding … well, Mum had a total meltdown, didn't she? She stood right in the middle of the hallway and yelled at us all to shut up so she could have a little bit of peace and quiet.

Ewan stopped drumming and stuck his head out of his room, and I gave him a look, because I was worried he was going to say something stupid like, 'Don't be such a Karen, mum.' Which would have been funny, because her name actually is Karen, but it was pretty obvious she wasn't in the mood for laughing.

So instead, being all diplomatic-like, I patted her on the arm and said, 'It's okay, Mum, think about Grandma. She's all by herself. At least you've got your family for company.'

But she didn't appreciate that comment at all.

So yeah, I'm not the only one to lose it.

* * *

Lockdown has finished and we're back at school. Hooray!

Most things have resumed, like sports and music – with COVID-safe restrictions of course. However, today I heard the best news ever: the formal has been rescheduled for the end of the year.

It's not going to be cancelled after all! There won't be any dancing, but at least we're still going to have some sort of end-of-school celebration.

I can't wait. Things are starting to look up.

* * *

I can't believe it, we're back at home, in self-quarantine this time!

Ewan went out with his friends to a bubble tea restaurant and someone who has COVID was also there at the same time. So he's now considered a casual contact. And because he's a casual contact we all have to get tested and quarantine.

Stupid Ewan! Stupid bubble-tea! Stupid COVID!

* * *

Okay, everything seems to be getting back to normal. Again. Our self-isolation period is over and none of us got COVID, which was good, although I feel like I've been kept prisoner in a psycho ward. Anytime one of us happened to sneeze, or cough, or even just clear our throat, someone else would call out, 'Corona!' Like we were a vampire or something.

It was totally mental.

I'm at Grandma's now. She's going to alter my formal dress because when I tried it on again recently, I discovered that it's a bit tight around the middle (probably from all those lovely, jubbly desserts). She also made me a headband with a feather to complete my Roaring Twenties look. Mum doesn't sew and, in any case, it's a good excuse to visit Grandma. I haven't seen her much this year.

James has tagged along because Grandma made some face masks for him and needs to check the size of his head. She's made heaps of masks already but they're only made to fit adults. I told her they should still fit James because he's got a big mouth, but she wants to check anyway, just to be sure.

Lots of people have donated odd bits of material for her to use and she's literally made hundreds of masks. She says it gave her something to do during lockdown. The mask she's sewn for James is apparently made from a Spiderman pillowcase.

While she's stitching the elastic loops on James' mask, he asks her if she was alive during the Spanish Flu.

I have to correct him, of course. 'She's not that old, James.'

But Grandma just smiles at him. 'Why do you ask?'

'Well, we were learning about the Spanish Flu and how this pandemic is a lot like it and I was wondering, Grandma, if you were alive back then and if it was the same, really.'

So Grandma sits back in her chair, and I know from the look on her face that she's about to embark on one of her long, story-telling sessions.

'Actually James, your sister is right. I wasn't alive back then, but I was alive during the Second World War in England. I was only really little, but we had masks back then too. They were different to the masks we have to wear now. The masks we had to carry around were gas masks. They were big and black and covered our whole face, even our eyes!'

James raises his eyebrows at this.

'And do you know what, us children had little, round, sticking-up ears attached to our mask and a big, red tongue under the snout. We called them Mickey Mouse masks.'

'Cool,' James says.

'But you didn't have to wear them all the time, did you Grandma?' I ask.

'No,' she shakes her head.

I feel a tiny bit smug about this fact, because we have to wear them all the time if we go out.

But then she adds, 'But they were quite heavy and you always had to have them with you. And we still went to school, we didn't get to stay home like you. And sometimes, when we heard the air-raid siren going off we had to grab our masks and run into the shelter under the school.'

'Were you scared, Grandma?' James asks in a whisper.

'Oh, no,' she laughs, 'it was all just an adventure for us children. Probably the same as what lockdown is like for you. A big adventure.'

James nods and happily tries on his Spiderman mask.

Grandma looks at me and winks and I smile back. But deep down I feel bad about all my complaining.

I'm pretty sure lockdown is nothing compared to hiding in a bomb shelter and these face masks are really nothing like a gas mask.

***

At last, it's here! The formal is on tonight – for sure. No cancellations. And I've finished all my exams. My last year of school is almost over. Forever.

Mum and Dad haven't stopped taking photos of me and my friends. Mum even got a little bit teary and hugged us all, but we told her not to make us cry because it would ruin our makeup.

But we did anyway, so we all ended up huddled in the bathroom, reapplying our fake eyelashes.

My dress looks really great and thanks to Grandma it fits me perfectly now. The funny thing is, when I told my friends about it, everyone admitted that they had to get their dresses altered too. So we had a good laugh about that.

Dad's going to drive us to the formal in our old, crappy car. It's not the vintage car we were hoping for but at least we have a vintage driver now. Ha ha.

The best thing is, the Queensland government lifted restrictions again today, which means we can dance at the formal tonight. The timing is perfect for once! I've never felt so happy to hear an announcement.

Also, there's been lots of talk in the news lately about vaccines. Apparently, they should be available next year – so more good news. Everyone will get vaccinated and this horrible pandemic will finish very soon! Maybe I'll even be able to go travelling next year.

It's going to be a great night. The perfect end to a crazy year. One that I'm pretty sure I'll never forget.

Goodbye school. Goodbye 2020.

I'm so looking forward to 2021.

RACHEL BRISCOE is a mum of three boys and spent much of the pandemic homeschooling them against her will. Two of her sons are teenagers, so she was aware of the growing concern in the high school community regarding the possible cancellation of the Year 12 graduation and formal celebrations. This story is based on a fictional teenage daughter's experience during those anxious periods of lockdowns.

To breathe or not to breathe

YVONNE FEIN

1 January 2020
Okay Rose. Listen up. Only three resolutions this year. Last year you made eight and kept, well – I can't lie to my own bloody diary – none. So here goes:
    Sign up to the gym – three sessions a week
    Water aerobics at Harold Holt pool, Wednesdays
    Enrol in Hawthorn Road watercolour class, Tuesdays.
    Oh, and better do something with the kid.
    Take him to library story time, Thursdays.
    Feeling good. Feeling great. This is going to be *the* year!

15 January 2020
Something came up, missed first week of gym. And library story time. Dropped the kid off at his nan's instead. He loves going there. Calls her scary old lady. Crying hysterically when I left.

25 January 2020
Big argument trying to get a refund on my gym membership. They were pretty snooty about it seeing I hadn't even been there a week. Bethany keeps her jogging up four mornings a week. Don't know how she does it, but she also keeps her nagging up. Says I

should join her. That's never going to happen. For a best friend she can get pretty annoying. But probably the fittest school librarian around, though she complains a lot. Always telling me how the bratty third-graders make every book they touch sticky. And that whenever she mentions it to Mr Hodson, he just laughs and says, Why don't you wipe down the covers with a damp cloth? I'm sure you do that sort of thing at home … I say, That's misogyny. She says, For someone like me, misogyny's got an awful lot of syllables. Especially seeing as I do all the housework, take care of the kid twenty-four-seven and serve Truelove dinner every night the moment he walks through the door.

Later that night
Washing the dishes. Truelove calls out, Hey Darl, come watch this. He does that whenever he thinks there's something on the telly I'd be interested in. Seems some lurgy from China made its way down here to Oz, to Victoria, even. They're saying some tourist brought it with him and it's like the flu, only more contagious.

30 January 2020
Hey Darl, come watch this. I dry my hands. Seems the lurgy's spreading around the world and the WHO's declared it's something they're calling a Public Health Emergency of International Concern. I say, Are they going to write a song about it? He says, No Darl, not *that* WHO and I'm starting to wonder where his sense of humour went. It's been MIA for a while now.

20 February 2020
Finally got round to taking the kid to story time. Remembered why I used to hate going. Other people's kids.

29 February 2020
Watercolour class a bust. Could not stand the teacher. Week 3

and she started rabbiting on about painting nudes rather than landscapes. I've always wanted to do those pastel-y colours over pencil outlines, sort of pale and sad and lovely. Nudes not what I signed up for. Truelove said, I don't know Darl. I wouldn't mind a nude or two here and there. He thought that was funny.

11 March 2020
Not sure about this water aerobics thing. Water's freezing and all the people doing it are at least eighty-five not-out.

Later that night
Okay, now Truelove says the lurgy's official name is COVID-19, and the WHO has declared it's a pandemic. It's gone right around the world, he says, from one little germ in Guandong. I say, The WHO's got a long way to go to the top of the charts from number 19. No response. Hey, I say, that was a good one. Not even a smile for my trouble.

26 March 2020
We've gone from zero to over five-hundred cases in two weeks and three old people have carked it. It spreads from droplets of other people's breath and saliva or something. And it gets on things you touch. So everybody's been buying up this hand sanitiser and now it's scarcer than swearwords in church. You're supposed to stay home except for the supermarket, doctor, school and exercise. Don't get why exercise is okay. When Bethany jogs she spurts out enough droplets to infect everyone from here to Tasmania.

Scarcer than swearwords in church. I like that.
Scarcer than meat in a meat pie.
Scarcer than ham sandwiches in a vegan's lunchbox.
Scarcer than unicorns in Noah's Ark.
Scarcer than red blood cells in a leukaemia patient … that got dark quickly.

31 March 2020
Okay, now we've done it. We've pissed off Headmaster Dan because not everyone's *obeying the rules.* LOCKDOWN. No visitors to the home so can't even drop the kid off at his nan's. All parks and beaches etc. closed. Even gyms. Should've waited longer to ask for my refund. No footy. Truelove's beside himself. Kids have to learn from home by computer and Truelove's even saying it's too dangerous to send the kid to childcare. He'll be working from home too, so that means I'll be making him breakfast, dinner *and* lunch.

18 April 2020
It's like Harry Potter waved his wand in Woolies and Coles and all the toilet paper disappeared. What is *wrong* with people? Back in the day when we still knew how to have fun, Truelove and I used to spend a couple of weeks camping in the Grampians every year. We only took two six-packs with us, and one of those was beer.

30 April 2020
Could really get into that Brett Sutton. For a Chief Medical Officer he's pretty cool. Sometimes when he's had a few days of high numbers he comes on the telly looking exhausted with this three-day stubble. Even cooler. But best is that photo of him floating around on the internet. He looks about in his early twenties, got the best long hair, a knockout smile and I reckon I can smell the weed from here.

27 May 2020
Truelove only comes out of his man cave to eat and sleep. And complain. Today it was, The house is a pigsty, when was the last time you gave the kid a bath and would it kill you to run the vacuum cleaner under my desk?

    Me going quietly crazy.

Kid going noisily crazy.

Not much fun writing these pages lately. Not much of an urge.

10 June 2020
Suppose I should have written earlier because restrictions eased halfway through May and even more ten days ago. Hardly makes much difference except, wait for it, we can go fishing. The only fishing I do is down at Stavros's shop. He has great blue-eye. And now I suppose I could drop the kid off at his nan's if I wanted to, but Truelove says he doesn't want his mum exposed any more than she needs to be. Still, to be honest, I wouldn't have the heart to leave him there these days. He's even started crying when I leave to go to the supermarket. He only knows about two-dozen words but he really knows things aren't right.

25 June 2020
Things are seriously opening up – cinemas, restaurants, bars. Not like before, but still. I want to take the kid to see Peppa Pig but Truelove says no way. Too dangerous. Suppose he's right. I do take him out in the pusher most days – the kid, not Truelove – when it's not raining. It's *some*thing to do and usually I'll buy him a treat from the 7-Eleven. Kid's putting on weight, Truelove says, himself always trim as a frenched lamb chop.

My fault?

I didn't say that.

He didn't have to.

1 July 2020
I've taken to making sure I've got plenty of $2.00 coins in my purse. Every time I take the kid for a walk, I see these mainly guys, but sometimes women, sitting on the footpath holding up signs asking for money for a bed for a night or for food. Makes me feel like shit. Found myself tipping three coins, $6.00,

into their caps in one go. Got to be a *little* bit careful. Some dick-brain walked past me one time and said loud enough for everyone to hear, He'll only spend it on drugs or booze. Not your business, I say, but under my breath because he looks kind of big and nasty. Just don't tell your dad, I say to the kid. I think I'd keep doing it whatever Truelove said, but what if the kid caught it from one of those guys. They don't wear masks. Neither does the kid.

15 July 2020
Really getting into reading stuff on the Internet. Nothing much else to do. And watching the news on the telly from start to finish. Hey Darl, I call out to Truelove, come watch this. He doesn't hear. Hiding in his man cave. Seems they're cutting JobSeeker back to $400 per week. Cannot believe it. I google stuff. I'm getting good at it. Seems Treasurer Josh is on $8,500 per week while PM Scotty's on more than $10,500 per week. What's wrong this picture, I ask the kid. He doesn't answer but looks disgusted.

Later that night
This is inedible, says Truelove. I think he's saying incredible until he tips his dinner along with his plate into the rubbish bin.

30 July 2020
Best yet. Now they're locking up people in their commission houses without enough warning for them to stock up on necessaries from the supermarket and chemist. Only they don't call them commission houses any more. It's all, 'public housing' or 'long-term rental social housing.' Everybody knows it's housing for poor people, mainly migrants or jobless. Truelove says they're lucky not to be on the streets. I go a little bit looney tunes. How'd you like to be shut up in a one-bedroom house, five kids and a dog you can't even take for a walk? Truelove says, Who asked them to have 5 kids and why would people like that even need a bloody dog?

10 August 2020
I'm reading to the kid more than I used to. Well I never really used to, and now I remember why. That stuff is boring as. I look online for funny books to order for him but they take ages to get here. I do find some pretty crazy stuff on the National Geo site ... Hey kid, listen to this: did you know that the Common Swift never leaves the sky, not even to *sleep*. The kid samples a bit of crusty pumpkin from the corner of his high chair. Spits it out. Well how about *this*? More male giraffes are gay than straight. He shrugs. So I try with, You know when they say 'out on a limb?' Well it comes from when girl koalas don't want to play mummies and daddies with boy koalas so they try to escape by running right to the end of the branch – get it? Out on a limb. He gets this expression on his face that says, You made that up, and starts to laugh like a drain. Sometimes I wonder about him. Don't tell your dad about the gay giraffe thing, I say. He goes back to the dried pumpkin. We have a secret life.

Later that night
Kid starts to cry. He's been nightmaring every so often for the last few weeks. I bring him into our bed and we cuddle up. Truelove says I'm spoiling him but I think I'm needing to hold him as much as he's needing to be held.

Even later
He's settled down but now I can't get to sleep. Start thinking that anything with more than two legs isn't under lockdown. Except for zoo animals. They're always under lockdown. And then I think about those half-drowned refugees who once paid some crook their life savings to bring them over here by boat. And now they're locked down too. Me? I'd choose the zoo. Truelove says I'm reading too much, says my brain's not cut out for it.

19 July 2020
Masks compulsory everywhere. Bethany's spitting chips. Says there's no evidence that masks help reduce infection. I send her a couple of links; she says I'm just being deceived by big business and the mask-producing industry. Apart from the fact that she's a bloody idiot, I'm seriously scared to take the kid just about anywhere anymore. They say kids hardly get it and if they do, it's never that serious. But kids have *died*.

26 July 2020
People wearing masks under their chins, under their noses, on their foreheads. Brett Sutton has a real go. Says, you wouldn't wear your bicycle helmet on your elbow, would you? Is he terrific or what?

2 August 2020
LOCKDOWN. Again. For at least six weeks. Thousands sick, hundreds dead. How's it all going to end? When's it all going to end?

13 August 2020
They're talking about this vaccine that could actually knock COVID on its head. Some mob at Oxford called AstraZeneca is getting together with the Americans.

31 August 2020
They've started clinical trials. For some reason our overpaid PM seems to think he should get the credit.

8 September 2020
Stopped trials. I think someone died.

13 September 2020
Started trials again. Said it was safe now. If they could just make *some*thing to cure this thing. I'd take the kid to story time,

to the park, to kiddie swimming lessons, to Gymbaroo, to the Collingwood Petting Zoo, to Maccas – you name it. I'd take him everywhere and anywhere every day of the week, including Sundays, just so long as I could stop thinking he might get it.

15 September 2020
Nan's got it. She says it's not serious. Not that she'd know but the GP agrees. She's a pretty fit old coot and he's organised the council nurse to pop by every morning. I reckon she'll be fine.

21 September 2020
She's recovered, tested negative but says she can't taste or smell anything. That sounds pretty grim. Truelove wants to go over there. I say he'd be putting us all at risk. He says you only care about yourself. I say what about the kid? He says what *about* the kid? And rolls the rock shut on his man cave.

26 September 2020
Bethany says you don't know what chemical poisons they're putting into those vaccines. No way I'm letting any of that stuff into my body. It's all about the big bucks and Big Pharma. You'd be crazy to trust them. Still trying to work out who the big farmers are.

10 October 2020
Exhausted! Kid started crying in his pusher about twenty minutes before we got home. Wouldn't stop. Had to pick him up and carry him the rest of the way. Both of us covered in snot and melted choc. I go to the bathroom to wash us down and see Truelove's shaving kit and toothbrush not there. Wander out and see his laptop's not there, his Black and Decker tool-kit's gone and his golfclubs also AWOL. I guess that means Truelove's AWOL too. My Mum (RIP) used to say you can marry 'em, feed 'em and fuck 'em but you can't ever trust 'em. You open your own bank account Rosie my girl, make sure

you do. And she put her money where her mouth was. Sent twenty bucks my way every week. And before the kid, when I worked at Myer, I put away some money too. Even managed to scrounge some from the weekly housekeeping. I've got a fair bit salted away.

28 October 2020
Kid's got COVID. He could hardly breathe last night. I called triple zero but had to wait twenty minutes before I got through to the ambulance. Scariest thing I've ever done, sitting next to him in the back of that van, siren blaring. They took him straight to Emergency and I'm running behind a nurse who's saying you're not allowed in here. I'm yelling I'm his parent, his single parent, his mother. I'm all he's got! And she finally twigs and lets me through. The doc doesn't take long to decide. They anaesthetise him and intubate him. At about 4:00 am I fall asleep holding his hand. In the morning, through half-closed eyes so they won't know I'm awake, I watch and listen to the doc consulting with the nurses. He's shaking his head. He says the kid might not make it. His name's Elijah, I whisper.

4 November 2020
Still in ICU. I don't wash or eat or even sleep anymore. The nurses tell me I need to take a break, that I'm no good to the kid if I crack up. But there's nothing they can say or do that can make me leave him alone with just them.

10 November 2020: Midnight
Machines and screens start to flash and beep. Someone yells Code Blue! Like on bloody *Grey's anatomy*. Nurses rush in followed by a doctor I've never seen before and then a whole team of experts comes in. They start working on the kid too. I know what they're doing. They're trying to bring 'the patient' back to life, restart his heart. I shut my eyes. Can't watch. But he's been that sick for that long his heart stops a second time.

11 November 2020: 2.00 am
Now the nurses find the one thing they can actually say that will make me leave. He's gone dear. We're so sorry.

Later
I go home. I drink half a bottle of Truelove's good scotch. Then I vomit and vomit and can't stop vomiting. And when I ring Truelove I'm still drunk. He comes straight over and we cry and hold each other. Then we stop and look at each other. There's nothing left. He leaves. I don't try to stop him.

23 November 2020
Funeral.

14 December 2020
Can't write.
   Just.
   Nothing.

1 January 2021
Elijah, I whisper.

YVONNE FEIN holds a BA (Hons) in Literature, an MA in History and a Diploma of Creative Writing. She has had two adult novels published (*April Fool*, Hodder Headline, *The Torn Messiah*, Hybrid Publishers) and one YA novel (*Rachel Racing Time*, Third Space). Her collection of short stories (*Choose Somebody Else*) was recently published by Wild Dingo Press. She has written scripts for film and theatre, as well as editing two literary journals. Her commitment to social action saw her conducting creative writing workshops for people with mental illness and advocating for those with disability by writing and performing stand-up comedy to raise public awareness.

Moth drift

KEREN HEENAN

There are empty buses in the quiet, empty streets. Trains rocking by, heard but not seen, yet she knows they would be quiet, empty train carriages. There is something sad about those buses and trains, their hollow intention, futile repetition of well-worn paths. She feels for the drivers. Then remembers, at least they have a job. Her own job reduced to one day hunched over the computer screen, scrolling through emails for *essential communications only*. But she's not sure what *essential* is anymore.

Life in the time of pandemic isolation lends itself to contemplation, but contemplation without form. She wonders about this – can contemplation have form? Thought on a trajectory of discovery. In which case there is potential for form, or change of form. Or could it just be random thought? Then, as if on cue, her thoughts dissolve into a blur of meaning and she has no clear understanding of the path that had taken her somewhere – partly there at least.

The balcony allows her to sit back in the shadows and watch. But there is very little movement today. The newsagent at the end of the street has a few customers. One at a time they enter and leave with their paper or some stationery item. The florist, dress shop and travel agency opposite are closed. She stands and leans on the railing, looks in both directions. The street is still, the air cold. An empty chip packet tumbles along the footpath gathering speed, then stops suddenly against a pole. Hangs there wrapped around the metal. Wind moves on and the packet falls limply back to the pavement. She watches a while to see if it continues on its way, wonders who'd eaten the chips, were they alone, did they toss it aside or was it blown from a bin? Then she realises the nonsense value of those thoughts, randomly taking her nowhere. She strokes her arm lightly with her fingers in large, slow circles, floating briefly in a dream-like haze.

Last night she'd watched the moths at the porch light after dark, moth dust drifting down. *Moth. Drift.* She'd said the words slowly on an outward breath, soft and whispered words like the silence in the room. These are the days of moth drift, she thought, of dust settling quietly through the filtered light, silence humming around her. She has made them her words – *moth, drift* – special words to allay anxiety, to feel one with this new small and quiet world. She says them now, in her head, drops her shoulders which she realises have been hunched up towards her ears. Leans for a moment breathing quietly, then pushes herself away from the balcony.

Inside, she pulls on runners, drags her hair up into a ponytail, and stretches her calves, palms against the door. She's not a runner, but today she will run through the quiet streets to the park a couple of blocks away. It seems an easy thing to do – run. There may be others there. Keeping the regulated distance, of course. People who will smile, say hello, throw a ball for their dog.

It seems a lifetime of practising the skill of communicating with others has disappeared. How does one do it, that social chat. So long now, wandering from room to room, speaking her thoughts out loud, to the walls, to the cobweb in the corner that she should get rid of but can't work up the interest now.

In the bathroom she looks in the mirror, pulls a face twisting her mouth to one side, puffs out her cheeks, moves her jaw from side to side. Sighs. She notes the mirror needs cleaning. Later, she'll do it later.

She wonders, how do you think about things that no longer happen. There used to be longing, hope, desire for something possibly out of reach unless you take action, or give up on the wanting. But now, there is no point to wishing, to longing for something that could be. Now, everything slides away into uncertainty so that the longing is made sad instead of hopeful. How to think about the things that cannot be now, without a wave of melancholy floating you into no thought, so you can be saved from yourself, your own annihilating grief. Grief comes from *something* happening. This grief is from nothingness – from stillness, silence, inaction – from that *thing with feathers* that has long flown away.

Around her the walls seem to encroach, wrapping about her like earth, like she is far beneath the surface. She lies on the carpet, makes herself long, arms stretched out above her head, and wormlike she moves along the floor.

Until she remembers: she has something to do; she is going for a run. She will also check on the gnome. Some neighbours have a gathering of gnomes in their front garden, the little figures always standing stiffly in a huddle, as if in conversation. When the pandemic first hit and isolation and social distancing became the norm, the gnomes were placed further apart. Then one or two were placed face down. As restrictions eased, they recovered and stood tall again. She's been noting the movement of the gnomes when she passes by on her walks. Last night she'd taken an old chipped and paint-faded gnome from behind the pot plants on the balcony, tied a face mask on him and placed him amongst the gathered gnomes, but at a distance – a stranger, looking for company. She'd given him a tender pat, adjusted his face mask and left. Later she stood for a moment in the quiet of her kitchen and imagined some sort of gnomish welcome and initiation.

Outside, she turns left, slows her steps past the gnome house, sees her little fellow, mask slightly askew, but still there. And someone has moved him closer, placed masks on a couple of the others. She smiles, gives a little fist pump and moves away. There is a steep rise up the street towards the park. She does not run up the hill, waits until the footpath flattens out, sets up a slow jog. She feels her calves, her thighs, already signalling their annoyance. Looks down at the path in front of her, not at the distance yet to be covered. Leaves in the shape of letters of the alphabet lie flattened on the concrete. Leaf shape shadows remain on the pavement where a leaf has blown away, the pattern like bird-prints on sand. She stops, squinting at the pavement to better take in the shapes and patterns. One shape is less leaf-like, perhaps small wings outstretched. She imagines a moth, the rain-dampened wings anchored to the concrete. And the wind, drying, restoring flight. She glances up at the sky, as if to see the moth rising from its damp limbo. *Mo-oth – dri-ift*; the rhythm of the lengthened syllables thrums in her head. She moves on, watching her feet, the scattered leaves, broken twigs.

At the park there are people and dogs, people with children, couples strolling, boys on bicycles flashing past or splashing through puddles around the oval. The play equipment is taped off like a murder scene; no one defies the *do not use* signs. Everyone stands in conversation, 1.5 metres apart, unless they are family. She stretches her quad muscles the way she has seen footballers stretch before a game. She knows she is fooling nobody. Half way around the oval she will slow to a walk, her breathing will be ragged and she may be coughing, which will alarm people nearby – *don't cough, don't blow your nose, don't puff,* she reminds herself.

It is possible that sometime soon everyone will need to wear a face mask when they are out. She cannot imagine what that will look like – streets of masked people. Anonymous people. She feels anonymous now, even without a face mask. Invisible, overlooked, lurching around the oval and trying to set up a comfortable rhythm. Even the dogs ignore her in pursuit of their sticks or balls. Groups of parents with prams stand talking; people are still being *social*, and they still will be social with their masks on – respectfully social.

In preparation for retirement, she'd cut her work hours back to two days. But she doesn't like to use that word, *retirement*. Makes her feel old, no longer able to offer anything to her colleagues. The reduction in her work load shrunk her social life in ways she'd never seen coming. And now, with her hours cut back to just one day at home, the pandemic has tightened that shrunken world, shifting the walls in closer, boarding up the windows.

She looks down at her feet, first one then the other passing into and out of view, metres gained. There are puddles and patches of bald, slippery surface, dog droppings and sticks to dodge. She focuses on the ground in front, keeps the rhythm of breath and footstep going: one breath in, three out with her steps. Reaches the point where she'd promised herself a rest, level with the line of scraggly wattles, and stops, breathing hard. Looks up to the low-slung clouds, a convoy of birds passing in a V. She imagines the traces they would leave in the air, if they could, like footprints on sand – how the air would be filled with their wing-swept trails. She watches until the birds, still in formation, pass out of view.

A kelpie dog chases a ball, leaping dramatically to the high point as the ball bounces. Its compact body arches and hovers in precision-perfect motion. A young man in a hoodie has a plastic implement, like a long-handled ladle, and he's scooping up the ball and tossing it relentlessly, the dog returning in a rush to deposit the ball at his feet. *Get a dog*, they'd all said, when she'd cut her hours back. But she'd never had a dog, wasn't sure of what it entailed – the costs, the barking, she'd need a larger garden. The perceived problems overwhelmed her and she'd left the thinking for *later*. There's always *later*.

Others had urged her to go on a dating site, get out, meet someone. But she hadn't asked for advice, had felt perfectly fine about all this new time on her hands. 'I think I rather like my own company,' she'd said to one friend. But that was before the pandemic had slammed the door while she was still testing out the waters of her new quiet life.

In the shadow of the trees her skin is tingling with the chill, the sweat drying. She listens in to conversations of those nearby, hearing the pronouns – *ours, we*. Imagines, if they spoke to her she may conjure a partner, perhaps adult children, grand-children, it won't matter, they don't know her. She will be, in their minds, going home to plan dinner, phone the grandkids, wait for her partner's return from work. She will be just like them – wings clipped by the pandemic, struggling along, *but it's okay, we have each other*.

A couple are teaching their young daughter, all in pink on a pink bike, how to ride – 'That's okay, you're okay,' when she falls, and the encouraging, 'Yay, you're doing it,' when she succeeds. 'Just keep pedalling, that's all you have to do,' and she does.

A man, two children and a dog stand nearby in a patch of pale sunlight. The dog prances lightly from foot to foot anticipating some stick-throwing action. The man tosses the stick and the dog races away, swoops on the stick and sits gnawing. The man laughs, shakes his head, looks across at her and shrugs. 'Loves the chase but hasn't learnt the next step,' he says. She nods, smiles. Wonders again about having a dog, a sizeable backyard.

The man squats and rummages around in a large bag, brings out drink bottles for the kids. A train rushes by behind them and she turns to watch it pass – empty carriages gliding by. The man takes out a bag of lollies. 'Snakes!' the kids shriek. He opens the packet and holds it out for them. They take one each, clamping teeth over the colourful sweet, stretching it out in front of their faces, laughing. He takes one himself, pushing it into his mouth, looks

Moth drift

over at her again and holds out the bag then pulls it back. 'That's probably not allowed, eh. We'll make it a virtual offer,' and he holds the bag open but close to his hip. She smiles, mimes taking the sweet, putting it in her mouth and chewing. He laughs, his eyes crinkling as he throws his head back a little.

Her mouth floods with saliva at the thought of a lime green snake, her favourite. A warmth rises in her chest. These are the days of moth drift, she thinks, and she is the moth, rising to the light.

KEREN HEENAN has won several Australian short story awards, placed second in the Fish Prize, and was a winner in the Griffith Review Novella Project VII. She has been published in *Griffith Review, Overland, Island, Award Winning Australian Writing,* and others, and in anthologies in the US, UK and in Ireland.

Unmasked

KELLY SIMPSON

'Do you have anything in charcoal?'

I swallow my impatience. 'Nope.'

'Beige?'

I shake my head at the webcam.

My mother sits back on the couch, and stares off into the distance. My dad readjusts his iPad. It must be propped up on their coffee table.

'Whatever you have is fine with me, bloss,' he says.

'Yep, I know.' And I do.

I hold up the fabric I thought might work. It's a neutral off-white and denim blue *shibori*-style print.

'I know this is blue and white, but I thought it might end up being quite neutral, and it's the right weight.'

A few seconds pass.

'Kathy?' my father prompts, as her gaze remains off to the side.

She shrugs her shoulders.

'Well, I'm making them up tomorrow, so how about I do two for you and post them. Up to you if you wear them.'

'Thanks bloss, that would be great.' My father's eyes slide quickly sideways. Still nothing.

'Okay, well see you next week.' I close down the Skype call.

My dad answers, wearing his new mask.

'Ah, they arrived?'

He removes the elastic strap from one ear. 'Yep, very nice, thank you. I wore it to the shops, and to get your mother's coffee.'

I don't say anything about the coffee. I learned that the hard way during the first lockdown. She doesn't drive, he's eighty-three, and I thought a home coffee machine would reduce the need for a daily trip to get a takeaway skinny cap with two sugars. I found a very smart-looking one, and offered to have it shipped to them.

Nope, that's about as insulting to my mother as suggesting we sign them up for online grocery deliveries. It's a freaking global pandemic, and short of being actual health workers, they cover every one of the high-risk categories.

'So, does the plainer one work for Kathleen?' I ask. I'd carefully contemplated the pattern placement before cutting.

'I can't breathe in them.' Her voice comes from out of shot.

'Okay ...'

My dad slightly shakes his head at me.

I can't help myself. 'Well, we find the pleats quite comfortable. They sort of blouse a little to give you some breathing space. It does take a bit of getting used to, but I'm even fine wearing them on my early morning walk now.'

I think of powering through six kilometres of fast walking and energetic breathing, compared with a twenty-minute trip into the supermarket.

'I guess we have to understand they're part of our lives for the next little while,' I continue.

I can hear the harrumph from off screen.

'Look what Gina sent me,' my mother excitedly exclaims. She holds up a black and ecru mask in a bold Aztec pattern. 'It's nice, isn't it?'

I can't see much difference between my neutral off-white and denim blue, and this, but I go big picture.

'That's kind of her.'

'Yes, well I told her that I only have blue, so she sent me this, and this one.' Another boldly monochromatic patterned mask is flashed across the screen. They are not in the least my mother's greige style.

But hey, if it gets her feeling happier wearing a mask, I can suck it up.

'Great!' I exclaim, summoning cheer squad enthusiasm. I don't ask if she can breathe in it.

I make another batch, and send two more in the controversial fabric to my dad.

My little family is going full colour. We raid my fabric stash for one with a multi-hued rainbow design, and another with Australian banksia in reds, oranges and pinks. We uncover some good-sized remnants of a bold IKEA print with floral shapes from a teepee project. And we find my favourite. A bold fruit pattern filled with grapes, kiwis, pomegranates, watermelons and more.

My daughter is excited and shows her grandparents on the weekly Skype. My dad smiles, but my mother is stony faced. They're not to her liking.

Another week, and I'm surprised my mother is on Skype looking at the screen. Usually the TV is more interesting, or another cigarette over her kitchen bench.

'Look what Maria made me,' she says, holding up a charcoal linen mask.

'Very smart,' I say, nudging my daughter. She catches on, adding her feedback. 'I like the buttons, Nana.'

The edges of the mask fold forwards and are secured with a co-ordinated grey button.

'She's selling them for $35 in a shop in Ivanhoe,' my mother adds.

'Well, that's a great use of her skills,' I say. My mother's friend is a talented seamstress.

'I just wanted charcoal grey,' my mother adds.

'We've gone for lots of colours,' my daughter says, and she dashes to our little stack. She starts holding them up one by one. Vibrant purple, cheerful orange, and hot pink sing out. We can't help but feel good looking at the colours and patterns.

The post arrives. An envelope with padding and lots and lots of sticky tape has my mother's writing, and is addressed to my daughter. She opens it curiously. A tailored face mask. A beige background with a soft, sweet print of a girl in red bathers and a straw hat. Matching buttons.

'Ermm,' my daughter says. 'I mean, I like the girl in the red bathers, but we have a lot of masks, don't we, Mum?' She's puzzled.

'Look what Maria did!' My mother is animated. She holds up one of the masks I made to the iPad camera. The edges have been changed. Instead of pleating sewn into a fixed channel for the elastic, the channel has been re-sewn so the elastic gathers the fabric.

'Your mother finds it easier to breathe in this,' my dad explains.

Same fabrics, same layers. It's the most minor of cosmetic changes.

But it's not her any more. It is me now, who can't seem to breathe.

KELLY SIMPSON writes short fiction and has previously won Stonnington Untitled What's your story and been published in *Award Winning Australian Writing*.

The promise

ZARIN NUZHAT

The plane descended into a thick grey cloud overhanging Hyderabad. Baba pressed his fingers against the window. Alia and I, sixteen and fourteen at the time, leaned back in our seats and gripped our armrests. My stomach dropped. My ears were overcome with a sharp, full sensation. There was a mechanical whir beneath me, and then suddenly the wheels skidded against the runway. 'Welcome to Hyderabad. The local time is ten o'clock …'

Before the plane could come to a halt, a chorus of clicking and shifting filled the cabin as everyone stood up. A flurry of Tamil and Hindi and English and other languages I could not name collided against each other. Baba pulled out his phone. 'You can't do that yet! They said to wait until the plane completely stops,' protested Alia.

Baba waved his hand around the cabin. Most of the other passengers were also yelling into their phones as they shuffled out of their seats. He put the phone to his ear. 'Ma, I'm home.'

* * *

Our home phone rings.

The promise

I turn on my lamp and look up at the clock with bleary eyes. 4 am. No one here in Australia uses our home number any more. My chest grows cold and heavy as someone in our flat picks up the phone. I lay on my back in the still darkness and strain my ears. The minutes tick by.

There is a light knock on my door. I hold my breath.

'Zainab?' My mother's voice is shaky. 'Zainab? There's been a call from India.'

* * *

'I'm never coming to this place ever again.' Tears of frustration were burning behind my eyes. The air was heavy with the sweat and anxiety and excitement of hundreds of strangers.

We stood outside the airport in front of the main gates. In front of us, there was a little driveway where battered taxis and sleek European cars lined up to pick up the incoming travellers. There was a press of bodies all around us. I clung onto Amma's dress in front of me. She in turn kept a white-knuckled grip on Baba's backpack as he waded through the throng of bodies. 'There! I can see Irfan!' he yelled, craning his neck.

Eventually the crowd spat us out and we followed Baba to a silver Toyota. A vaguely familiar man with fuzzy strips of hair on either side of his otherwise bare and shining scalp pulled Baba into an embrace. He blinked down at me and Alia and patted our heads. 'You must all be starving. Amma's cooked up a feast, let's go!'

* * *

My cousin posts a Facebook status. 'Dadi is no longer with us. Please keep her in your prayers.' As I watch my phone screen, the comments section comes alive. Sad reacts galore. OMG! I'm so sorry. I hope your family is doing okay.

Baba's grief is a foreign creature. It seems wrong that the sound of his sobs should slide under the bedroom door. I have never seen Baba cry. Sometimes, when the home phone rings and delivers us the news that a distant relative has passed, he shakes his head and says, 'We are all heading that way.' Then he would put on his uniform, pick up the keys to his taxi, and go to work. Today, though, there has been no pause in his sadness.

I take a breath and step out of my room. Soft blue-orange light filters through the curtains on the kitchen window across from my room. Somewhere not too far away, birds begin their morning song, unfazed by the grim darkness that has settled into our flat.

I knock briefly on my parents' door. 'Come in, Zainab,' Amma replies.

My parents' room is dark, cast in a dim yellow haze by two bedside lamps. Bills are piled in a neat stack on both bedside tables. A garishly colourful floral screensaver flashes on the monitor over on the computer table squashed into the corner of the room. The room is too small to begin with, but with all four of us in it now the air is stale and stifling.

Baba does not look up as I come in. He sits on his side of the bed. His knees are drawn up, and his eyes are fixed on his hands resting on them. Tufts of dark hair stick up haphazardly on his head. Sitting there, with his shoulders folded in and his eyes wide and dark, he seems unbearably young. I want to leave the room.

Alia is sitting at Baba's feet, tears streaming silently down her face. Amma sits by his side and rests a hand on his shoulder. 'Come sit,' Amma says softly to me. Baba looks up around the room, startled, until his eyes fall on me. He looks at me blankly for a moment and I stand there, stuck in place with my hand on the cold doorknob. 'Zainab.' His voice breaks as he says my name. His face crumples in on itself. 'Zainab, where is Dadi now?'

As Baba cries, something unlatches within me. When I say, 'I'm so sorry Baba,' my words are broken. There is an aching numbness

The promise

in my chest. I walk over to him and sit next to Alia. He clasps my hand in both his own and holds it to his forehead. His chest heaves as he says – pleads – 'I just wanted to see her one more time.'

* * *

I was covered with sweat by the time we had heaved all our suitcases up the stairs to my grandparents' apartment. The door opened and a young woman with a thick gold ring in her left nostril smiled shyly up at us. '*Assalam walaikum*. Sorry – Aunty was waiting for you all but since you were running late, she just stepped into the shower.' She ducked her head and pulled my suitcase away from me.

'*Walaikum salam*. That's okay, we'll get settled in. Alia, Zainab – this is Rohila, she helps your Dadi around the house.'

My breathing seemed to settle as I stepped into the apartment. The black and beige speckled tiles beneath my feet were cool and calming. The heady scent of beef curry and freshly cooked rice drifted enticingly down the hallway. As my family began pulling out clean clothes and washing up, I followed the scent down to the kitchen. Several melamine plates were stacked on the bench. Old newspapers were taped to the wall behind the gas oven, blackened with age. Countless Horlicks jars and biscuit tins lined another bench. Some of their lids were slightly open, revealing spices in all shades of brown and yellow and red. Amongst the biting fragrances of the spices and the smell of lunch, there was also a dancing tinge of coconut oil and baby powder. I closed my eyes and breathed in deeply. The chaos of the morning had been worth it.

'Zainu, my little Zainu!' called Dadi's laughing, lilting voice. 'You are home!'

* * *

The space between the news and whatever comes after is an uncertain, thorny one. I feel clumsy and heavy as I follow Alia to the kitchen to help get something ready for lunch. The fridge whirrs in the corner; it is a trusty old thing that has followed us from flat to flat for as long as I can remember. The tiles sitting around it are chipped and dark with age.

I open up the windows and blinds in the living room. Clumps of dark grey gather in the sky, threatening to unleash a torrent at any moment. The road is dark and slick with rain that has already passed. The sibilant whoosh of cars driving on the wet roads is comforting.

I envy how easily Alia gives into the sadness. As I watch her pull pans out of the cupboard, her bottom lip trembles occasionally. Her dark eyes are distant as she pours oil into a pan. I rifle through the vegetable drawer for onions and potatoes and hand them over to her. Leaning against the bench, I try to conjure images of my grandmother.

A cream-coloured sari with a baby blue border. It is light between my fingers, made soft by washing over and over again throughout the years. Thin, slightly deformed fingers press firmly into my scalp. My knees ache as I kneel on hard tiles, warm legs at my back as someone parts my hair and rubs at my temples. The sweet coolness of coconut oil fills the air around us. I crane my neck back to look up at her face.

'I can't see her.'

'What?' Alia turns around.

'I can't see Dadi. I'm trying, but I can't see her face.'

Alia nods and looks down at the tiles. 'After you were born, we only went back what, twice? Three times at most? You were so small the first couple of times, you wouldn't be able to remember much from then.'

* * *

After lunch, I scrabbled through Amma's little purse of medications and the odd lipstick in search of the key to unlock my suitcase. Amma frowned down at me and told me to be patient. I pulled my purple suitcase, with the dent in one corner, onto the bed. I threw open the lid. Mixed in amongst my clothes were biscuits, chocolates, perfumes, little purses, make up. My suitcase had the most room, so Amma shoved most of the gifts in with my clothes. I pushed aside all the items and threw them on the bed. Amma groaned with frustration. But I'd found it. A tub of peanut butter – the smooth kind, because Dadi didn't like the crunchy kind. I clutched it to my chest and jumped off the bed. I ran to the kitchen, where Dadi was spooning ghee out of a giant vat into a pot filled with steaming rice. 'Dadi! Look what I got you, it's your favourite!'

A soft laugh. She turned around and cupped my cheeks. Her lips were slightly wet as she pressed a kiss to my forehead.

* * *

A cacophony of ringtones echoes throughout our flat, almost without reprieve. I hate the piercing shrieks of my parents' ringtones. My mother often steps out of the room to answer the calls in hushed whispers.

'Yes. Thank you. Please keep her in your prayers.'

'Jamal is so upset. I don't know what to do.'

Joanne is the first to call me. 'I'm so sorry, Zainab. Are you OK?'

'Yeah, I think I'm OK.'

'How is your dad?' Her voice is high-pitched with concern.

Alia walks out of my parents' room and closes the door with a soft click. She holds a plate heaped with food, the spoon still tucked neatly on one side. 'Um, he's struggling.'

'Do you think he'll be able to get an exemption or something to go over for the funeral?'

I try to do the maths. Some of my parents' friends have been trying to get exemptions to see their families as well. At the dinner table, Amma would shake her head and say, 'Lalita's application was rejected' and more recently, 'Muni has been waiting for two weeks; she still hasn't heard anything.'

Three nights ago, Baba sat with my laptop at the dining table. He slammed the lid shut without warning and buried his head in his hands. 'Tickets are $5,200 dollars. Each. One way.'

Even in the best-case scenario, I know that there is no way Baba could get there soon enough. I know that in the old family apartment, Baba's brothers have gathered to discuss arrangements for the *Janazah*, the final prayer. Somewhere in Hyderabad, a stranger may already be marking out a grave site; soil is being lifted in the air and pushed aside to make room for my Dadi.

'Probably not. My grandma has to be buried by sunset today.'

For a moment, there is silence on the other end of the call. Finally, Joanne says, 'Oh … I didn't realise it all happens so fast.' There is more silence, and I don't know how to fill it. 'Let me know if you need anything, okay Zainab? I'm always here if you need to talk.'

I want to tell her that I can't see my Dadi's face. I am afraid that the memory of her had started to fade long before today. 'Thanks Joanne,' I reply, and hang up.

The home phone rings. Alia and I watch the little orange light flashing on the extension set in the living room. My fingers are clammy as I press the answer button.

'Hello?'

'Bhabi? *Assalam walikum*. It's Irfan.' The words are rough and clipped. I do not recognise the voice, but I know the name belongs to Baba's younger brother.

'Sorry, it's Zainab. I can give it to Amma.'

'Oh.' An awkward laugh that sounds more like a cough. 'Do you remember me? It's Irfan Kaka. Listen. It's very important you pray for your Dadi, at least, if you're not here.'

The promise

'Yes Kaka. I am. We're all praying for her.'

I knock on the door and go in. Baba has stopped crying. He sits cross-legged on his side of the bed, staring down at his clasped hands in front of him. I tell Amma that Irfan Kaka is on the phone. She closes her eyes for a moment and inhales sharply, before reaching a hand out for the phone.

'Do you want to talk to him?' Amma asks Baba, who shrugs. She takes the phone and puts it on speaker.

'*Assalam walaikum*, Irfan bhabi.'

'*Walaikum salam*, bhabi. Ma is no more.'

'I'm so sorry. We're all devastated, and Jamal is still shocked.'

The line crackles, and when Irfan Kaka's voice returns, it is piercing and loud. 'Yes, well we're all together at our house and we've been praying all morning. Jamal, are you there? Ma was unwell for so long. She just wanted to see you one last time.'

Amma and I both look at Baba. His hands are shaking in his lap. Amma takes another deep breath and replies in a low voice, 'I know. There's not been a day that Jamal hasn't tried looking for flights. But Australia is locked down, it's so hard to—'

'I'm not just talking about the pandemic, bhabi. Jamal has a good job. He should've come twice or three times even before the pandemic.'

I want to tell Irfan Kaka that last night Baba came home at 2 am, even though he was due to finish at 11pm. When I called him to tell him it was unsafe, he said, 'Just a few more rides won't hurt, Zainab.' Each night that he takes his shoes off at the front door, the dark creases under his eyes are deeper and his grey driver's uniform hangs more loosely on his shoulders.

'With all due respect, Irfan Bhai, Jamal has been sending back money every single week. He always tries his best and—' Baba puts a hand on Amma's, and takes the phone from her.

'Forgive me, Irfan. It has not been easy for me, but I know that is not an excuse.'

'Yes, well, I wish you could still ask Ma for forgiveness. But she's gone now. The *Janazah* will be after the afternoon prayer, at 1 pm our time.'

'Will you video call us during the *Janazah*? Zainab will give you her WhatsApp details.' Baba pleads into the phone. 'I just want to see her one more time.'

* * *

The camera shakes in time with my uncle's footsteps. The images pause and distort in zig zags without warning. 'I don't have much data,' he warns. 'I don't know when the line will cut out.' As he approaches I see something white and thin laid out on the floor. I see the narrow end of it first, two feet pointing towards the sky.

My uncle stands still and swings the camera up to the face. I almost see it, a flash of something yellow-white, before I whip my head to the side.

Baba grips the phone in his hands and cries, 'Allah! Allah, take care of Ma. I'm so sorry. Forgive me, Ma.' From the corner of my eye I see him press his fingers to his lips, then to the phone screen. He passes the phone to Alia and Amma to say their goodbyes.

When they pass the phone to me, I shake my head and push it away. The air in the room squeezes me from all sides. There are shards of glass in my throat. I step down from the bed and stumble out the door. The wall is cold against my back as I crouch against it, my knees against my chest. My hands shake. My face is hot with tears. I can feel my face twist into the ugly crying I didn't know I was still capable of. I lean my head back against the wall and close my burning eyes.

* * *

The promise

I succumbed to the smell of coconut oil. I did not fight or try to look back as calloused fingertips pressed into my scalp. Our flight back to Australia was booked for tomorrow; I knew this would be the last time in a few years I would get to sit at Dadi's feet like this. Her voice washes over me. Her village accent never fades, no matter how long she lived in the city.

'There, doesn't that feel nice?' she asked. She grabbed a comb from beside me and began to brush my hair. 'Zainu, can you promise me one thing before you leave tomorrow?'

'Yes, Dadi?'

'Come back to me when you've finished high school. Show me all the beautiful things you've accomplished for yourself. I will have a big hug saved up for you.'

I tipped my head back and grinned. Her hazel eyes twinkled back at me. 'Of course I will, Dadi.'

ZARIN NUZHAT is a Bangladeshi Australian writer currently residing in Queensland. She is inspired by the beautiful, sometimes heartbreaking, but always inspiring tales of bravery and hard work that are the bones of her community. When she is not reading or writing stories or drinking tea, you can find her working as a doctor at a local hospital.

Bearing up

FRANCES SENSI

Bears on chairs
It started as a 'Spoonville' moment. An action to jumpstart me from the pervasive *Groundhog day* inertia, an after-effect of the long Victorian lockdown. I placed a teddy bear on a child's chair at the end of my driveway. Mr Bear held a cheery sign, 'All the best for the next week. STAY WELL.'

Why did I do that? 'You have always said you need time to write,' I conversed with myself. 'So, here it is', I continued. 'Go USE this pause in your normal busy-busy life,' I told Me sternly.

I moved my desk and computer to the front room as, from its panelled window which creates framed living 'pictures', I could view the increasing foot traffic and less-frequent motor traffic. I also needed to expand my involvement in a suddenly reduced world. I began to notice people stopping to read the sign. I need more 'interest' in my day, I thought, as I slogged to keep motivated to write. So I decided to develop the project.

I unpacked our children's toys, finding the dress up box with the nurse cap and aprons which I had sewn for my girls. These, combined with the medical case, outfitted a nurse. During an easing of the number of kilometres allowed from home, I met my daughter at a park halfway between our homes and got her firefighter bears. My police officer niece gave me her police bear. A neighbour doing a clean-out gave me two huge bears, one wearing a hand-knitted Australia jumper. On hard waste, I found more children's chairs.

Soon, I had up to six bears across the end of the driveway. I knew they would venture no further as they, like us, were under CURFEW – OMG, who would have thought we would experience this in our lifetimes!

My brain cogs kept 'oiled' to provide cheery, inspirational signs for each of the bears to hold. I swapped signs every few days. If I found anything that might add to the diorama, I would add it to the scene.

For instance, I found a good sized, bright-yellow tip truck, so a small bear sat in that.

When the mask mandate came in, my bears responded appropriately to show good example. They realized that compliance is not resignation nor a sign of weakness, but part of an arsenal of preventative and protective practice.

I watched the dog walkers, pram pushers, couples of all ages out and about. Most smiled, nodded, thanked the other for moving aside, even off the footpath. Where did they all come from? I've never seen so many new faces – and no, that's not just me being 'Mrs Mangells' as my daughters call me; I have lived in this house for over thirty years and feel I know the regulars. I see politeness and humour – 'Oh, it's you again!' 'You do the circuit quicker than us.' We apologise if we haven't noticed someone walking behind us causing them to move over.

I grasped that most of us do not physically explore our neighbourhoods. Yes, we have driven many times, around the five, ten, twenty, kilometre radii of our homes, to shop, schools and work. But we were intent and focused on the destination and upcoming task at hand. But now we are walking, ambling, strolling. We are going slower. We wander into courts, local parks, playgrounds, walkways; really view people's yards.

We notice the increase in the rejuvenation of yards and renovation of houses, and some delight in examining the hard waste put out. Is it all because we want to make the most of our 'two hours allowed out', or are we re-learning how to apply our senses to our ambulatory experience?

We wait our turn to go into the shops, then observe till we see a less crowded aisle. I was waiting once in an outdoor queue, each of us appropriately distanced, all wearing masks. A lady turned and exclaimed – to no one in particular – 'God, we're good, aren't we.' My personal thought is that we comply not because we are mandated to, but from an innate consideration of others.

Share bears
From my vantage point behind my one-way view tinted window, I watched children, grandparents, joggers, walkers and delivery persons all stop to point, admire, chuckle and take photos. I delighted in hearing mums and dads exclaim, 'Hey kids, look at this.' And I am thrilled when the toddlers tentatively approached my 'characters' and touch and whisper to them.

I was out the front once when a jogger stopped short when she saw me. She said breathlessly, 'I want to thank you. I've changed my running route, just to see what these guys are saying today. It cheers me up no end.' Another time a passer-by called out, 'Love your bears!' A complimentary note was dropped in my letterbox and then another.

A neighbour knocked on the door, stepped back keeping great distance, and asked if she could photograph the bears occasionally. I knew she was an innovative and energetic school principal. She told me she would like my 'display' to be part of a project of building resilience during the pandemic. Her students and staff had been asked to submit their own pandemic experience photos.

As the months passed, our world contracted, but our vocabulary of words and phrases expanded. Yes, some of these already in our lexicon but their meanings differed radically in our new milieu. Coronavirus, COVID-19, pandemic, social distancing, flattening the curve, face masks, N95, mandates, Telehealth, (7 am) pensioner shopping hour, density quotients and limits, remote learning, homeschooling – uuuurrrgh, Zoom – anything including funeral services, working from home, PPE, frontline workers, anti-vaxxers, clusters, the ring of steel, donut days. Later came variants, air purifiers, Delta, Omicron, RATs and boosters.

Who would have thought that so many of us would almost become addicted to the daily press conference? Really! We turned on the radio or telly each day to hear and watch a group of 'talking heads' (albeit knowledgeable ones), especially one led by a politician. In true Aussie fashion, we lightened the sombre content by debating the Premier's clothes and need for a haircut. And don't get me started on some of the arbitrary 'in' or 'out' exclusions for various industries and workplaces!

Continuing with words, that great oxymoron 'By keeping apart, we are staying together' appeared to become the state's theme. We came quickly to know, via the world's media, of the soaring and frightening infection and death rates of other countries. We were shell shocked by distressing images on the nightly news as we realised how dire the situation overseas had become. I realised that our country's perception of disadvantage caused by our 'tyranny of distance' had now become a massive advantage. The time-worn adage 'the lucky country', a description of a long-past era when our wealth once 'rode on the sheep's back', now took on a personal, poignant meaning.

The lockdowns continued, sometimes briefly punctuated by relaxing of restrictions, during which we would hold a family gathering and visit our loved ones. Case numbers grew and we worried. I worried about my grandchildren's thoughts and reactions. After five weeks of bedtime stories and 'nighty night' kisses, our three-year old granddaughter had had enough. 'I don't want to say good night to Nonna's face, I want to see all of her!' she screamed, pulling away from the screen. I broke the rules the next morning, strongly feeling a 'guilt trip', and drove directly to her home, to offer care and cuddles. She grabbed my knees and dragged me to her bed, then snuggled in with books for the next few hours. 'But no face kissing Nonna because of the virus.'

We try to stave off boredom by varying our routine down to having morning and afternoon teas in a different part of the yard; planning meals; writing 'to-do' lists; filing, sorting and labelling years of accrued photos; tackling long-procrastinated projects; and, like many, many others, cleaning out cupboards and wardrobes. We try not to get on each other's nerves – he to the garage, me to the front room for extended periods.

We know it's Monday – Zoom exercise class, just as Tuesday evening is putting out the bin night! I learn how to do on-line click and collect orders from Officeworks. Likewise, to Bunnings, to keep hubby sane and yes, how to set up PayPal, to pay for our distractions. Zoom is used for a few meetings for which we would have had to travel into the city and to participate in a writing course. Mastering these technologies, I felt buoyed that I was offsetting separation 'downsides' caused by the pandemic. I perused Facebook, perhaps a bit too much, but the comedians who came out in force there – Sooshi Mango, Jimmy Rees, Sammy J. – lifted my spirits and made life bearable.

But back to my bears. My signs went from a simple 'Thank you for wearing your mask,' to 'Well done everyone! A little longer with the rules.' I started putting the words into conversation balloons and adding colour to the text and inserting a background colour – more business for Officeworks.

I wanted my bear signs not only to be cheery, but to have meaningful words, responsive to the changing goalposts. 'We're getting there. You've been great,' 'Let's keep the good vibes going,' 'We're going well. Everyone has been doing their part.'

I noted events such as Mother's Day, and for the children finally returning to school, a simple but brightly coloured, 'ENJOY SCHOOL.' I would acknowledge setbacks – 'We're getting there – maybe not as quickly as we had hoped.' Similarly, they welcomed any easing of restrictions.

Bears that care
But it was on receiving two significant comments that caused me to 'raise the bar' from lighthearted, community chatter to offering significant and meaningful comment. After these conversations, I knew my little community might have to 'watch my words' as the saying goes.

A lady walked slowly by and saw me watering the front garden. 'Do you do these?'

'Yes.'

'These bears mean a lot to me. I work full time but I am having a few … mental health days off. Your messages cheer me up so much.' With that she walked briskly off.

I hoped she was going to be OK.

Two men who live nearby regularly pass by with their sturdy dogs. This one day they looked so 'down.' 'Are you OK?' I asked without hesitation, such was the look of distress and their 'beaten' demeanour.

The older man replied quietly, 'It's just this whole thing … and someone had a real go at our dogs.' Now, *I* know their 'middle aged' dogs are as quiet as. You never hear them and at most, they amble as they are well fed by their equally quiet masters. So, I would warrant the diatribe would not have been deserved.

'We won't let him crush us.' 'The dogs actually stop here, sniff out your bears so we have to read your uplifting messages.'

'Good', I said emphatically. 'Keep bearing up.'

With that, they smiled tentatively and strolled on.

And theirs were not the only dogs who scrutinised. No daily walk was complete without a 'welfare check' on each bear, conducted by Missy, the aged (and again well-fed) blue heeler. Missy's companion, a sprightly eighty-one-year-old, stopped compliantly with her. She knew I was most likely to be in the front room and would wave to the window.

It was quite an obligation putting out the bears each day, rearranging their positions, securing them to their chairs or propping them to stand and making sure their messages could be easily read. I had to rush out if the weather abruptly changed (ahh, Melbourne); and of course, to bring them in each night. Late one night I had a text from my friend across the road.

'Your bears are still out and it's too dark for them. PLEASE bring them inside!'

It was with considerable regret that I had to decide on the last day of the bears along with their cheery and encouraging signs. I knew, from the beautiful feedback I received, verbally and from notes left in the letterbox, that they were well loved and much anticipated. But the time had come, I thought (incorrectly, as it turned out); that we had 'turned the corner' and perhaps they were not as 'needed'.

My final message was written as winter was well upon us with the bears having to shelter more and more inside or perhaps on the verandah. It also stemmed from an enquiry from a grandchild as to when their bears would be returned to them.

And I can tell you this for sure, the bears leave-taking did not go down too well. Their departure saddened some, and I felt guilty.

But I hope everyone remembers them that as part of our collective pandemic lived experience.

I have not been the only person to have been proactive in providing goodwill. All around the streets of Melbourne, at letterboxes, signs and boxes: free plants, books, lemons, collectibles – 'Take only what you need.'

My daughter and her friends got together to think of ways to keep motivated and upbeat as some were buckling under the homeschooling regimen.

They created 'dare-you-to' activities, which involved 'runs' into the yards of neighbours whom they didn't know. You had to disguise yourself and drop two toilet rolls at their front door.

The ladies said it was a lot of fun and they were mostly 'caught'; as so many people (like myself), were spending more time looking out their front windows! Their fun led to some introductions and chats.

My girl also fixed a massive chalkboard onto her fence and each day, she and her little ones collaborated to write inspirational sayings, to find quotes and jokes.

One of the recipients of her 'stealth run' toilet rolls, a pensioner whom she hadn't known very well beforehand, photographed each and every one of the boards. He gave the photos to her husband who sent them on to a graphic-artist friend. She arranged these as a collage, mounted on a large canvas, which became a present to his family from hubby.

In summary, what do I think was the effect of my bears on chairs?

I hope that: they helped acknowledge that ordinary human beings should be celebrated.

I hope that: they applauded the public for just 'clocking-on', every day, while struggling to cope with an unrelenting and unpredictable situation.

I hope that: they cheered people up.

My final words come from my favourite left-of-centre person, Michael Leunig, to whom I turned for inspiration when the lockdowns seemed interminable:

Dear Vasco,

In response to your question, 'What is worth doing and what is worth having?' I would like to say simply this. It is worth doing nothing and having a rest; you must rest Vasco – otherwise you will become RESTLESS!

FRANCES SENSI is a long-time Ferntree Gully resident. She loves her family, writing, reading and helping people. The activity on which this story was based was one to 'cheer up' and 'cheer on' neighbours and passers-by. Frances is currently editing a series of life stories, each presented within its historical context, to gift as a book for the next generations of her family.

Anywhere but here

MARISA BLACK

At night I think of Dad, alone in his apartment, the city around him emptied, desolate. In my half-dreams, I take him back to the beach he loves. We float on our backs, away from the sounds of the shore – the shrill calls of children playing, the seagulls overhead – wherever the current takes us. Drifting back in time to when the world hasn't yet been fractured.

* * *

He stands in his doorway now, the last remnants of sleep washing over him. 'Come in.' He turns, expecting that I will follow. 'Tea?'

Shaking my head, I try to raise my voice. I shouldn't. I peer into the small space beyond the doorway. The racing channel hums on, the soundtrack of my childhood. Photo frames sit atop every surface, the past spreading back in time. It's neat, orderly. Dishes washed and drying, bed made. But the floor, it is filthy. Vacuuming now beyond him with his bad back, his weak knees. I try and remember if this fits into some exception. Caring for those who need our love. Or has all humanity been stripped from us, the sacrifices we make to save ourselves, each other?

'I'll quickly vacuum,' I say as I squirt more sanitiser onto my angry skin. 'Then we'll go for a walk, get some fresh air. And then I'd better get back to them. The homeschooling.' I raise my eyebrows, offer a grimaced smile. Pressing firmly on the wire of my mask with one hand, I tentatively step inside with the bags of shopping in the other.

Pushing the stick of the vacuum over and over the same small piece of carpet just seems to move the debris about. It feels like my days now, all our days – shovelling things around without achieving much at all.

We walk along the river, side by side. He deviates in exaggerated arcs when maskless walkers approach. We pause to look for the duck he befriended during last year's endless winter, but it's gone – along with all the eager beginnings of things we thought would sustain us, leaving in their place this new winter, where we all just drift through our days, sleepwalking.

He slows as we climb the grassy hill at the periphery of the gardens, points to a statue sitting on the park bench up ahead. 'I couldn't work out why that man was always there. I'd made up a story about him – before I realised.'

Before, unlikely that a man would be there, day in, day out. But not now, not anymore.

We make it to the shops, and I ask if he feels like a sandwich.

He nods. 'And a beer if they've got one.'

'We can't drink anymore – at least, we can't remove our masks to drink alcohol, not quite sure what that means. Perhaps a straw,' I add, shrugging my shoulders, a smile twitching at the corners of my mouth. It reminds me of the press conference where a journalist asked whether a runner could stop for a kebab. That such things would ever need to be considered.

Dad shakes his head slowly, his eyes set somewhere beyond. I cross the road and stand in the queue for an overpriced pastrami-and-Jarlsberg panini, ask for it to be toasted to justify some of its cost. An assortment of drinks is arranged around the till. 'And a can of this too, please.' I glance about me before popping it into my shoulder bag.

We sit on a bench under a tree, eating our half-paninis, resting from the long walk. Dad takes furtive sips of his beer as we chat about the kids: online Auskick, Saturday mornings spent dodging my daughter's goals kicked across the living room into the washing basket; the Peppa Pig my youngest has started watching in Mandarin, perhaps because he has seen all the English ones or perhaps because at least it's something different, this foreign sound; my eldest and his grace when told that his birthday, his double digits, will be celebrated without his friends, yet again – so devastatingly accustomed to disappointment.

I tell Dad about when the army came knocking, too. Checking that we were isolating, confined to our homes after being notified we were 'close contacts'. Great hulking men in dark glasses and camouflage and boots that seemed to fall too heavily. 'The kids peered out the windows, standing on furniture, craning their necks to get glimpses of them as they walk the deserted streets. The squealing began as they approached. "They're crossing the road towards us! They're at our gate!" And then there was a knock at the door.' My youngest had stood beside me, wide eyed and silent as he wrapped himself into the folds of my skirt, transporting himself to some other place, a safe place – perhaps back in time to how the world once was.

On the winding road ahead of us now, two police vans begin to unload. Within moments, eight officers are striding towards us. I spring up, willing Dad to hurry. 'We're not allowed to sit down. Quick, grab your things. We're going to get fined.' I try to talk without moving my mouth, try to enact a casualness to my movements, as if acting independent of their approaching footsteps. 'Also, I think I'm slightly more than five kilometres from home. Two fines. Shit.' As I take a step, I remember the beer. Swooping his scarf over the top of it, I wrap it around and bring it into me, walking gingerly away to stop the swell brimming over. Dad is still sitting there as they get to him and for a moment I wonder if he's going to resist – not because he disagrees with the laws, or the police enforcing them, just in grief that he cannot sit in the sun with his daughter, after everything. But he soon stands, nods and they turn their attention to a mother and child lying in the shade of a gum tree, his little head resting on his mother's chest.

On the way back along the river, Dad tells me he fell in the rain at the tram stop. His pants slashed, his legs bloodied, the guts of his stopping trolley expelled violently across the road. 'Everyone helped me, retrieved the potatoes, got me up.'

'I'm glad they were kind. I feel like people are running out of it or something. Too exhausted. That it's becoming a bit *scary* – out there.' I gesture towards the looming buildings. 'I got out of the car the other day, right outside our house. The kids were screaming, my arms full of shopping, someone needed the toilet. I took one step and saw two men approaching. Quickly scrambled around for my mask. But one of them glared at me with his beady little eyes, shaking his head as if I'd just committed some sort of heinous crime. I couldn't let it go. I let the kids inside and marched back down the street calling after them, "Excuse me! Excuse me!" I thought maybe they didn't realise I was just coming from the car. I wanted – needed – to explain myself. But they realised all right. One of them – beady eyes – turned around, gave me the finger and told me I should have put my effing mask on. I cried. Sobbed. I couldn't stop. Then a man, getting into his car with his heavily pregnant wife, told me to let it go, that it wasn't worth it, to think of my kids. Of course he was right. But it just felt so unfair. After everything we've done, been through. To have his judgment reduce me.'

I glance over at Dad. His attention is elsewhere. Following his gaze, I see it's the rowers he's watching, mesmerised by the two boats gliding down the river, with speed and precision and something more. Purpose, perhaps. I bite into my bottom lip, embarrassed by my monologue. But it spoke of something I could not let go: the shattering of my belief that we were all in this together.

* * *

Dad rings to tell me that his brother has died. He tells me stories of this man I never really knew, while the kids scream in the next room. 'They'll send the funeral link.' I had imagined a room full of family and friends and love, buoying the grief, just slightly. But a link, of course. They hang on the line, these words, the weight of them.

I tell him I have a new niece, 'They're doing well, Geelong Hospital.' So close. In under an hour, we could have been there, holding her, marvelling at the size of her toes, the shape of her nose, the smell of her. And yet, now we just get a photo that I stare at as I lie in bed, trying to get a sense of her, this new little soul in this strange, strange world.

We talk about the case numbers, up and up they go. I tell him he needs to get vaccinated – now. And this time, he doesn't disagree. After I hang up, I leave the phone resting against my ear, incredulous that lives are still ending, beginning.

* * *

Dad rings as I'm cooking dinner. I put the phone on speaker as I try ineffectively to push spaghetti strands into a too-small pot of boiling water. He hasn't been outside, he might get out tomorrow. I tell him I'll bring over some more masks.

'I had my shot,' he tells me, 'I feel fine!'

My jaw stings, some knot I hadn't known was there begins to loosen.

Just as the pandemic began, I lay in hospital fighting severe pneumonia and sepsis. The infection was like a weed through my lungs, poisoning my blood, setting in motion a cascade of consequence: liver, kidneys, electrolytes. On every television channel there had been a cruise ship. Stories filtering through, a strange energy building.

In the depths of this pandemic, when memories of those days in hospital gripped me in terror, the idea that science might save us kept me afloat. It seemed inconceivable that a vaccine might be created when only so recently this virus didn't even exist. But I kept hoping, an agnostic prayer at bedtime, before dawn, under the streaming water of the shower. Because what else to do as images came of mass graves in New York City, overwhelmed hospitals in Italy, masses of burning funeral pyres in India; the endless, impossible decisions as to who gets to live and who is left to die.

And now, finally, Dad has his cloak of protection against this wretched virus and also against the insidious fear that runs alongside it.

'It's going to be hot on the weekend,' he tells me and the conversation drifts to summer, a mythical place I can't really imagine reaching. He wants to get a fishing rod, take the kids to the beach, sit on the pier, sun on our backs, can in his hand, radio on. Then come home, cook it all up on the barbeque, sit at the table. 'Together.'

The line goes quiet for a moment. Then, 'And I'd really love to get to Williamstown.' The home of his childhood. He wants to drive around with us, point out the landmarks of his life, tell us stories from long ago, about a time and a place when life happened. He wants to go back, or forward – just anywhere but here.

MARISA BLACK is concentrating on writing after seventeen years as a practicing lawyer. Her non-fiction has been published widely in *The Age* and *The Big Issue*, among other publications. Her fiction has been twice shortlisted for the Nillumbik Prize for Contemporary Writing, the Alan Marshall Short Story Award's Open Section, and commended in the Eastern Regional Libraries Competition, among other awards. Marisa is currently working on a memoir.

The deal

ELAARA WYLDER

Jeremy crouched in the shadow of the towering apartment block. A faded, discarded sheet of newspaper blew across the bitumen and tried to wrap itself around his leg. He brushed it off, watching it tumble away with a number of its brothers and sisters. It eventually came to rest on a pile of refuse that had been pressed by wind and rain against the mesh fencing that surrounded the carpark.

Beyond the fence stood another high-rise apartment block, and beyond that, another. All of them a uniform dirty-grey and crumbling, with the occasional bright swirl of graffiti.

With a furtive look over his shoulder, Jeremy tucked his right jeans leg into his striped football sock. Gran would be annoyed if he ruined another pair of pants. He rolled his shoulders as he stood, his nerves jangling. 'S'okay, s'okay' he muttered over and over, mostly failing to convince himself.

Squaring his shoulders, he took hold of the handlebars and threw his leg over his bike. One of the rubber handgrips fell apart in his hand.

Of course it would right now.

He tossed the perished pieces of rubber to the ground, cursing as he gripped the roughened metal bar in his left hand and pushed off. The rusting bike groaned as he put his weight on the tattered seat. Ignoring it, and the squeal from the dry chain, he steered for the exit of the carpark.

He pedalled furiously, trying and failing to keep pace with the rushing cars of harried commuters on their way home from their pointless jobs. He hated riding on the streets at this time of day, but today he had no choice. He zigzagged from road to pavement and back again, narrowly avoiding the smelly old lady who wandered the neighbourhood, known to everyone only as 'May'. Her usual low muttering grew louder as he ducked around her and the wheeled bag full of who-knew-what that she dragged along behind her.

Ahead, a group of dogs ran loose on a piece of open land where an old tumbled-down cottage had once stood. He guessed not everyone had got the memo about not being allowed to keep pets in the apartments. Several people lounged around, watching the dogs, talking, smoking, just hanging out.

Ugh, those dogs.

His bike wheels, and his legs, had been a target more than once. He threw a quick look over his shoulder, shot between two parked cars, and barrelled for the other side of the road, leaving a trail of squealing brakes and shaking fists behind him. He shrugged.

Oh well, guess they are angry commuters now.

At least he avoided the dogs this time.

Jeremy lowered his head, pedalling faster. His pride and joy, a large black jacket, flapped out behind him like a cape. His dad's jacket. It still smelled like him if Jeremy buried his nose deeply enough in the lining or draped it over his pillow at night. Not that he did that. Ever. He just wished he had something of his mum's.

High-rise apartment blocks and dingy stores gave way to dirty factories that churned out foul-smelling smoke and foul-tempered workers. Run-down tyre- and service-stations gave way to abandoned factories and empty stores. No one lived here, as far as he knew. Jeremy eyed the smashed windows, the piles of refuse, and the offensive slogans and pictures spray-painted across almost every wall and door. He shivered, hunching deeper into his jacket. The wind was less kind here, howling between or sometimes through the blocky buildings, trying to push him from his trusty, rusty steed.

It took Jeremy more than an hour of hard riding before he reached the muddy, trash-filled laneway that was his destination. The sun had lowered, its bottom rim hidden behind the imposing building at the head of the lane. It would be dark before he got home again. Gran was going to be pissed.

He squinted at the bent and rusted street sign.

Garlan Lane.

Yep, this was the place. He wrinkled his nose at the rubbish, boxes, and other indescribable bits of refuse that were stacked up against the walls of the empty building. He stepped down from the pedals, the bike still between his legs, and stared down the short length of the lane. He couldn't see anything suspicious, but there were more stacks of stuff, bins, and skips scattered haphazardly down both sides of the lane. Jeremy stepped back up onto the bike, his reluctant feet pedalling forwards, turning into the lane. He had to do this.

The front wheel of the bike slammed into a pothole hidden by sludge and wet newspaper. The bike stopped suddenly. Jeremy did not. He slid from the cracked vinyl seat and landed solidly against the handlebars with an 'Oof'. He sent a silent, sour thanks to the group of bullies that had ripped the men's bike frame from his hands, forcing him to build his franken-bike with a girl's bike frame. At least it wasn't pink. Actually, he wasn't sure what colour it had originally been as there were so many layers of paint on the rusting frame. He had added his own touch with a half-assed coat of dark blue.

Jeremy swung his leg over the bike, dismounting completely, not wanting to chance another injury. He limped forward, wheeling the bike deeper into the laneway. He halted when he reached a line of skip bins that had been pushed against a solid brick wall. He dropped the bike, rubbed his hands down his jeans and then popped the collar on his jacket. The swagger that he had intended became a scuttle as he scurried from skip to skip, making his way still-deeper into the laneway.

Heart pounding, Jeremy peeked around the last large skip bin in the row. A large, solid metal door stared impassively back at him. Jeremy straightened, pressing his back against the rust and flaking paint of the skip. He glanced back up the laneway, at the heap of mish-mashed parts that he had scrounged over several months. Anxiety clawed at his insides. He could just get on it, ride the hell out of there, and go home. He grimaced; Gran was going to kill him anyway. He straightened shoulders that didn't quite fill out the jacket and stepped around the end of the skip.

He dug his hand into his pocket. The money was still there, rolled up tightly with an elastic band twisted around and around it, but he resisted touching it. He had counted it over and over at home, in the darkness of his tiny single room. He knew how much was there. He fingered the tightly-stretched elastic nervously as he looked toward the road. No cars passed the end of the rubbish-filled laneway.

There were no artfully designed window displays here, no smiling baristas to ask what you wanted. There was no welcoming scent of baked goods and fresh coffee to draw people to friendly cafes or lunch spots. There were only boarded-up windows and padlocked doors with warning signs and threats. Should a person even chance this part of town, they didn't look up as they made their way swiftly from wherever they had come from to wherever they were going There were only hunched shoulders, caps pulled low over faces, and masks hiding the rest.

Pretence at bravery gone, Jeremy slunk into the shadow cast by the last skip, his back against the rough brick wall beside the massive handleless door. Movement on the opposite side of the lane caught his eye. Jeremy froze, his heart pounding in his chest. A rat leapt out from between two decaying boxes with a thin, scruffy tabby cat in hot pursuit. Jeremy drew a deep, shuddering breath, willing his pulse to slow. He ran a grubby hand through his equally grubby ginger hair. If he had to do this too often, his nerves would be shot.

He had been told not to draw attention so he tried to relax back against the wall, but an attempt at casual leaning was the best he could manage. He rapped once on the door, as instructed, and waited. He tried not to fidget, but his fingernails nervously dug at the mortar between the bricks as he waited. Five long, nail-biting minutes passed.

'What?' a deep voice said from the other side of the door.

Jeremy jumped for real this time, his feet actually lifting from the mud beneath his scuffed third-hand Converse, his hand clutching at his chest.

It felt like hours before he was finally able to speak. 'I–I've come to buy.'

'You got cash?'

'Yep,' he squeaked. He cleared his throat and tried again. 'Yes,' he repeated in his deepest voice.

There was a long pause before a *click* was heard. That was a chain. Deadlock. Another deadlock. Jeremy counted off in his head. Seven locks, bolts, and chains. Impressive. Also, scary. Terrifying, really. The door swung open on silent hinges. Toward him. Oh. Whoops. He slithered out of his corner before the door could crush him between its solid weight and the side of the skip.

Turning toward the doorway, he was met with a pair of folded arms at eye height. Very muscular arms. Very muscular tattooed arms. A skull with bloody fangs sneered at him as he raised his eyes to look at who he could only assume was a guard of some sort. Skull, as Jeremy immediately and silently dubbed him, was wearing a plain black T-shirt with matching black sunglasses. Jeremy couldn't see the man's eyes behind the glasses, so he could only assume that he was staring down at him, the rest of his face expressionless.

'Err … hi?'

Skull curled his lip at Jeremy and turned, walking into the pitch-black darkness behind him. Jeremy scrambled to follow him. The idea of walking into the darkened interior terrified him, but he had come so far, and he was desperate. The guard's long-legged stride meant that Jeremy had to awkwardly jog-trot along behind him to keep up.

Skull made his way across a vast open area that must have been the work floor of the factory when it was still in use. Jeremy had no idea what it was used for originally, just that the heavily graffitied sign over the entrance that faced the street said 'D'Amelio and Sons' in an elegant, if faded, script.

Overhead, a web of steel supports, cables, and the odd piece of decrepit hanging machinery decorated the ceiling of the factory. Dust motes swirled lazily in shafts of light from discoloured skylights. The occasional stack of items loomed at him from the darkness, but none of the boxes or barrels had labels, just a plethora of spider webs and a thick coating of dust. Jeremy shrugged and tried to keep up with Skull's long strides.

Jeremy heard movement far from the pools of light cast by the skylights, far from the broad back making its way deeper into the factory in front of him. He hoped it was simply a rat or two that had successfully escaped from the cat, and nothing more sinister. His neck began to ache as it twisted from side to side, his eyes wide, alternately trying to watch where Skull went and goggling toward every tiny noise.

Skull finally halted before another door. This one had a small square window with wire-reinforced glass in it. The glass was shot with a spider web of cracks and covered with a thin film of dirt. Skull knocked once. Mere seconds passed before a blurred face, also wearing black sunglasses, peered through the glass. The sunglasses turned briefly in Jeremy's direction before nodding once. The sound of locks could once again be heard on the other side of the door.

Do banks even have this much security?

When the door finally swung open, Skull stepped through and disappeared behind the open door. Jeremy stepped forward but the second guard, who also had his arms crossed over a plain black T-shirt, stood in his way. This set of arms was just as muscular as the previous pair, but somewhat less decorated. A single dagger ran the length of the man's left forearm, the ink so lifelike that Jeremy half-expected the blood that decorated its point to drip onto the floor. He looked up at the black sunglasses.

'Money.' The dagger moved to point at him as the guard opened his palm expectantly.

'Urm … can I see …'

'Money.' The hand was still in front of him.

Jeremy dug into his jeans pocket and then dropped the roll of cash into the palm that looked almost as big as a shovel. The cash disappeared as Dagger stepped back. Jeremy guessed that was permission to enter, so he did.

Behind the door he found himself in a dimly-lit office of sorts. Right in front of where Jeremy now stood with his eyes wide open and his mouth firmly shut, crouched a large, ornately-carved wooden desk. Behind the desk sat an elderly woman with curly grey hair and bright, coral lipstick caked haphazardly onto her half-smiling lips.

The top of the desk was almost bare, with only a lamp, a blotter, and a fancy stand with fancy pens standing up in it. Beneath the lamp – the room's only source of light – was a photo in a silver frame of a smiling man with a neatly-trimmed moustache. The wooden top of the desk gleamed where the lamplight touched it.

The deal

Jeremy's nose twitched. He had no doubt it would smell like the same lemon furniture-polish that his grandmother used.

Jeremy stepped toward the desk. 'G'day.' Yep, he could smell lemons, and … mothballs. He wrinkled his nose at the combination. 'I'm Jeremy C—'.

The woman cut him off, her pudgy hand making a chopping motion. 'No last names.'

He nodded and swallowed hard.

'Pleased to meet you, Jeremy. You may call me Marisol.'

'P-Pleased to meet you, M-Marisol.' He ducked his head and received a return nod for his politeness. 'I've c-come to buy—'

Marisol held up the same hand, palm forward. 'I know what you have come to buy.' She turned toward Dagger and lifted an eyebrow that was drawn on heavily with some sort of black makeup, also crooked. Jeremy was afraid to look for Skull.

Dagger stepped forward, bent, and began counting out the unfurled notes from the roll that Jeremy had given him onto the desk. Most of the notes were fives, some tens, very rarely a twenty, so the counting took some time. '… Nine-seventy, nine-ninety … a grand.' Dagger gathered up the notes and, at Marisol's nod, stepped through another door behind the desk that Jeremy had not noticed.

'Uh … where's he goin' wi' me money?' Jeremy peered past Marisol at the door that banged shut behind Dagger.

'*My* money,' she replied mildly. 'Are you here to buy or not?'

'Yes, but—' Jeremy swiped at his nose with the sleeve of his jacket. 'Do you actually have … you know?'

Marisol's coral lips thinned. 'What are you implying, boy?'

'Oh … n-nothing. I jus' mean it's near impossible to get, and well, me Gran would kill me, if she knew I was here, ya know?'

Marisol smiled at him, a dimple appearing on one wrinkled cheek. She tilted her head to one side. 'I do know indeed.' Skull appeared out of the darkness and took one step closer to Jeremy.

Jeremy took a matching step back. 'I di'n' mean nuthin', jus' checkin' where me money was goin'.'

Marisol stared silently at him. She bent forward slightly, pushing her sizable bust against the desk. She reached into a drawer with her right hand. When she placed her hand on the desk again, her fingers were curled around a tiny silver handgun whose barrel was pointed directly at Jeremy.

Jeremy squawked and took another step back. 'Your money! Your money!' He tried to scramble further back but slammed against something hard. He twisted his head wildly. The entire wall behind him was taken up with a series of mismatched filing cabinets; some metal, some wooden, all with padlocks on them. The tops of the cabinets held a wide variety of photo frames, each containing a smiling face, or a group of smiling faces. Jeremy could see the similarity between the faces in the picture and Marisol, who no longer reminded him of his grandmother. A heavy hand clamped tightly to his shoulder. He twisted his head back to find Skull towering above him, holding him in place with that single, very large hand.

Oh shit.

Marisol smiled at him again. This time it didn't crinkle the edges of her watery blue eyes, but her dimple made a reappearance. Jeremy was surprised that a dimple could show through that much powder and rouge. The handgun had disappeared. 'You can't go without your merchandise.'

Jeremy gulped, the weight of Skull's hand on his shoulder was terrifying. 'Uh, o'course, o'course,' he babbled.

The door behind Marisol swung open. Dagger reappeared carrying a small cardboard box. He lowered it for Marisol to inspect. At her nod, he placed the box on the desk in front of her.

Marisol beckoned Jeremy forward with a crook of one arthritic finger. 'Here you go, dearie.' She pushed the box toward him.

Jeremy stepped forward, Skull's hand vanishing from his shoulder. He stared down into the box. He hadn't seen anything like this in a long time and he had been expecting a much smaller package. Nestled in the box were eight individually wrapped rolls of toilet paper.

Gran might not be so pissed after all.

ELAARA WYLDER lives with her husband, a cat, a dog, and some-or-all of her children depending on the day, or sometimes the time of day! She writes young adult fiction under the pen name 'Ellie Wylde'. Her debut book, *Silver Horn,* will be published before Christmas 2022 and is the first in a young adult trilogy. Elaara hopes to publish more books in both the adult and young adult genres, and to share the lives of all the people living in her head with people in real life.

Surviving from home

ALYCE CASWELL

Content warning: suicidal ideation, postnatal depression

The pandemic saved my life.

I spent nearly nine months trying to prepare for postnatal depression – my predisposition for mental health issues made it almost certain. We were all at ready stations: my husband amassed six weeks of leave, my parents knew what symptoms to look out for, a psychologist was lined up, and the GP was on standby. There wasn't much else we could do but wait out my textbook pregnancy. I even started to think it wouldn't happen to me.

But for a month where I wore P2 masks because of the dense smoke smothering Sydney, everything seemed to be on track.

I had no idea I'd be wearing masks again in a matter of weeks.

One evening in February, after more than twenty-four hours of contractions, I gave up on my dream of a 'natural birth' and consented to an epidural – I can't believe I didn't want one initially. It made childbirth the most relaxing event of 2020.

Darkness coated the windows of the room I was given in the maternity ward. My little boy was spirited away after some bonding time, allowing me to rest. In the morning he returned to me, having transformed into a sweet little burrito, wrapped up inside a stripy hospital blanket.

I thought I was fine. I had to be fine. My son was counting on me.

But the days I spent trapped in the maternity ward made me feel like I'd slipped into a whitewashed hell instead of a dreamless sleep that first night. I was bombarded by doctors, nurses, a photographer, orderlies, and family members. It was so exhausting I barely remembered to make a post on social media celebrating *the arrival*.

I had no idea how to handle the burrito-turned-baby.

Breastfeeding in particular was a disaster. I never made it to the class held down the corridor, because I was still sore and faint. The lactation consultant seemed to be covering the entire ward – she barely had any time for me. Why didn't it work? Why couldn't any of the women in my family give me useable advice? And why did none of them remember those crucial first weeks?

Nothing helped. I was constantly in tears and knew I was dropping, fast, into the dark cracks where I'd already spent many years of my life.

I told the nurses about my past depression, and they immediately closed ranks, telling me that if I was reacting like this already, I'd best switch to formula.

It was the right call.

On my last day in hospital, my nanna came to visit. She was in Sydney for a whirlwind trip to say goodbye to everyone. For months, we had traded news: a promising ultrasound, a prescription for chemo pills. My pregnancy progressed faster than her cancer, thankfully.

Nanna held my son. It was the first and last time he ever saw her.

The last time *I* saw her.

I left the hospital and ignored the whispers about a pandemic overseas. It seemed so insignificant when I had to focus on cramming sleep, food, hygiene, and a good book into those short hours between my son's frequent bottles. My mother-in-law was the first to bring up COVID-19 during a visit – unbeknownst to us, she wouldn't be able to return for months. Her home, on the other side of the Blue Mountains, would soon feel as far away as Perth.

I dismissed all discussion on the topic of pandemics. She was an unapologetic conspiracy nut – what did she know? Humans are bright sparks, I thought, we'll get on top of this just like we did with SARS. Disaster movies always show the worst-case scenario, or else no one would see them. This was boring real life and not a spectacle designed to put bums on seats.

I trusted the world to keep my baby safe.

I should not have. I couldn't even trust myself.

Prior to our son's arrival, my husband and I had rented a townhouse with a high staircase that plummeted from first-floor bedrooms to living area to basement garage. I envisioned throwing my son down there so many times. I'm sure the staircase is not as dark as I remember it being. I do know that my arms were rigid around a colicky baby that refused to settle. Those memories are often difficult to access and now I understand why so many women can't remember those first weeks.

Interrupted sleep was the least of my problems. My carefully curated routines, which had been my coping mechanism for so long, were destroyed. Babies, I discovered, will slowly settle into a routine of their own; rarely the one that works for you.

I'd had depression before, but this ... this was something else.

My own thoughts horrified me, and I decided that I'd end myself before I had a chance to enact them. I had grown up in this area, so I knew the movements of all the trains. I had a plan.

My husband spent a good chunk of his leave talking me out of the car or trying to get me off the floor, where I'd sat so I could bang my head repeatedly against the wall. The rest of the time he was looking after our son and ensuring that I was able to read my book, that tiny paperback island where I could find respite. I began to think everything would be okay.

And then my husband went back to work.

In a world without COVID-19, he would have walked to the station and sat on a train for forty-five minutes, departing at Wynyard in Sydney's CBD. If he was lucky, he'd get out of the office at 5 pm and jostle for standing space on yet another train. He might be home a little after 6 pm. I'm not sure what he would have found upon opening that front door.

For an entire working day, I would have been left alone in that townhouse with a vulnerable little boy. Despite my family insisting that I ring them and ask for help, I would not have done so. I would have convinced myself, without someone to stop me, that I had only one option.

But none of that happened. My husband was told to work from home. He left the office in February – the day before my contractions began – and did not return for many months.

When my son's rear end splattered faeces all over me during a nappy change, I screamed. My husband ran down the stairs and took care of him while I shook inside the shower. When I was sobbing on the floor and could take no more, my husband left his home office (which had been my study for writing – we'd always had this space, but others weren't so lucky) and took my son away to watch a screen filled with lines of text.

My mother would ring to see if I needed her. I'd say no.

My husband would pipe up and make sure my mother heard him – she was needed.

My son was difficult to understand, the colic especially confounding. I panicked and thought I was doing something wrong. So I took him to see a doctor. I should say we took him to the doctor, because without my husband sneaking out of his so-called office to accompany me, I would never have been able to manage it.

My son was fine. But I wasn't. The doctor, who was easier to get into than my usual GP, could tell. My psychologist hadn't noticed because I was good at putting up a front if I had advance warning and time to prepare. The doctor informed my GP, and I was called in.

Reluctant, angry, I took the antidepressants. The pills didn't stop the depression, but they dulled the edge of the blade scraping at the inside of my skull. My husband was there to make sure I didn't miss a dose.

Meanwhile, there was a pandemic going on.

The cafés offered takeaway only. This changed nothing for me, the former café aficionado, because leaving the house with a baby was still too hard. Other people seem born to this, I despaired, capable of quickly adapting to lugging an infant along to all their favourite places. I was someone who had worked myself up into a tizzy over buckling my son into his car seat for the first time. I also had trouble tamping down on my anxiety if I was near too many people – the shops were bad enough *before* I had a baby!

Eventually, I managed it. After a few trial runs on the footpath outside the townhouse complex, I was able to walk a whole ten minutes with my baby in a pram – or a baby carrier – to the shops, where I'd order a matcha latte from a café. My usual anxiety about crowds was missing; most people were staying home unless absolutely necessary.

In any other year, I might have not found the courage to push that pram into a packed-and-seething shopping centre. But a quiet, empty one? That, I could do!

The rules that restricted me from visiting anyone were a godsend, since my pulse would race at the thought of navigating a friend's house with a baby and a heavy nappy bag. Lockdown gave me a convenient excuse to stay home. I know my friends would have talked themselves breathless trying to get me to leave the townhouse, thinking that I would get used to it, that I just needed a push. But all a push would have done was trigger a panic attack.

I was barely able to make it to Mum's house. These small trips, without pressure, with someone on the other end to feed and look after my baby, were what helped me get out. And get out I did. Mum was often looking after grandson and daughter at the same time. Whenever she came over to help me, or whenever I went to her in tears, we made sure our doctor's notes about my postnatal depression remained in the glove compartments of our cars – in case someone pulled us over and wanted to know why we were on the roads during a pandemic.

It was becoming clear to me that I needed space. Time to be *me* again. I so badly wanted to use day care, but how could I send my son somewhere he might catch COVID-19?

My family banded together to give me two days a week to myself and my neglected work. On Tuesdays, my husband took a day of leave. On Wednesdays, my mother cared for my son. The new system worked so well, restoring me almost overnight, and I didn't want to think about what would happen if something interfered with it.

Nanna took a turn for the worse in May. There was a flurry of activity as my mother sought permission from the Western Australian police to fly from one end of the country to the other. She'd need to quarantine for two weeks, but she was allowed to spend it in Nanna's tiny retirement villa. I panicked. Oh God, I couldn't stop her going – I needed my mum, but she needed to be with hers. How was I going to keep my head above water?

Dad stepped up. Work had slowed down for him during the pandemic, which was why he could take Wednesdays in Mum's place. I had never thought about trusting him with a baby for a full day before, but he must have done it at some point! I'm happy to report that both grandad and grandson survived.

Video calls to Perth were arranged: my son's chubby, fresh face in the corner of the screen, Nanna's haggard, thinning one dead-centre. This was how we visited her, when her state's border was closed. Once again, I had the perfect excuse to stay home.

Boarding a plane made me anxious and it had nothing to do with a certain contagion. I was afraid of leaving my son – what if I never wanted to go back to him? My family would have judged me in different times, I think, for not flying over. I could not have borne that judgement. My mental health was tenuous enough as it was.

God, when was Mum coming home?

In June, my aunt in Queensland passed away. The cause was also cancer and we'd expected it for so long, but still it was a shock. My cousin – her daughter – had a son the same age as mine. How could my cousin handle losing her mother, especially now? It made me realise that I could live a few weeks without my own mum, because she was coming home.

There was no funeral, since so many people were not able to attend.

Ten days later, Nanna also left us. I'd sent her a letter, thinking we had more time, but due to postal delays it arrived the day after she died. It was placed inside her coffin. For months afterwards, I was haunted by the thought of that unread letter.

My mum flew back to Sydney. So did Nanna, after a fashion.

A funeral was arranged and by then the restrictions governing the number of attendees were more generous. There would be enough space for every Sydney-based relative.

Mum brightly told me that family would be there in spades, with someone always able to look after the baby. I should go! But by then, we'd established a comfortable routine at home, one that allowed me to catch my breath. I had needed to draw those breaths for so long that I didn't want to risk emptying my lungs now. I kept quiet about the real reason for my absence and blamed my son's vulnerability to COVID-19.

I still got to farewell Nanna, however.

While my son napped, I watched her funeral via the Internet (just as my relatives in Perth did) There were malfunctions and audio problems, but I was there.

I marvelled at this new way of doing things. People were more connected than ever. Later in 2020, I attended a wedding that was streamed to friends and family (some too infirm to travel at the best of times), the tablet responsible sitting in its own chair like an honoured guest.

How many treasured events will no longer be missed because we learned to adapt?

Other aspects of our lives also benefited.

On the days when I couldn't physically take myself to my GP, I could instead arrange a Telehealth appointment and 'see' my doctor while my son played on the floor. While I wore clothes covered with suspicious stains. While I caught up on chores. Without this method, without my GP being able to remotely check up on me, where would I be? I don't know.

I still use Telehealth, scheduled around my busy life. I've never been good in queues or waiting rooms, so being able to spend that time (sometimes up to ninety minutes!) at home has been so helpful for me. Since my psychiatrist also uses virtual visits when necessary, I've finally been able pursue a diagnosis for my autism and ADHD. I'd 'got by' before I'd had a baby, using strict routines to manage my mental health, but one small breeze could have toppled that house of cards at any time.

I am most grateful, however, for the changed attitudes towards working from home. Having my husband close at hand in those early months of 2020 was literally lifesaving. Two years later, I continue to benefit from this. Some days he only commutes down the hallway, able to give me respite on particularly challenging days.

We survived. We braved day care. We bought our first house. We rolled up our sleeves for vaccinations – three times so far. I gained access to Ritalin, which helped to chase away the last shadows left behind by my postnatal depression. I still know the movements of all the trains, but now it's because I need to make sure there will be one at the station when I take my train-obsessed son for a visit.

It's strange to think that a devastating global event could yield so much good. But it did.

And I'm alive because of it.

ALYCE CASWELL is a self-published author who has written several novels, including the pandemic romance *Love and Lockdown*. She currently resides in Sydney with her husband, her son, and a wallaby who has decided that the backyard is a great place for a nap.

Small things

L. E. MORGAN

The fence between them is flimsy and steadily succumbing to the pull of gravity, but means as much as a wall of concrete. To visit would be against the rules, so they steal glances at each other throughout the day, as if looking at each other would force them to acknowledge the truth: they're neighbours, who live *right next to each other*, and they can't go any closer. What if they catch the virus from each other?

She's out gardening, getting her hands dirty, mud under the nails refusing to wash out with repeated scrubbing. She didn't know it would be like that, before this; she's never taken the time to improve her garden, sad plants sagging and drooping in the harsh sunlight.

He's focused on his laptop, squinting in the brightness, and probably struggling to see it even with the screen turned up all the way. Probably using up his battery quickly because of it, so that he'll have to charge it more often. It would be so much easier inside.

They're both sick of inside.

They've patrolled the entirety of their blocks twice today, probably making mental notes for all the improvements they can do – won't do – once the lockdown is over and they can get supplies. They keep away from each other, because after all, even though they're neighbours, there are rules and they ought to stick to them.

He clears his throat, and she glances over at him, half expecting him to speak. The other part of her is wondering what she'll do if he *does* speak – she has no idea how to socialise with real people who are actually there anymore. But it was just because his throat needed clearing, she realises, not to talk to her.

They never talked before the lockdown, anyway. Why should it be any different now?

It's lunchtime for her. It's strange, keeping a routine that used to exist to have other events fitted around it and now is the only routine left. She cleans her hands and prepares her lunch. After this she'll probably have a bath and then go around in her pyjamas for the rest of the day. Who's to stop her?

He continues working through her lunch, head down and focused. At the end of it she cleans up her crumbs by tossing them into the garden. Maybe they'll attract a few birds. She says, 'Hey birdies, here are crumbs!' and it earns a look from him. They both know the reference, surprisingly.

Then he gets up and goes inside. She waits, not sure why she's waiting for him. He's a neighbour, nothing to do with her. She pretends to admire her faded flowers – she's not much of a gardener, after all; only learnt when there was nothing else to do – until he returns, his own lunch in hand. Nothing to do with her. She ignores the disappointment it brings in her, and goes inside.

Midway through her needlessly-elaborate preparations for a bath, her phone rings. It rings all the time except when she wants to talk to somebody. Sighing, she takes the call. Another person ringing around generically to ask how she's going. She doesn't think they care, but she answers anyway as if they do.

Despite how much she wants to talk to people, social interaction has tired her out and she determines she does deserve a bath after that. Maybe she doesn't know what she wants, really.

She glances out of her window at her neighbour. He's finished his lunch, and is focused on picking up every tiny crumb and eating it. He's probably already put in five or six hours today; he was up early. So was she. Even sleeping gets boring sometimes. And she's read all the books she cares for. He's probably the same – if he likes to read at all.

A new idea occurs to her, and she abandons the bath idea for this infinitely more thrilling one. She goes outside empty-handed, and says, 'Hey!'

He looks up as if he was waiting for her to say something. 'What?'

'Do you like to read?'

He goggles at her as if he's forgotten how to comprehend the spoken word. 'Sometimes.' There's an awkward pause before he adds, 'I've been reading more, recently.'

She nods, scrambling for what to say next. 'Nice.' Trying to be subtle, she shifts backwards as the wind blows gently in her face, and she tries not to breathe. He might have the virus and she'd be breathing it in right now. Serve her right for going downwind. Is that how it even works?

'Do you want to borrow a book?' she asks at last, back firmly against the wall of her house.

His lips twitch. 'What book?'

'What books do you like to read?'

He shrugs. 'Fantasy, mostly. I don't like so-called "realistic" fiction or—' he shudders overdramatically in a way that makes her smile—'romance.'

'Most of my books are romance,' she says, disappointed. 'Read any old books? Dickens, people like that?'

He gets up, putting his plate aside. He's wearing pyjama trousers and a plain top; he had a video call earlier in the morning at some far-too-early time, or else he wouldn't have bothered to change at all. 'I've read some Dickens. I quite liked *Our Mutual Friend*.'

'Have you read *A Tale of Two Cities*?' She read it last lockdown for the first time; it had been a Christmas gift four years ago, and she'd kept it for the elegant look it gave her bookshelf, being a fine hardcover with gilt lettering.

'I've heard of it.'

'Want to borrow it?' She's not quite sure why she's offering, except as something to do. Maybe they could start talking about the books they've read, and so she could have a bit of social interaction, at least, with her neighbour, even though they're not allowed to visit each other. She can hand it over the fence, and they say that your arms' span should be enough, right?

A similarity to a scene in *Fiddler on the Roof* strikes her, but she's not looking to marry this man. Just to get through lockdown and be able to talk to people by the end.

'Sure, why not.'

She goes indoors and puts on gloves. One can't be too careful. What if *she* had the virus, and the faintly scratchy throat from yesterday that lasted only a couple of hours was really the first sign of it? Wouldn't want to give it to him. She pulls out the book carefully, knowing without looking that it has her name in it. She won't forget that he's borrowed it; there's very little to keep track of at the moment. She's got work tomorrow, but that's about it.

She comes to the fence holding it, and after a moment's hesitation, he does too, reaching out as far as he possibly can. She holds it away from her like it's got the plague. Figures of speech are funny. She's *dying* of laughter.

'I haven't touched it for more than two weeks,' she assures him as he takes the book carefully. 'I put these gloves on just now and washed my hands beforehand.' She's probably sounding like a health freak, but she takes this stuff seriously. She has to; after all – her friend's sister's boyfriend is a doctor, and she hears about the awful toll it's taking on the healthcare system.

'That's fine.' He cradles the book as if it's made of gold. 'I'll return it once I've finished it.' There's another moment of hesitation. She wishes she could invite him in for a cup of tea, but she knows the rules won't allow that. Maybe someday. Maybe not. At last, he shifts away from the fence, and she does too, shedding the gloves with the dexterity of practise. You never know when a surface might have the virus on it, and she prefers not to take chances.

She goes to have that bath; nothing else to fill her time, after all. As she finishes setting it up, she glances out of the window again. The sight of him sitting down in his chair and opening the book causes a warm feeling inside her. She gets into her bath slowly, but then her curiosity gets the better of her, and she gets out again and looks out of the window at her neighbour, like a peeping Tom.

He's reading it now, and he's smiling.

L. E. MORGAN is an aspiring Christian author who started writing when she was very small and never quite stopped. She writes in a wide variety of genres and has far more ideas than she can keep up with, despite yearly November shenanigans. You can generally find her hibernating at home wrapped in a teddy bear blanket.

Animal adaptation

KAT BEATON

Animal Adaptation, remote teaching, day twenty. Miraculously, all twenty-three of my Year 7s are there for Science by 10:05 am. PowerPoint on Animal Adaptations ready to go. I sip the coffee Luke just brought me, push aside the toast. Nothing worse than on-screen crunching.

'Just let me know if you can't see it,' I say as I hit 'share screen'.

'Can't see anything,' Ruby says.

A stream of thumbs down emojis appear in the instant messaging.

Shit! I spent so bloody long on that PowerPoint last night.

'Okay, guys, trying again.' I breathe in and try again.

Nothing.

Question marks and emojis with confused faces.

Fuck!

'Okay, guys, just stay in here – I'm gonna go out of the meeting and then restart Teams to see if that works.' I wave as I leave the meeting, wondering if I'm breaking school policy by leaving them unsupervised in an online lesson.

I hit the control-shift-power keys and my screen goes blank.

Fuck fuck fuck.

Okay, so according to my phone that's the command for putting your displays to sleep. Fucking brilliant.

By the time I figure out how to get back in, eight minutes have passed, and eighteen students have disappeared.

'What happened?' Kobi asks.

'Well, I just, ah ... hit the wrong command to quit teams.'

A cascade of laughing emojis.

'The others all left?'

'Yep,' Rohan nods.

'Oh. I'll try to invite them back in,' I say as I click away, knowing it will be futile.

'So. Okay. I'll try to share my screen again ...'

'Yep. Got it!' Ruby announces excitedly.

'Can't see anything,' Zara says, and shrugs.

Thumbs down from Rohan and Kobi.

'Okay. Right.' I glance up at their faces. No one else has rejoined. It's just Zara, Rohan, Ruby, Kobi and Theo. Theo – with his camera off.

'Theo, can you put your camera on please?'

Silence.

It's school policy to have the camera on but how much do I push it?

'Theo?'

Nothing. Then a neither-happy-nor-sad-face emoji appears from him in the chat.

Okay, well that's something, I guess. Then I remember something about Theo from parent-teacher interviews last term: only child, lives out of town. Remember how quiet he has been lately in online lessons.

'Hey Theo, can you show us around your property?'

A thumbs-up appears from him in the chat straight away, followed by some clapping emojis from the others. Theo turns his video on and points his camera out. Chatting away, he shows us an enormous burn pile, the front paddock that's so wet he can now kayak on it, the shed he's helping to paint, and his one-eyed cat.

I've never heard this kid talk so much. Now the others are saying they want to show their places too.

'Sorry, guys, we're out of time.'

Sad emojis.

'Miss?' asks Kobi.

'Yep?'

'What even was this lesson meant to be?'

'Umm. Animal Adaptations. Sorry.'

'Don't be,' Theo says as he smiles, camera on.

KAT BEATON lives in Beechworth in Northeast Victoria with her family, and works as a classroom teacher with grades 4 to 6. When she's not teaching, Kat enjoys writing, reading, playing violin and getting into the outdoors on bike or on foot. She has been writing stories, songs and poems throughout her life and has just finished the first draft of a novel set in 2035 for middle-grade readers. Kat is currently completing the Write Your Novel course run by the Australian Writers' Centre.

The animals will save us

CATHERINE EDWARDS

It is the middle of winter.
Annabel asks again, but this time accompanied by a PowerPoint presentation she has titled, 'The Nitty Gritty of Getting a Kitty'. We have talked about getting a cat for years. Annabel's presentation is comprehensive and convincing. We know how much a cat will cost to feed and care for, and she has put together a Click-and-Collect cart with the essentials. All we have to do is hit 'checkout'.

My husband, Andrew, crumbles, despite his allergies and a deep-seated distrust of cats since he suffered from a bout of toxoplasmosis when he was a kid. 'Might as well, might be a good distraction,' he says with a shrug. 'But I'm not feeding it'.

At each day's end we sit together on the couch, the five of us, and watch old episodes of *Midsomer Murders*. We sip cups of tea and eat our way through another cake that was baked out of boredom. We are resigned to this predictability and soothed by the familiar. But its cost is our joy and spontaneity. Lockdown has stolen our daytrips to visit family, and the choice to do anything on a whim. It is all the same. Maybe a cat to love is what we need.

And so we trawl through the RSPCA and The Lost Dogs Home sites. We judge their offerings by colour, age, and name.

'"Bobbykins" is a ridiculous name for a cat,' I complain, and keep scrolling.

'How about this one? She's lovely,' Annabel exclaims, pointing at the screen, already half-in-love with the scrawny creature.

'Annabel! It's fifteen! It'll just sleep all day.'

We apply to adopt a fluffy grey kitten but before we hear back the site tells us her 'adoption is pending'. Annabel will not be defeated, and the search goes on.

* * *

Work is monotonous. My desk is shoved in the bedroom corner, and I have to keep the door open to ensure internet connection. My husband's voice booms through the walls from his makeshift office in our eldest daughter's room. I have started grinding my teeth at night and I wake each morning with an aching jaw.

Some days I prefer to work among the chaos of the dining room with three kids floundering around their Google Classroom meetings trying to learn something. Anything.

The days get darker and colder. We don't want to leave the house. We are not allowed to leave the house. We are stuck beneath a ceiling of grey.

We fall into an uncomfortable rhythm. I am lethargic and slow, and the kids mirror my mood and movements. We crawl through each day like we are coated in honey.

Every few days, a surge of guilt floods my system and I force us all outside into the drizzle with raincoats and umbrellas. I stomp up the street, nose running and shiny with cold. The kids lag behind, and I get an uncomfortable look into the future.

I mark the days by press conferences and statistics.

At dinner each night we hold a vote for what we are going to name the coming cat. We start with a list of twenty or so and whittle it down. We each have one veto, apart from me – I get two. Because I just can't abide having a cat named Frodo. We all have strong opinions and arguments for and against. We narrow it down to four possibilities: Toast, Usnavi, Araminta and Sherlock. We don't have a cat, but we have a name.

* * *

Annabel texts me from the other end of the house, with a link. 'Mum, this is the one.'

I close my laptop and click the link. This cat stares straight into the camera. Through the screen I can feel the force of its anger and disappointment in the humans that have come before. It's like he's daring me to adopt him. Something about his defiance creeps into my heart and I know this is the one, too.

I apply straight away, barely registering that this cat has some kind of eye condition and has been in foster care for six months.

The adoption site calls, and explains that he needs drops in his eyes twice a day for the rest of his life; that he needs tablets and check-ups.

'Fine, fine,' I say. 'When can I meet him?'

We organise a time, and as I drive to the appointment I am fizzing with nerves and hope. I haven't told Annabel. Her heart has decided that this is the one, and I can't bear to disappoint her. Or the cat. I want this cat to come home with me. I want this cat to love me. I want it to fix something in me that has cracked from endless locked-down days. I know this is unfair. I know this cat owes me nothing. And yet ...

They take me to a small 'cat meeting' room. I see him for the first time, and I bite my lip to stop from crying. He stalks around the walls, not acknowledging my presence.

'We'll leave you here to get to know each other,' a chirpy volunteer says.

'Can I take my mask off?' I ask, hearing a shake in my voice.

'Sure. Just wait till I've closed the door.'

She leaves, and we are alone.

He is beautiful. His dark fur is long and silky. He has matching ginger circles on either side of his ribs. I can hear the soft thud of his paws as he walks. He is big – bigger than I expected. And his eyes are seafoam-green, bright and clear. His eye condition is a hidden thing.

Do you want to come live with us?' I whisper.

He looks up at me, seeing me for the first time. We hold each other's gaze and I try to imagine what he's thinking. He turns away and meows at the door. I take it as a sign.

The volunteer returns and I tell her, 'This one's mine.'

She claps, and trots away to sort out the copious admin that is required to adopt a cat.

We name him 'Araminta'; 'Minty' for short.

They tell us to keep him confined to one room for the first few days.

'Let him acclimatise and get used to the place,' they suggest.

That lasts about an hour. Minty scratches at the door and demands to be let loose. We are weak-willed, and bend to his demands. He cannot be contained.

That first night, I can't sleep. I wonder aloud if Minty is happy to be here, with us, and Andrew says, 'It's a cat. As long as it has food it's fine.'

All night I can hear Minty rustle under beds and thump along the corridor, and I don't know what that means.

* * *

Minty's eye drops become a thing of contention between him and me. I have to hold him still with one hand, and aim and squeeze the drops with the other. I am clumsy and he is skittish. He has to trust me, but he doesn't yet.

The animals will save us

* * *

I stop watching the press conferences and the days become longer and lighter.

Like he has always been here, Minty claims spaces as his own. We delight in his confidence and in the absolute subjugation of ourselves. When Minty wants to play – we play. When he wants to eat – we feed him. We are being ruled over by a cat and we don't care. The promise of time with Minty galvanises the kids' online efforts. They rush through classes and produce more work in less time.

Annabel's love for Minty is immense. They develop their own private language and games. They chase each other up and down the hall.

She makes up a song about him. The first line is, 'Minty's a cat, he's not a brat'. There are multiple verses and choruses. I hear her sing it to him when she thinks I'm working. I hear her whisper, 'You're the best cat in the world, Minty.'

* * *

We find a new rhythm to our days. One that includes Minty in every way. Everyone gathers to watch me put his eye drops in. They cheer when the drops slide in easily. Feeding Minty has become an enviable task. The kids fight over who gets to do it and how many treats he should have. The refrain, 'Where's Minty?' echoes constantly through the house.

Joy has crept back into our lives.

* * *

At night, when the kids are in bed, Minty jumps onto the couch and curls up near me. He stays close, but never touches. He watches me as I watch TV. Eventually he tucks his head under his paws and falls asleep. I was not prepared for how Minty would save us.

CATHERINE EDWARDS is a writer from Melbourne. Her poems and creative non-fiction have been featured in multiple anthologies and magazines. Catherine's love of nature is often present in her work. She is currently working on her first novel.

The stranger

ROANNA MCCLELLAND

The screen of her door is filthy. She doesn't own the property. The tell-tale signs of an overused welcome mat, zigzagging cracks, watermarks staining the portico. People who own houses don't run them down like this. They buy fancy door mats with quippy slogans, paint their houses crisp white, and spend their Sundays pressure cleaning. When I pull into their driveways, they continue gardening with beetle-like headphones wedged firmly in their ears. I place their parcels on spotless porches, next to the cast-iron loveseats, and they throw unfriendly glances at me until I move on. Their deliveries consist of organic market produce, and alcohol; endless cases of wine rushed inside so the neighbours don't see how much they have ordered this month.

I already know her doorbell doesn't work, so I rap loudly on the screen, upsetting clouds of grey dust. Casey Marone, Unit 5, Castermaine Street. Always a delivery of books from the local bookshop. I drive past its shuttered windows sometimes and wonder if she used to go there in person, back when we used to go places in person. I wonder if she misses those excursions. I know she lives alone.

She opens the door a crack, enough to whisper, 'just leave them on the porch', before waiting for me to back away and lift my body creakily into the van.

It's her regular wave as she stoops to pick up the brown box that I like. Not many people wave to me. Most of them don't even answer the door, even though they are all stuck at home. I can feel their eyes peering at me through venetians, waiting until I have reversed the van before they emerge. Sometimes I feel rushed, knowing they are waiting impatiently for me to leave while my clumsy thumbs struggle to hit the links on my terminal inside the van. Judith would laugh if she saw how much I resemble my dad these days, club fingers punching the wrong numbers, old eyes squinting at the screen. I don't even know where the information goes after I press 'submit'. My boss is as invisible to me as I am to the people in these houses. In fact, we could pass each other in the street – if such a thing is ever allowed again – and never know.

* * *

My big white van grumbles after idling for so long and I wonder if I can put off servicing it another month. The man who services the few remaining taxis in our neighbourhood does a cheap deal for me as well, but I suspect he runs solvent through the engine. I don't know what I will do if the van carks it.

A van was never in our plans. Judith and I weren't to be the grey nomad couple, permanently shackled to folding chairs with cup holders. We were going to be sophisticated retirees, drink good coffee, maybe go to the occasional writers' festival. We would live easily on the pension despite our lack of Super; we didn't need much. Judith would wear those flowy dresses that made her look like an eccentric art teacher. I would wear jeans because I never had to go into an office again.

* * *

David P lives up the road in a large, white townhouse – the kind that screams 'bachelor's first home'. He never has his full name on the delivery label. I pile multiple boxes onto his porch every day, mostly from that global corporation I hate even though they keep me in business. I often arrive at the same time as the food delivery chap who looks harried as he remounts his bike. He nods in my direction but never has time to say 'hello'. I don't remember Judith and I ever having 'take-out', but we always ate well. Perhaps Judith always cooked. Perhaps I never noticed. Did that frustrate her? She never seemed frustrated, but she did have a tendency toward passive aggression.

David P doesn't answer when I buzz his large intercom. I move back into my van, which is starting to smell damp inside.

* * *

When Judith first left me, and I looked around the house I could no longer afford, I wondered if I could drive a rideshare like those chappies who ferry drunks around the city. But I did the math – still a business-brain buried under the fog – and I was better off delivering parcels. I start delivering at 8 am and, despite assurances of a reasonable load, often deliver until evening, my coccyx sore from sitting and an angry nerve twanging in my left hamstring. Delivery covers the bills, covers what is left of Judith's medical costs, and at least I don't have some young punk telling me what to do after forty years running my own firm.

* * *

Maria at number 52 always opens the door as soon as I pull up to her bungalow. I see the frazzled desperation in her eyes, looking not at me but at the parcels in my arms, hoping they are a dopamine hit addressed to her and not another member of her ungrateful family. She is still in her dressing gown, and visibly deflates as she reads the label addressed to her teenage daughter. She manages a curt smile, says, 'have a good one,' before walking slowly back to the house, sounds of sibling squabbling floating down her garden path. I chuckle a bit. Poor Maria. If Judith and I had kids, perhaps they would have cared for me after she died. But they could have turned out a-holes like Maria's kids, too.

The glare from the setting sun blinds me as I turn back down the street. I say the names as I pass the houses: Dimitri Hellos, Number 10: meal preparation boxes. Helen and Sylvia Arnold, 5A: fresh flowers every Friday. Sigourney and Walter Macdonald, Unit 5: care packages from their worried adult children. Tai and Lydia L, 12: endless identical boxes of designer sneakers. Peter Bellucci, Number 34: cheap toys to entertain his brood of bored kids.

I turn right from Castermaine Street and onto the still-quiet freeway, shielding my eyes from the white light streaming through my windscreen. A violent screech of brakes and my foot is slamming on my own brakes in slow motion, heart pounding loudly between my ears.

Bloody idiot almost t-boned me.

The hotted-up orange car is off in an instant with another squeal of tires, leaving my van stalled in the service lane. I take a few breaths, take a rear-view look back at Castermaine Street to confirm no one has ventured from their house to check what the racket is about, and shakily turn the ignition back on. I wonder if any of them would notice if a different person knocked on their doors tomorrow. I turn onto the freeway toward my empty apartment, joining the sea of strangers in vans crisscrossing across the city.

ROANNA MCCLELLAND is an emerging writer of fiction and non-fiction, with a background spanning law, politics, media and research. Her work explores conceptualisations of climate, the environment, identity, and human nature in modern society.

Week eighteen

MARIAN MATTA

For the previous seventeen weeks, he'd risen with the alarm as he had done for every day of his long working life. Each weekday of that seventeen weeks, excluding public holidays, he'd put on his suit and tie, picked up his briefcase, kissed his wife at the door, and walked to the train station. For Stephen, routine was everything. Routine kept the worries at bay for a few precious minutes, granted him a small, constrained place in which to breathe.

Towards the middle of week eighteen, Janice brought up the dreaded subject of their annual holiday as she turned her face up to Stephen's morning kiss.

'Any chance of bringing it forward this year, love? It should be a gorgeous autumn for caravanning.'

Her bright words felt like cold, hard fingers reaching in to twist Stephen's guts. He kissed the corner of her mouth then turned his face away. 'I'll check. No promises. You know what Gillespie's like, especially when things are tight.'

And all the way to the station his heart crashed against his ribs as he recalled their beloved Bessie, their Beston Carnival caravan, no longer safe in storage, no longer theirs.

The journey into Flinders Street would have taken close on an hour but Stephen bailed out at station five. He'd travelled in the last carriage, as had become his new habit, and now waited until the train cleared the platform before making his slow ascent up the ramp. No need for hurry, no need to join the crush of bodies in the city. There was a quiet park nearby, plenty of shade against the late summer sun, bench seats, even a toilet block which wasn't too appalling. If nasty weather threatened, a small shopping mall was within comfortable walking distance, but that noisy, echoing place was full of babies and mothers and unemployed men who nursed coffees for hours while ignoring the piped *muzak*. He'd stick with the park until the time came for his homeward train.

For seventeen weeks his mind had focused on the problem at hand – how to eke out his severance pay and the sale money from Bessie until he could find another job, then airily announce to Janice that he'd decided on a change of career after two decades at the same old daily grind. The scene had played out in his mind again and again: her face would crinkle up with surprise, concern, deep worry, and just a hint of disappointment that he'd not discussed it with her first, but he'd laugh her cares away, enfold her in his arms and spin all the advantages for her delight. There were bound to be advantages in any new job. Closer to home, more freedom, better pay, better workmates, better boss. She already knew how he felt about Gillespie and his new band of go-getting underlings. 'Just keep your head down for another few years, love,' she'd say when the subject came up. 'Then it's the open road for us.'

Despite his current dreadful situation, he wasn't oblivious to world events, especially the galloping spread of a new disease that caused people overseas to be barricaded behind locked doors, leaving the streets to the plague. That, and the wild animals which were timidly returning to reclaim their usurped territories. Every day Janice tut-tutted over the news then went into the study to have a worried video chat with their daughter, Deirdre, all the way over in Texas. *How's our little Jordan? Enjoying playschool? Can't wait to see him again; give him a big, squeezy Grandma-hug from me.*

How are you and Brett? Are you being careful about this virus thing? I've seen the footage out of New York, dear, and it looks dreadful. Yes, I know Austin's a long way from New York but still… You really should come home.

In a strange and disquieting way, the troubles of the outside world calmed Stephen. No one would be paying attention to his recent change of circumstances, Janice included.

But in the middle of week eighteen, when the issue of the caravan had arisen, there also came a new sense of concern among his fellow train travellers on his homeward stretch. He picked it up in the short trip: worried tones, physical wariness, even a couple of makeshift face coverings. When Janice greeted him at the door she didn't ask if he'd spoken to Gillespie about his annual leave. Instead, she hugged him tight and whispered, 'Where will it all end?'

He murmured soothing, meaningless words into her hair while his brain scrambled to latch onto whatever had happened between his morning departure and his evening return. The TV was on in the lounge room, so he assumed something big had happened. Janice wasn't one to fritter away valuable hours in front of the box.

'Let's sit down, love, catch our breath, hey?'

He gently steered her to the couch where, with his wife's hand clutching his own, he caught up on the news which had entirely passed him by during his hours on the park bench. The World Health Organisation had officially declared this new virus a pandemic, the Australian Grand Prix was in imminent danger of being cancelled, people were being warned against mingling in large groups and – in the most perturbing news of all – it was being suggested that working from home would be a good idea where possible.

'It's all right,' he said, but his voice quivered just like Janice's.

Working from home. It was at once a thrilling and terrifying prospect. Instead of the daily charade of 'going to work', he could retire to their study and spend his day sending out job applications. So much easier than his current method of visiting a library a couple of times a week. Yes, it could work. Janice had little idea of what his working day used to be, in the same way that he didn't have much of an idea about how her part-time job as the local Community House office manager worked.

But what if she twigged? Could he keep up the facade? And assuming he managed it all the way through to his November holidays, there would still be the issue of the sale of the caravan.

He became aware that Janice had perked up a little, was saying something about buying a second laptop 'so we can both work from home when the time comes'.

'If it comes.' A new laptop? Half a week's non-existent wages frittered away on a nonessential item? 'Let's worry about that later, shall we?'

By week twenty-one, Stephen was ahead of the curve. He assured Janice that, while not amenable to an autumn holiday, Gillespie had been uncharacteristically obliging about the new working-from-home arrangements. Worried about Stephen's age and vulnerability, he'd said. Just a daily video update and everything else could be conducted online. It was perfect. While the rest of the workforce was scrambling to adapt to the new normal, Stephen was slipping into it with consummate ease. He rearranged the room so that the computer screen faced away from the door. 'Better background for video calls,' he assured Janice. 'More professional than a view of photo frames and knick-knacks.' He adopted the 'suit-and-tie upstairs, pyjama-bottoms downstairs' fashion as his own, ensured there was always an incomprehensible spreadsheet open on his computer in case Janice ventured too far into the study with yet another cup of tea, and found a long-discarded set of headphones to apply to his ears when the boss was supposedly making his daily call. Meanwhile, Janice set up her own home office in Deirdre's old bedroom with a laptop from the

Community House. Each respected the other's privacy. They were both working professionals, after all, even if Janice's job consisted mainly of keeping the House's unchanging files looking spruce and acting as a conduit and sponge for all the sorrow and loss suffered by their community-in-limbo.

Stephen thanked his lucky stars that his wife's now-on-hold job qualified her for government support. He gave himself a small tick of approval whenever he landed a writing or clerical job on Airtasker. How pleasant it was to hammer out a resumé for some poor sap who'd suddenly found herself on the scrapheap thanks to this microscopic enemy. It gave him a tiny feeling of usefulness which working for Gillespie had never done. He monitored the bank balance every day just in case an online purchase tipped them over into the red and revealed his deception. And he and Janice agreed that this new normal was a normal which suited them very nicely.

As winter deepened and their world shrank to a five-kilometre radius, the couple found more positives.

'We could just pack the work thing in and hit the road once this is over,' said Janice as they completed a quick circuit of the deserted golf course and sat on a bench to get their breath back. 'Is this allowed, by the way?'

'What?'

'Sitting down instead of exercising.'

'Goodness knows. If we're asked, we could always claim you twisted your ankle or something.'

'Good thinking. Or say our dog ran off and we're waiting for its return. Everyone's got a dog these days, it seems.'

'What sort of dog do we have, love?'

'A bitser for sure. Black and white thing called … called …'

'Ethel. Spritely for an old girl, Ethel is.'

'Ethel it is. Anyway … hitting the road. With Ethel, of course.'

'We could,' Stephen replied, forgetting for a moment that there was no caravan to be hitting any road with, let alone a dog to share it. That moment of happiness was all the more delicious for the thud of reality which followed. 'But let's not get ahead of ourselves. No good hitting the road and getting only five kays away. And even when this lifts, we'll still be stuck in the state.'

'Nothing wrong with holidaying locally. Businesses will be grateful for the customers. Perhaps we could take Bessie out of storage and holiday on our nature strip.'

Stephen laughed at that but only on the outside.

'Perhaps it's time to upgrade from Bessie.'

The words fell out of his mouth before his brain considered the financial implications of buying a new caravan with a dwindling pot of money which existed only through the sale of the old one.

'I like Bessie.'

End of *that* conversation.

* * *

Shopping trips got reduced to one person per household per day. Janice happily volunteered, 'Because you have more work to do than me'.

Stephen found her absences weirdly relaxing. Even when he was ensconced in the study, he always felt the strain of wearing his mask of normality, and yet, as they watched news clips of people working from home or struggling to make ends meet, he slowly started feeling like one of the gang. What did reality mean when an entire world was tumbling in a maelstrom of unprecedented confusion?

* * *

With winter receding, the prospect of a lifting of lockdown was rapidly approaching. Even with a so-called 'Ring of Steel' surrounding the city, keeping its residents' plague-carrier bodies out of regional areas, there was a sense of hope abroad, a feeling that the worst was behind them all. It was as if there was a city-wide sigh of relief.

Going anticlockwise around the golf course, arms linked, they walked in silence. Two varieties of silence.

'So,' said Janice at last. 'I'm guessing it's the usual holiday break for you. You haven't mentioned anything.'

'Mmmm, I expect so.'

'And if we're able to travel further than five kays we could pop over to the storage place and give Bessie a spring clean. That'd be legit, wouldn't it?'

'I suppose so.'

'This whole thing getting you down? Strange, isn't it, how nobody's quite the same any more.'

'Janice, love.' He stopped in his tracks, pulled up every ounce of courage he still possessed, took a deep breath, and began. 'Something I have to tell you. No, lots of things. There's nothing normal about our new normal. I haven't worked in nearly a year, not for Gillespie anyway. We've been living off my severance pay. And,' he finished in a rapidly descending mumble, 'about Bes—'

'What? But you've been working from home like everybody else.'

'I haven't, love. He "let me go". That's the expression. As if I wanted to go.'

'And when was this?'

'Right before we went on holidays last year. He said my annual leave would serve as my month's notice. I didn't want to spoil our trip so I kept quiet.'

'And then walked out the door that first morning back as if everything was the same?'

'Yes.' His voice held all the misery and self-loathing which he'd carried for so many months. 'I was hoping I'd get another job but it turns out that firms aren't all that keen on hiring sixty-three-year-old suburban accountants, or sixty-three-year-old anythings, as it happens. And then this COVID thing happened and, oh, I don't know, it gave me a chance to play along. I'm sorry.'

He moved towards her, arms outstretched. She moved away, eyes unblinking above her flower-patterned mask.

'And Bessie? What else were you going to say?'

'There's no Bessie. I had to sell her.'

Behind her mask it was obvious to Stephen that his wife's mouth had dropped open.

'Say that again?'

'Love, the van was the only big asset we could live without!'

'You didn't think to consult with me?'

'This blasted virus, the world on its head.' He shrugged, studied his shoes.

Now she did reach out – but only to pull his mask below his chin.

'Stephen, you had weeks, months even, to tell me before this pandemic got really serious—'

'Eighteen weeks. It's all on a spreadsheet.'

'—so don't you dare use it as an excuse. You should have told me straight away. What on earth did you think I'd do? I know what a prick Gillespie's been to you. I would have understood. Might have personally gone in there and shirtfronted the bloke.'

Stephen ventured a weak smile in response, but his wife's angry eyes indicated that no joke had been meant.

'It's about to rain,' Janice said, turning away in the direction of their home.

He scuttled after her, wondered about linking arms again, decided against it. An elderly man passed him, glaring, and a red-faced Stephen pulled his mask back up.

'What are we going to do?' Janice was asking. She covered another hundred metres in silence before turning to face her fearful husband. 'Who did you sell Bessie to?'

He mumbled the name of a local RV dealership.

'Here's what I think,' Janice continued in a tone which brooked no disagreement. 'We go back there and see if she's still for sale. I'm thinking with lockdowns and what-have-you, van sales won't have been good this past year. We buy her back – Wait! I'm coming to the money side – or at least put a deposit on her. And if she's gone already, then we pick out a new Bessie, maybe even a better Bessie. We put our house on the market and hit the road. If we're forced to live with a new normal, I think it's only fair that we have a say in what that new normal is. You know,' and her voice was gentler, softer now, 'I would have understood. I don't know why you felt you had to keep me in the dark. This is 2020 not the 1950s.'

Stephen made the sensible decision to let Janice talk this all out in her own good time. She'd have the answers, that much he knew for sure, and right now, with the burden of his secret shame out in the open, he wanted only to relax into her caring arms. She was saying something about the awful year everyone had suffered through, about not crying over spilt milk, about pulling together and soldiering on, about lights at the ends of tunnels.

When he tentatively slipped his arm around hers again, he met no resistance.

* * *

Across the globe, optimists were convincing themselves that they'd weathered the storm. Between Melbourne and Austin, London and Rawalpindi, Auckland and Sao Paolo, smiling faces beamed at each other across half a world. Christmas lights twinkled and anxieties were pushed back into their boxes.

'Merry Christmas, darlings!' an excited Janice said to her distant loved ones. 'What's the weather like? Any snow? ... It doesn't snow in Austin? Fair enough. Lucky we didn't give you a toboggan, hey, Jordan! ... Sorry about just sending money, Deirdre. The parcel post has been useless here. No planes in equals no planes out. Funny how you don't think of all the knock-on effects. … Yes, we've finished lunch here. Nothing special this year, keeping it simple. Anyway, we have some big news. Do you want to tell Deirdre and Brett, Stephen? No? Okay. Thought everyone would be sick of the sound of my voice by now. So, darlings, we've made a huge decision. Your dad's going to retire, we're going to sell this place, buy a new caravan – yes, Bessie's done sterling service but it's time for her to retire too – and then we'll become grey nomads. We've got our eye on a Beston Delta Four, very swishy compared to Bessie … No. no; state borders still closed but that shouldn't last much longer. There's a bit of an outbreak up north but we'll be sticking to Victoria for the time being. Better safe than sorry, I always say. The thing is, we've knocked this virus on the head down here. No new cases in the past couple of months. *And* Australia's apparently at the front of the queue with vaccinations. So it's looking like 2021 is going to be the year we get back to normal … yeah, that's right darlings, the new normal.'

MARIAN MATTA is an award-winning writer of short fiction, whose first short story collection, *Life, Bound*, was published by MidnightSun Publishing in 2020. She also writes non-fiction articles and historical novels. Her home in the Dandenong Ranges is a constant source of inspiration. As well as a writer, she's a great-grandmother, circus student and ineffectual gardener. Optimism is her watchword.
https://marianmattawrites.wordpress.com/

The lockdown diaries

KRISTY RHOADES

5:00 am. 'Mum! Mu-um! Jade isn't social distancing!' Skye (age seven) screams.

'I … do … not … have … cowon-a-viwus!' Jade (age three) bellows.

5:30 am. I get up from reading stories on the lounge and open the curtains. Another bright-blue cloudless day with the birds singing sweetly. I step in a puddle of cat vomit next to the curtains. Hobbling to the kitchen on one heel, I knock down a Lego tower Skye is building.

'Mu-ummm! It's ruined! It'll never be the same again! You did that on purpose!'

Copious crying. I take a breath.

6:30 am. Breakfast done. Dishes overflow in the sink. We get dressed.

7:00 am. Todd's up and starts work in the kitchen while making his toast. His earbuds are in and he mouths, 'I'm in a meeting,' over piles of debris on the kitchen counter.

8:30 am. School day starts. Skye uses dry pasta to measure objects around the house for Maths. Jade sticks dry pasta up her nose.

9:00 am. We do Art on the balcony. Painting portraits. Skye paints one of herself and the cat. I paint my own portrait. I look mad. Jade is painting the actual balcony.

10:00 am. Music. The girls are somehow both nude. Sitting on green plastic stools at the adjustable table, they sing to a video sent by Skye's music teacher.

'En-gine, en-gine, num-ber nine; go-ing down the rail-way line. Woo-o-hoo.'

Bo-ttoms wi-ggle on the stools; as en-gine goes on down the line. 'Poo-oo-pooh!'

What? Oh.

We sprint to the toilet. Just in time. Jade has accidents since lockdown; and Nanny doesn't come anymore; and we don't go to parks; and she's told not to touch anything when we go out; and she has to wash her hands and sing happy birthday; and Daddy's home but in a meeting.

She is only three.

10:30 am. I get morning tea ready. I look from the kitchen to see Jade holding the cats' tail between a pair of scissors. I sprint to the living room. Just in time.

11:00 am. Trampoline bounce. The hose sprays up underneath the trampoline and splashes the girls as they giggle and squeal. The laughter tumbles out of our backyard.

12:00 pm. We cook Anzac biscuits, following Miss M's video teaching fractions. ½ cup of flour; ¼ cup of oats. Skye's loose tooth falls out in the batter.

'How will the tooth fairy find my tooth? She'll never leave me any money!'

I'm thinking of making a new word: 'Scryming' – it's screaming and crying at the same time.

We find the tooth. We send photos of Skye to her teacher: toothy grin holding a finished biscuit in one hand and her tooth in the other. I don't eat the biscuits.

1:00 pm. School can be done for the day. I'm covered in paint and flour and sit in the house, noise, and mess, and the afternoon stretches beyond me like a decade. I feel like scryming.

KRISTY RHOADES lives in an old double-storey brick house perched on the edge of an ancient rainforest by the sea. She lives there with her two spirited young daughters, her strong man of the sea, and a cat made of white snow. When life affords her a moment, she can be found gazing into the forest watching wildlife and listening to the wind for stories to tell.

The little C

T. J. ROWNTREE

Not sure why I couldn't stop blubbering when I heard about Warney. I hadn't even met the bloke, but each greedily consumed, syrupy tribute served to deepen the distantly personal connection. Something to do with mortality? Just my weakened state? I wasn't unfamiliar with hangovers but the virus coursing through me felt like a doozy and left my brain in a permanent state of fade. The tears flowed like I was on a long haul flight watching some sentimental dog-dies-at-the-end movie. I tried to reassure myself they weren't tears of self-pity, but I couldn't rule out that possibility.

I'd done everything right. I listened to the alleged medical experts and sleeve-upped, QR coded into each and every slowly-dying venue, compromised my breathing with an overpriced mask and even stayed home when Auntie Anna told me to. It didn't matter; the virus will take you down if and when it wants to. The bloody thing had taken me as soon as I'd been ambitious enough to book an overseas trip. *There's always someone worse off than you.* The platitude played in my mind accompanied by an orchestra of other overused clichés designed to guilt-trip us into some sort of action. We pretend to overcome, but the sneaky bottle of selfish within can smash at any time, cascading bitterness and outrage.

The little C

I flicked on another Warney special to force the bottle back onto the shelf. His *Top 50 wickets in Australia*. By number forty-five, the blubbering ceased, and I was on the edge of my seat. It wasn't like I hadn't seen the dismissals a hundred times before, but the back-to-back format elevated the genius. It also brought warming nostalgia and I found myself attempting to calculate the year of each dismissal based on King's hairline, styling and yo-yoing physical condition.

Some sort of understanding emerged through the brain fog. The reason for the blubbering wasn't because I did or did not know the man, nor was it some sort of imagined friendship or connection. As his glorious 300th dismissal played, I realised it was all about stones: milestones, touchstones, and headstones.

Amidst the carnage of his broken-stump milestones, I could situate my own life. The triumphs and the failures; the unexpected and the inevitable; the endings and the new beginnings – each meaningful event in my own life could be matched to a wicket or series. The man was a deeply-flawed but omnipresent touchstone for my generation. Pretty soon, though, he'd be another headstone in a field of bones and ash. Not forgotten, but a sometimes-recalled part of the past that seemed so much more meaningful and tangible than the present, let alone the dark possibility of the future.

The realisation seemed to quell the fire of what I supposed was grief. Understanding and acceptance now walked hand in hand, and my mind shifted gears into appreciation. *Here for a good time not a long time.* Another overused cliché but admittedly apt for King. I needed to take a leaf out of his little black book. Just had to beat the 'Little C' first.

I cheered aloud as the number one dismissal (Warney's 700th) rolled around, and took a satisfying sip of electrolytes – as recommended by the Chief Health Officer of course; no way I could possibly make my own plans or decisions. I adjourned from

Warney and warily flicked on the news channel. Heartbreaking floods intermingled with a despot dropping missiles on a sovereign nation. Bloody hell! Combined with Warney, it really was the coronation moment of a piss poor couple of years. Hard to imagine the world not being in a more perilous place but that was egotistical thinking. We all think we're important enough to still be here when things go to shit, hence the proliferation of post-apocalyptic productions streaming across the various time bandit services.

Judging by the doom-porn news, it was hard to imagine the Little C even existing anymore. I shook my head; just my luck to pick it up when it appeared as though it was no longer relevant. I decided to call Mum. No better person to provide a bit of sympathy, and one of the few people left who accepted voice calls rather than text messages or posts.

'Hello, Georgina speaking.' Mum picked up almost immediately. I could picture her lazing in her recliner, dog at her feet and word search book on her lap.

'Hey, Mum. How you doing?'

'Flynn! Don't worry about me. How are you feeling?'

'Bit surreal today. Feel a bit better, but Warney's departure has knocked me for six.'

'Who's Warney, Flynn? Is he a friend of yours?'

My hand involuntarily clenched around the phone as I shook my head. 'Shane Warne, Mum. Haven't you been watching the news?' I replied in my most impatient patient tone.

'The overweight blonde guy who's always in *New Idea*?'

Fair to say I'd not inherited my love of cricket from Mum, but she definitely had her finger on the pulse of trash magazines. 'Yep. He played a little bit of cricket too,' I said, deciding a change of subject was in order. 'Today's my last day in isolation. I'll retest myself tonight and come round on the weekend if it's all clear.'

The little C

'That's great, Flynn. Do you still have the RATs I gave you?' Mum was immensely proud of the fact that she had somehow secured RATs at the peak of their demand. It didn't matter that they were now freely available; in her mind they were still the most valuable and sought-after commodity on the planet.

'Yes, Mum, one left here. Hopefully that's all I need.'

'Okay, make sure you let me know how you go.' Her labrapoodledoodlenoodlador barked in the background. 'I'd better go, Flynn, someone's here.'

'Bye, Mum, hopefully see you soon.'

'Bye, love.'

I checked the time as I put my phone down. Only 3:00 pm. Jesus, it had been a long week. I was certain I'd seen the old-school analogue clock on my lounge room wall ticking backwards at one point. It reminded me of the time I had chicken pox when I was a kid – on the bloody school holidays. Buggered if I know how I got through it then. I vaguely remember being bored and sleeping like a sloth, but I must have watched a truckload of daytime television tripe. At least I had Netflix and Fox and all the rest as faithful friends this time around.

Through the whole ordeal, I'd attempted to divide my days into one-hour units. One hour Netflix, one hour reading, one hour failing to complete a crossword, and so on. The problem was, the old grey-matter didn't want to cooperate. Even an hour of concentration was too much, and I'd increasingly felt like a mental pygmy. Bingeing Netflix certainly didn't help the intelligence quotient. The disturbing notion that Warney carking it had helped me through the final twenty-four hours occurred to me. Another reason to be appreciative.

Looking around, I conceded that I probably should have allocated more time to housekeeping. Empty takeaway boxes and coffee cups were the most conspicuous contaminants, but half-filled bottles, newspapers and magazines also held pride of place. I rejected the tired cliché that it looked like a bomb had hit – that particular simile wasn't holding water in the current geopolitical climate. I told myself that I'd sort it out if the test was negative. I'd told myself I'd do a lot of things if the test was negative. The big IF.

My intention was to take the test at about 6:00 pm, so I considered how to fill the next three units. Remote in hand, I began to surf. News – flick. Sandra Bullock movie – flick. Some English game show – brief contemplation, then flick. *Seinfeld* – I took the wave. The show about nothing seemed especially relevant in my current circumstances: my days about nothing, my week about nothing, my life about nothing. I snapped my fingers aloud guiltily, raising myself from the toxic self-pity.

Two episodes and one unit later, the mind started spluttering and I switched off the idiot box. The daily journey to the letterbox had become a real highlight and I decided it was time for today's adventure. A bold explorer, I stepped out the front door and very nearly went ass-up. Why hadn't I heard the courier? I looked more closely at the box that had just about brought me undone and understood immediately that it had been hand delivered. A mystery box from whom, I wondered. Mum was the obvious guess, but she probably would have asked about it when I spoke to her on the phone earlier.

Seriously considering the possibility of an act of anthrax terrorism, I carefully hauled the potential treasure chest, or death trap, inside. I noted it was about the size of a smallish moving box and estimated its weight at no more than a couple of kilograms. The first thing I spotted as I ripped it open was the familiar handwriting scratched on a pristine white A4 page. Trent; no one else I knew wrote like a drunken doctor. The scrawl was his distinctive trademark. I squinted and did my best to find some sort of meaning.

> Hey Mate
>
> RIP Warney. Genuinely irreplaceable.
>
> Few medicinal goodies to help you through what is hopefully your last day in iso.
>
> Enjoy and see you soon.
>
> Trent

At least, I thought that's what the mishmash of alleged vowels and consonants said. Fortunately, short and sweet was Trent's style. I peeked further into the lucky dip and smiled. A four-pack of my preferred pale ale stood impressively on top of a magazine. I lifted the glorious tinnies and there he was: Shane Warne, circa 1993, on the cover of Inside Sport magazine. The image of Trent getting lost in his 90s sports magazine archives as he searched for the elusive King cover solidified in my mind, and my smile evolved into a quiet chuckle. Beneath the magazine, a paperback revealed itself. Bloody smart-arse – a Mills & Boon pulp special. I guess I could use a little romance in my life, I pondered, particularly within the vivid realism of quality literature. Then, finally, I spotted Trent's crowning achievement: protected within a small, clip-top microwave-container was a perfect, triumphant joint. Trent had even thought to include a lighter. The man was truly a care-box artist. Medicinal indeed.

As I more closely examined my treasures, a single silent tear of co-mingled gratitude and grief trickled down my cheek. Trent had lost his uncle to the Little C about eighteen months previous. It was pre-vaccine and, burdened with a thirty-darts-a-day habit, it was no great surprise that Uncle Ted succumbed. Like Warney, he was a larrikin and had lived an amazing life. The tragedy wasn't his passing; it was the pathetically inadequate send-off imposed by our esteemed elected dictators. My mind flashed to a Little C news stalwart – interviews with self-absorbed twenty- or thirty-something couples complaining that they had to postpone their wedding. I shook my head. Such humans appeared to operate under the assumption that the world spun purely to cater for their whims and special occasions, that nothing bad could happen on days that are important to them. Funerals aren't like weddings; there is no option to postpone. I knew Trent had been shattered he couldn't mourn properly with loved ones, and concluded the brilliant care-pack gesture was an act of uncommon wisdom and newfound sensitivity.

I grabbed my phone, deftly manoeuvred my thumb, and hit send.

Thanks mate, ur a deadset genius

Almost instantaneously, a thumbs up appeared in response. Sometimes brevity runs deep, I thought to myself as I checked the time. Again. Trent's lucky dip had consumed nearly a full unit. I glanced over at the kitchen bench where the RAT sat enticingly.

Not yet.

Instead I somehow found space for my newly acquired four-pack in the freezer, then connected to my headphones. Pearl Jam would provide the soundtrack for the last unit. But which album? I deliberated, then pressed play on their sophomore effort and was quickly lost in gorgeous, gargling grunge. Another touchstone, I reflected, this one still very much alive fortunately. I followed the lyrics and sang like a deranged, flu-riddled angel, all the while lamenting that it's all about singles and playlists in 2022. The true album experience is in the rear-view mirror for most.

The little C

With voice strained and final track playing, I re-engaged with my old friend. 5:45 pm now. Close enough. I almost knew the RAT instructions by heart but read through them again anyway. The last thing I wanted to do was bugger up this test, of all tests. While hating the stick up the nose treatment, I'd been advised that nasal swabs represented a more accurate testing option. Maybe more accurate but bloody uncomfortable, I concluded, as my nose twitched following its violation. Sample taken, and for a horrifying instant I was sure the test stick was going to slip from my grip. A dark vision of Warney dropping Pietersen in '05 moved through me, but luck or fate intervened and my fingers held firm. Instructions followed to-a-tee, all that was left to do was wait.

The next fifteen minutes was spent in a world of what-ifs and tenuous resolutions. A positive result was simply unthinkable, but I sensed a small pocket of brain tissue instinctively preparing itself for the possibility. Beyond that, I wouldn't allow myself to consciously consider the ramifications. Superstitious maybe, but acknowledging the worst-case seemed like a curse that would ensure it eventuated.

How to best utilise the potential freedoms associated with a negative result dominated my mind. It really had been a fucked-up couple of years and just as the tail-end appeared, the Little C had caught up with me. I tried to mentally articulate what I'd learnt in those two years. What I'd do differently in the future. How I wanted to live my life on the other side. The actions I must take to attain satisfaction. It really felt like there was potential for an authentic new dawn, and I didn't want to bugger it up.

Eat better, exercise more, go to the footy instead of watching it on TV, turn off the idiot box, quit the dead-end job, engage in more random acts of kindness, meditate, recycle, cut down on the booze, be a better friend, be a better person, be politically aware, live your best life, fight injustice, volunteer, ditch the social media, live in the moment, save the fucking pandas …

By 6:00 pm, I knew I could no longer distinguish between truisms and banalities. I stopped trying and thought about Warney and Putin and floods and Uncle Ted instead. About living a full life. What the fuck did that mean, exactly? I didn't know, but I was certain blokes like Warney, Ted and even Putin didn't suffer from paralysis by analysis. Courage was what I needed. And good people to steer that courage. I felt uncommonly certain that it might be that simple.

Time up and hypothesis in place, I examined the future. My heart sank into the deepest trench. Surely not? Panicked and failing to exhale, I re-compared my test result with the instructions …

Thank Christ, or whoever is the director of this shit show. Negative. I released a deep breath and cursed my carelessness. Medical test analyst I was not.

Glass full of pale, I reclined and took a moment before my mind was besieged by a familiar foe.

Eat better, exercise more, go to the footy instead of watching it on TV, turn off the idiot box, quit the dead end job, engage in more random acts of kindness, meditate, recycle, cut down on the booze, be a better friend, be a better person, be politically aware, live your best life, fight injustice, volunteer, ditch the social media, live in the moment, save the fucking pandas …

I took a sip and smiled ruefully. It was true. Another cliché. *Nothing worthwhile is ever easy.*

T. J. ROWNTREE is a Brisbane-based freelancer specialising in travel and craft beer writing – with a little fiction on the side. Follow his adventures at thetripologist.com.

A tale of twin towns

CHRISTINE E BETTS

On that chilly Saturday morning, Lily and Dave went about their business like two people who had no idea things were about to go sideways. Lily taught a class, then went to lunch with her friends. Dave had a busy day at the café, then went for a surf. Dave missed the news that the border was closing because he didn't have Twitter, such was the ridiculous nature of existence in 2021.

By three that afternoon, Lily was hiding in a wardrobe. The dog sniffed at the door, confused about the turn of events. Dave, oblivious to the impending nonsense, was lying on the couch watching football.

'They're closing the border,' Lily said into the phone, her voice a fierce whisper.

Dave was silent for a beat. 'When?'

'Midnight.' Lily chewed on her cheek. It was a bad habit. She wasn't aware she was doing it. If Dave had been in front of her rather than on the other end of the phone line, he might have said, 'You're doing the thing with your mouth again.'

Dave clenched the phone to his ear with his shoulder and determinedly picked at his fingernails. Unlike Lily, he'd been aware of this bad habit, his own nervous tick, since primary school.

'They're slamming it shut in our faces,' Lily said.

'Whaddya mean?'

'They're not letting anyone from Tweed across. You won't be able to go to work. If I go to the studio, they won't let me come home.' The panic rose in Lily's chest. She wanted to cry.

'Where are you? Sounds like you're in a box.' He laughed.

'In the wardrobe. I don't want Mum to get upset.'

Dave nodded and went back to shredding his fingernails. 'I'll call ya back. I need to think.'

The line went dead. Lily pictured Dave walking down the hallway and turning left at the bathroom. The toilet was his thinking place, and the cats would take up sentry at the door.

Dave pictured Lily making her mum a cuppa and not mentioning the fact that life was about to get really complicated.

Lily's phone buzzed, a text from Dave.

WE COULD SWAP HOUSES.

He wasn't yelling; he used all caps, all the time.

Lily's TV was on mute, but that was the way her mum liked it. Lily's mum, Joyce, didn't have her glasses on but she wasn't really watching the telly anyway. Joyce wanted to know when life had gotten so boring. One minute she was busy with a job and a family, the next, she was in front of the idiot box all day.

Lily, with Bella the rottweiler at her heels, checked on Joyce, and was relieved the sound was still turned down on the Newsflash. At least Joyce wouldn't hear about the border closing until Lily had come up with a plan. Lily collected the used mugs and asked Joyce if she wanted another Monte Carlo.

'No thanks, love. Don't want to spoil my tea.'

Lily smiled at her mum as though she hadn't completely forgotten about making dinner. She took the cups to the kitchen and put them in the dishwasher. She and Dave couldn't swap houses. Dave wouldn't leave his cats and, besides, his house was definitely not set up for Joyce. It was a three-storey walk-up, for starters, and Joyce was just about to graduate from a walking stick to a wheely walker – not that she felt it was anything to celebrate.

Lily tapped out a text.

No can do. Mum can't move to your place.

The three little dots indicated Dave was typing something, but then they disappeared. He was busy pacing. His café, Cooly Beans, was doing well, considering he'd opened the place only a year before COVID had hit. Lily helped out when he couldn't get staff. It was at the end of her street, so sometimes she would take the super-slow walk with Joyce, old Bella shuffling at their side. Joyce would enjoy one of Dave's excellent coffees and whatever sweet thing he had in the cabinet that day, while Lily waited tables or washed dishes. Joyce loved Dave, and he lapped up her devotion and applause when he busted out some impromptu dance moves between serving customers.

After the slow walk home, they would spend the afternoon with Bella snoring on the back patio and Joyce wondering aloud why Lily had split up with such a lovely guy.

'We're better as friends,' Lily would say, for the hundredth time.

For a moment, Lily imagined Dave and the cats moving in with her and Joyce. And Bella. The pros were: he'd be close to the café, and he could come home to cook Joyce her favourite scrambled eggs. The cons? There were only two bedrooms and one bathroom. Oh, and the cats would not get along too well with Bella.

'Love? You there? The man on the telly said they're closing the border,' Joyce called.

Dammit.

'Yeah, Mum. It'll be okay. Dave and I are just coming up with a plan,' Lily said, trying to sound cheery and failing.

Joyce said something Lily didn't hear, and Lily wandered in to check on her. Bella hadn't left Lily's side since she'd come out of the wardrobe. The old dog always knew when something was up.

Joyce had the remote pointed at the TV, a look of concern on her face. 'What are you going to do about the studio?'

Lily was well versed in the keep-calm-and-carry-on routine she had going with Joyce. The 2020 lockdown had been rough. She had moved the studio in the Christmas break; the landlord for the old place had put the rent up. Dave had helped her find a bigger space in Tweed for half the price, in a commercial block behind his boxing gym. No one cared about the stupid border in 2019, but when COVID hit, that invisible line may as well have been a brick wall.

'Love?' Joyce said.

There was no point trying to tell Joyce she had it sorted. Joyce Peters had been a high school teacher for years, before she got sick, and she could smell a lie at thirty paces. Lily shook her head. She really had no idea what she was going to do.

'Don't chew your cheek, love,' Joyce said.

Lily opened her mouth and glared at her mother as though she had been unfairly accused. Then, knowing she was close to losing it, she went back to the kitchen and pulled out some dinner options. Dave had taught her to cook well over the years. They'd worked for years on cruise ships all over the world. Thanks to Dave, they'd always had healthy meals even when they only had a microwave or a single-burner stove.

'Curry for dinner?' Lily called, and Joyce replied with an emphatic 'yes'.

Lily prepared the curry and set it to simmer. A message popped up from Dave, but it was nothing useful, no all-caps outbursts; just a GIF of a man panicking, followed by a photo of the Berlin Wall. Dave always was dramatic. Lily started the rice cooker.

'Mum, you want to use the bathroom before dinner?'

Joyce thought about it and said she did. She hated being dependant. 'Useless' she called herself on a bad day, but Lily would reply that lifting Joyce helped her stay fit for her dance students.

'Davey's still a wonderful dancer,' Joyce said as Lily helped her up. Her voice suggested she was revealing a tantalising secret.

Lily nodded. 'He hasn't really danced since we quit the ships, but it's not something you forget. Muscle memory.'

Joyce said nothing else. She just smiled.

The whole house smelled of the delicious curry and they forgot about the border for a while. As though he had smelled his own recipe cooking, Dave knocked on the door and walked in. 'Is that my yellow curry?'

Joyce and Lily laughed. 'Pull up a bowl and a chair,' Lily said.

He went to the kitchen for some rice and came back with Lily's phone. There was a dozen or more messages from friends and studio clients. All asked variations of the same theme; What were they going to do when the border closes?

'I phoned too, but you didn't answer.' He spooned a mouthful of curry in and chewed then nodded his head and smiled. 'Damn, you're a good cook.'

'She had a great teacher,' Joyce said.

Lily rolled her eyes.

'You should run the café,' Joyce said. 'And Davey, you can teach at the studio.'

Dave nearly spat his mouthful of curry across the table. He swallowed and stared at his ex-mother-in-law. 'Joyce, I haven't taught in years. I hardly dance any more, unless you count trying to stay away from my boxing trainer.'

Silence fell for a few moments. Then Lily leaned towards the table. 'This is a great idea, Mum.'

Joyce nodded her head. 'I have a lot of good ideas, but I'm old. People don't usually listen.'

Dave put his hand on Joyce's arm. 'It is a great idea, and it might just get us out of this mess.'

Joyce beamed at him.

* * *

The first week of the Tweed lockdown was hard on everyone. Dave knew his café would thrive under Lily's caretaker management, but the unfairness of it all riled him. He was less than a three-minute drive from his favourite beach, his friends, his Italian coffee machine, but he wasn't allowed across the border, an imaginary line that lay between him and the people he loved. He didn't even try to cross. He'd heard that doctors, teachers, and paramedics had been turned away from the border crossing. 'Not Essential,' they were told. Imagine what they'd say to a barista.

Each morning, Dave and Lily facetimed. Dave talked Lily through the startup procedures and daily menu. Joyce was there with her walker, emptying the dishwasher and watering the plants.

Lily worried about her students, but there was nothing she could do. COVID cases 800 kilometres away meant the studio had to close. It made no sense to her, but then she was just a dance teacher, not a politician. She figured she must be missing something.

Dave filled his time running on the treadmill and smashing the punching bag in the garage under his apartment building. A few of the local kids hung around, so he said they could use the bag. He found a bag of old gloves in the garage from his coaching days.

'You need to start doing some of the dance routines I've got on the studio YouTube channel. So, you can teach them when the lockdown lifts,' Lily urged him one morning as he talked her through a new zucchini slice recipe.

Dave slumped his shoulders. 'It's never gonna bloody lift. Did you see the cases in Sydney today?'

Lily stopped squeezing the water out of the grated zucchini and frowned at the screen. What could she say to him? At least she had something to keep her busy. She was exhausted, but she was enjoying working in the café. And Joyce had left the walker in the corner of her bedroom that morning and was busy refilling the serviettes. Even Bella was trotting jauntily along when they walked in the afternoon.

'Of course it will lift, and they'll open the border, and we'll all laugh about this one day.'

Dave gave her a grim smile. 'No, we won't.'

'I'm sure the cats are enjoying having you home all day,' Lily said.

Finally, Dave laughed. 'Even *they're* sick of me.'

Over the quiet weeks, Dave learned Lily's dances and even started teaching them to the kids who came to smack their frustrations out on the punching bag each day. The cats learned to make themselves scarce when he put the music on.

* * *

When the lockdown finally lifted, Dave opened the studio, offering free classes to kids and their parents. His group classes were more fun than they were dance, but wasn't that what everyone needed?

One morning, Lily texted Dave:

You have mail.

Dave's texting etiquette hadn't improved:

MEET ME AT THE BORDER ON BAY STREET AT 3.

Dave bought coffees at Bread Social just before they closed, and wandered up the incline towards the ridiculous border wall at the top of the street. Lily had brought some of the slice from that morning's baking. They chatted over the orange bollards about the café, about the studio, about how Joyce was the new *maître d'*, seating everyone and taking their orders.

'That slice is delicious,' Dave said. 'Hey, can you help me with this step?'

He stood back from the row of bollards and performed a section of a routine from Lily's class. Lily's mouth dropped open and all the other people meeting with their loved ones and business partners at the orange wall cheered and applauded.

Dave had nailed the steps, but he was struggling with the turn. Lily showed him how it was done. He watched intently and they now had the undivided attention of the nearby crowd on both sides of the wall.

'Oh right,' Dave said, nodding. 'Like this?'

Lily clapped out the beat on the bollard between them, and Dave executed the routine perfectly.

'We should do this again,' he said, smiling at the happy people around them.

*　*　*

A couple of days later Lily received another text:

BAY STREET. THURSDAY 3PM. 80'S THEME

A slow smile crept across Lily's face.

Dave and a small group of others milled on the southern side of the border wall, looking like extras from a Janet Jackson music video. Lily had invited a couple of friends, but as they all walked up to the wall, she could see she would need to lift her game next time. Suddenly Dave lifted an old boom box over his head and the beat started. He placed the stereo on the wall and let the music take control. Dave and his crew moved in perfect unison, but Lily and her girls held their own. By the time they finished dancing, the two separate crowds gathered at that loathsome wall were laughing and cheering wildly.

'Next week we'll do Disco?' Lily called and everyone cheered again.

'Latin?' Someone called from the crowd and a few more people cheered. Lily grinned and blew Dave a kiss. 'I'll bring Joycey. The rate she's improving, she'll be high kicking by the time we get to show tunes.'

So, the worst of times turned, like gradual magic, into not-so-terrible times. Joyce gave her wheely walker away to an elderly neighbour. Bella had trimmed down but she was content to embrace her old age and her position on the patio.

Dave and Lily shared the running of the café and the dance studio and one day, after the border opened, found they could probably consider being more than friends again. One day. One day we'll all look back and laugh and perhaps we'll sing, dance, and make zucchini slice, too.

CHRISTINE E BETTS is an Australian writer who left her heart in Paris years ago. A keen traveller, her first two novels are set in France, with works-in-progress set in California, England, and Australia.

All the lovely eyes

P. S. COTTIER

We learn to read expressions by the eyes alone, or the eyes assisted by rivers of frown, hills of surprise. Gone are the clues of mouth, hidden behind the safety of masks. Turned-down corners of lips, or the display of teeth in smile or grimace, are erased. Talk seems gentler, less carnivorous.

The eyes tell; now words are muffled. I see grief in the deep eyes of one woman, telling of her family trapped overseas. She sheds no tears, possibly because she had cried herself dry, a fake drought breaking out in the corners of her telling eyes.

Some of us relish the privacy of the mask, anxiety clothed. Dreams of naked anguish have been assuaged, if not eliminated, by the sweet curtain between us, the nervous players, and an over-eager audience, all too likely to throw advice like overripe fruit. I know my eyes show relief, to be given this thin barrier. Designed against viruses, it protects against the nosey and over-assured.

Words uttered need more concentration to be deciphered, almost as if the wearers had broken into another language – say, Mandarin or French. Apart from English, I speak only *très* bad French. I rely on the accents provided by the eyes, the grave or acute eyebrow of humour or anger. The flatness of boredom, the glassy blankness of some eyes makes spoken language almost indecipherable. Blank pages of forehead provide no clues either.

I saw a young girl begging for a mask. Her mother gave her one, and her eyes became neon with joy. Adults are the ones decked in these blue rectangles, and she feels like a grownup, admitted to the ranks of the tall and masked. Her much-too-big mask, flopping under her chin like a bikie's beard, is a badge of honour. I feel myself smile at her sweet victory, wonder if others are reading the sudden outbreak of humour in the brownness of my eyes, the creases folding upwards like a quail's wings. Emotion flushed out, into readability.

When we no longer need masks, will we have to relearn the expressions that give meaning? The openness of mouths will seem somehow crude, after the gentle, fringed communication of eyes. It will seem as if we yell every sentence, shout every observation.

The strange beauty of these months should be remembered, amongst the loss and fear. Our mouths behind a blue mouth-lid, closed over, murmuring. Our eyes speaking, quietly requiring patience and trust, concentration needed for meanings to be met.

P. S. COTTIER writes poetry, the occasional short story, and book reviews. She is currently Poetry Editor at *The Canberra Times*. She completed a PhD at the ANU, on images of animals in the works of Charles Dickens, and has worked as a union organiser, lawyer, and tea lady (not all at once).

Woman sits at home

KATELIN FARNSWORTH

When I'm asked to write about the pandemic, I don't know what to write. The task is at once overwhelming and simultaneously full of nothing. There's a nothingness when I think about the pandemic. Endless days of sitting at home, staring at the walls in my house, watching the news and scrolling through news articles. Not going anywhere. There's greyness too. All-encompassing, a medley of varying shades. Fog grey, cloud grey, mountain grey, sky grey and concrete grey. I try to think back to what I call the *before* time, when everything was simple and made sense. But when I try to, my thoughts separate and scatter inside my head.

I think back to January 2020, just before the pandemic began. Bushfires raged across the country, glowing red and orange, fire glittering from every corner. Smoke curled in the sky. I could see it as I walked to the train station in the mornings, thick and heavy. At night when I fell asleep, I could still smell it, penetrating, pushing itself underneath my skin. I started to dream about bushfires. These weird fierce dreams I didn't understand. There was cracking, thudding. Darkness over everything. Everything was the colour of charcoal. Firefighters pierced my mind. I wanted to do something, to somehow plunge myself into the fires as well, although of course that made little sense. But the fires consumed me, these swollen images of red and orange, amber and black – all of the time. Fires spread out across everything, leaning and seeping into all my thoughts. Until suddenly they didn't. Until suddenly it all stopped. But that's the thing. It didn't stop. It's just that something else started.

I was meant to get married in July 2020. A beach wedding, the white sand curling underneath our feet, a fiddle playing as we took our first dance together as husband and wife. The wedding was meant to be in Canada, on Canada's tiniest province, Prince Edward Island, an island known for seafood, golfing, and for being the birthplace of the fictional Anne of Green Gables. Many years earlier my partner and I had both been travelling, exploring Canada independently when we had met, connected, fallen in love. It was – and is – a special place to us.

So, we had booked our flights, arranged accommodation, booked hair stylists and makeup. Everything was ready. All we had to do was get that flight. It turned out that was the only thing we couldn't do.

I grieved the loss of our wedding. I sat at the kitchen table and wept. I stared at my wedding dress, the colour of sunflowers, the dress I'd bought only a few months earlier, and suddenly hated it. I felt selfish, foolish, absurd, to be crying over a postponed wedding when there were real tragedies in the world. People were sick, people were dying, and all I could think about was myself. The shame burned in my belly. I threw the dress into the back of the closet and told myself everything would be okay again soon.

When the nation was plunged into lockdown in March 2020, it felt like a bit of a joke. Not a very good joke, not very funny or clever, but a joke nonetheless. Collectively, we baked bread.

Sourdough starters. We went for long, languid walks, surrounded by green. *This is a good thing, we said, this is a chance to rest, breathe, do all the things we never had a chance to do.* I remember lying on the balcony at home. Summer had just ended but it was still warm, and the sky was a mix of gold and amber, the sun pushing down slowly. I watched the sky and breathed in. There was a peacefulness somewhere, knowing that around the country everyone else was sat at home too. Stillness. A nice thought, a comforting sort of soft thought. But it wasn't true. So much of what I thought wasn't true.

We postponed the wedding. *This mess will be over soon, we said, and then we will go. We will do Canada in 2021 because COVID will be over by then. It will be perfect. It will be worth the wait.*

The nation came out of lockdown. Except we didn't. My state of Victoria, my city of Melbourne, my hometown stayed in it. At least that's how I remember it. My memory plays tricks on me. All I remember is one long continuous stretch of time, where nothing happened. Days after days after days of sitting inside, watching through the window as a magpie flitted from branch to branch in the peach-coloured sky.

We were given one hour to leave the house. One hour to stretch, to move and unfurl. One hour to awaken our limbs, to breathe the fresh air, to notice the trees, the bushes, the birds. I used to look longingly at the road, the shining tarmac, and imagine myself thousands of kilometres away. Sometimes I would stop and stare at bus stops, even run my fingers down the timetable. All the places I could go, if only I was allowed. One hour wasn't enough. But it had to be.

I looked forward to that hour every day. Even if it was dark outside, even if it was raining, even if the rain was big and dark and overpowering. I put on my rain jacket and I walked. I remember how, at first, I walked with purpose and then later how my strides became steps and then my steps dwindled away, and after over 200 days and six lockdowns, I stopped moving at all.

I was safe. The lockdowns kept me safe. I was physically healthy. But I was not happy. I began to think I would never be happy again. Lockdown had taken everything I knew, had mixed and bent everything out of its shape.

It's a deadly global pandemic, I would say to myself, in a bizarre effort to comfort myself, *and you're in one of the safest countries in the world. It will be okay. You'll see.* But as the days went on, folding under one another, I didn't see at all. In another way, I didn't want to see. I told myself obsessively, whispering it at night, repeating it, chanting it, my new mantra: *lucky.*

So, you're in lockdown? *Lucky!*

So, you're bored? *Lucky!*

Lucky, lucky, lucky! It was like a clock striking. I was one of the lucky ones. But no matter how many times I said it to myself, I didn't feel lucky. I was exhausted, this ugly fatigue running through my bones.

What is anything, I began to think. What is something, what is nothing, what even is a virus?

I looked up viruses on the internet. I went down the rabbit hole, head spinning. I read about pandemics, about vaccinations, about doctors and scientists, and I closed my eyes and prayed to God – something I didn't even believe in – but nothing happened.

I even typed into Google, *when will the pandemic end*, but it didn't give me an answer. I smashed the keyboard with my hands. I cried a lot, tears that made me feel as though I was going to throw up.

I don't know. I don't know. Soon, that became my new mantra.

What should we have for dinner? *I don't know.*

What do you want to watch on Netflix? *I don't know.*

How was work from home today? *I don't know.*

How are you? *I don't know.*

Tea, tea, tea. I drank a lot of tea. I still drink a lot of tea. Yorkshire tea, chamomile tea, rose-scented herbal infusions, Scottish tea, green tea. Cup after cup. There's something meditative, almost dreamlike about making a pot of tea. Scooping in the tea leaves, pouring over the boiling water, watching, waiting for the scent to unfold. Adding milk, sugar, honey. These tiny moments of tea began to mean everything. I bought a new teapot and took it out into the garden.

But then there was my body. I pressed my stomach with my fingers. Was I putting on weight? *How much weight have I put on*, I wondered, as I reached for the chocolate. I felt the most unattractive I had ever felt. I wanted to hide myself, to put on an oversized jumper, and pretend my body didn't belong to me. I liked wearing a mask, felt safe inside it, hiding my face. I could be anyone, anything. If I saw someone I didn't want to talk to, I could pretend I didn't recognise them.

I'm not sure which lockdown it was – there have been so many – but the day after we came out of one, I walked to my local shopping complex. It took me forty-five minutes. The day was blue. Even now I remember that blueness, like it's a part of me, stitched into my skin. My hands were sweaty. I hadn't been to a shopping centre in over a year. But I walked and when I arrived there were people everywhere. Big people and little people and in-between-sized people swinging in front of me, moving quickly and slowly, and then not even moving at all. Surely all these people couldn't be real. Where had they all come from? How had they gotten here? It was too much. I'd longed for this noise, this thrum and bustle of people for so long, but now that I was here amongst it, I just wanted to get away. I turned and scurried off, feeling like a church mouse, gone after only ten minutes.

Back into the blue, I breathed out. My pandemic – such a funny thing to write – has felt like a patchwork quilt. Made up of so many different parts, even though for the most part, I have only been at home. But I have had to learn how to rewire myself, how to sit inside days, how to be still, how to meet with myself.

It became increasingly obvious that COVID wasn't suddenly just going to disappear. The hope that it would all be over after a few months dissolved quickly. Canada and the wedding seemed like an impossible dream. *Why don't we get married here in Melbourne*, I suggested uneasily, nervously, not even sure I meant it. I didn't want to give up our dream of Canada but I longed to marry the love of my life. I was tired of waiting. We talked about it. We thought about it. We sat around and looked sad. Finally, we agreed. An Australian wedding wouldn't be the same, but we could make it work.

A friend from interstate – a state that had, at this point, experienced virtually no COVID – asked me how I was. I told her I was struggling, that every day felt like it was slipping away from me, that my life no longer seemed to belong to me. *It's just the same thing, over and over again*, I told her. *What do you mean*, she asked, *my life hasn't changed at all since this all began*. She didn't mean to be cruel or unfeeling, but her words stung me. Immediately I was red-hot, anger scorching my insides. How could I explain to her that I did nothing, saw no one, hadn't seen my work colleagues in over a year, didn't know how to be a person in the world anymore. It wasn't fair. Her life hadn't even changed – she was still going to work, seeing her friends for coffee and cocktails, dancing in nightclubs and lounging at the beach – and I couldn't even leave my house for over an hour a day.

The Prime Minster called the virus 'The Victorian Virus'. For a time, it felt like Melbourne was the butt of every joke.

Fading, fading, I was fading. I wanted my life back.

We set a new date for our wedding. A tiny bush-wedding. Finally, there was something to look forward to. I held onto that date, marked it up on my wall calendar with love hearts. Tentatively we made new plans, booked a bush cottage to honeymoon in.

But it wasn't to be. Lockdown struck again.

Everything changes all the time. All of the things I want to say about time, about happiness, grief and loss, feels like a cliché. My tale from the pandemic doesn't have a happy ending because it doesn't have an ending. The pandemic isn't over. People are still getting sick, and people are still dying. Grief exists everywhere. We can pretend it's over when we're at the beach with our friends, drinking beers over the footy, or sharing takeout with our family, but it is not over, and our lives will never be the same again. But nothing ever stays the same. Things will change again because things always change, even if you can't see it, even if you can't believe it, can't conceive of it. There's always movement; it runs under everything. I try to hold onto the movement now. I take my time when I walk. I look at things more. I do my very best not to take things for granted.

Happiness exists, nestled within things – bottles of wine, new books, smiling faces, long walks in the bush – a happiness that I had forgotten about, something I had given up on for almost two years. Sometimes I think it sounds melodramatic. After all, I have access to healthcare and am so lucky to be vaccinated. I have a job and a safe place to live. I have loved ones and I am loved. It is enough, *more* than enough, but it's funny how sometimes the things that fill you up, that keep you grounded, can feel like they're not enough. How easy it is to forget.

When the virus finally caught me, after so long avoiding it, I felt curiously empty. I stared at the text message from the Department of Health: *'You have tested positive for COVID-19. Please isolate immediately at home*' and wondered how it could be. Part of me wanted to be angry, after all, hadn't I done everything right? I had gone through every single lockdown diligently, I had obeyed every rule and restriction with painstaking obedience, no matter how harsh or unfair it felt. I had worn a mask every time I left the house, and checked in with Service Victoria meticulously. But in the end, the virus found its way to me, as severely infectious viruses do. I wanted to blame someone but what good would come of it? I had to get through the infection, had to monitor my symptoms at home, and trust that the vaccine was doing its job.

I have learnt more about happiness these last two years than ever before.

Finally, after postponing three times, we had our wedding.

We stood in the Aussie bush, surrounded by tree ferns and gum trees and a creek that warbled like a bird, and we said what we'd been longing to say. I wore a lavender-coloured dress and as I leaned in to kiss my now-husband, I realised something all of sudden: the pandemic wasn't over; COVID hadn't gone away; the world was not healed, but I was no longer a woman sitting at home; somehow, despite everything, I was happy.

KATELIN FARNSWORTH is a writer from the Dandenong Ranges. Her unpublished manuscript was shortlisted for the Penguin Literary Prize 2020. Katelin has had work published in various journals here and overseas.

Isolation

LAURA JAYNE

January 2020. Australia.
Sunlight fell in sharp, thin sheets through the slats of the little roof. It fell onto the chipping wood of the picnic table, onto the plates and playing cards laid out together. Warm bodies sat curved at the benches, listening to the radio. Eighteen-year-old bodies, sweating, two months out of high school and basking gloriously in their freedom and the summer scents of the campsite around them. Their tents, pitched a few kilometres away, were hidden from the reaches of wi-fi, but it could find them at this picnic bench. Here they played their music, and Ambrose read them the last few days' worth of news off his smudged phone screen. He listed the details of one article – a report of something that made his voice lower in concern.

Emma dismissed his attempts to raise alarm. 'It won't reach us.' Two or three cases, the report said. And Ambrose had never read from a reliable news source in his life. 'How's it supposed to get over here? Five cases, in one country. So few people have it, and they'll hardly be travelling. It's not even a worry.'

Ambrose was still scrolling. 'They reckon it's catchy.'

'And?'

'More people might have caught it already. They reckon

someone in Italy might have it, by the looks of him. It'll travel, just you watch.'

The air in Emma's lungs, scented with eucalyptus, turned sour for a fraction of a second. Her mind travelled from a sick man half-way across the world, to her mum, an hour's drive from where Emma now sat. To her cousin, much further away. To her own, tightened lungs.

'They're pretty strict about quarantines and stuff over there, though,' James said.

The eucalyptus scent was back, and Emma got up from the bench to lay down on the grass beside the table, the sun full on her face as she abandoned the sheltering roof, pointing at James as she did so. 'See, that's what I'm saying. There's no way it'll make it over here. It's a non-issue.' The warm light on her closed eyelids mingled with the voices of her friends, and the conversation moved on with the sun until evening began to cool the playing cards in their hands.

The summer sun lingered long that year and was still turning cars into saunas, at the close of March. Emma sat in the passenger seat of one such silver sunbox, her friend at the wheel. The light flickered through the trees as the young women drove through pockets of shade, comparing notes in raised voices about the shops near their homes.

'Dad went to four different stores,' Tahlia was saying. 'He got nothing. All the shelves were empty. Everyone's gone mental.'

They spent the day together, driving from place to place. Emma's arm grew sunburned where it rested next to the window. By the time Tahlia's car pulled up outside Emma's home, dusk was setting in. The friends were still talking as Emma undid her seatbelt.

'Well,' said Emma. 'We timed it well, at least, going out today. Imagine if we'd planned it for next week, we'd have had to cancel. I'd have been gutted.' Emma opened the car door and swung her legs out. 'I'll see you soon, though!'

Tahlia made a face. 'Not that soon, with all this.'

'Ah, it's only three weeks. And we can do video-calls and stuff. It'll go quick.'

Tahlia drove off as Emma walked up her driveway and into the growing dark. The first lockdown went into effect a few hours later, as Thursday ticked over to Friday.

April 2020. England.
Ten degrees Celsius. Liam had been in England for a year and a half, and his semi-permanent Australian tan had faded along with his accent and the novelty of snow. Six months now until he was due to go back home. He'd left the Yarra Valley the month before his twenty-first birthday, and this year he expected to be back with family when he turned twenty-three this September.

Not that he wasn't with family here in Leeds. His girlfriend, Saoirse, sat at her laptop, typing – whether for work or for her visa application he didn't know. Both were difficult for her at the moment. The events industry had ground to a halt the moment the virus entered England, and Australia wouldn't have her come home with him, not for good, until she'd jumped through their bureaucratic hoops and into some form of citizenship.

One of Liam's workmates, a fellow Australian abroad, had quit earlier that month. He'd be back in Brisbane by now, Liam knew, carried over by one of the last flights allowed to land before the Australian borders closed and the country entered the lockdown England had already begun. The call had gone out to Australian expatriates when the international state of emergency had been declared, the call to escape the lockdowns of other countries and return to Australia before they were shut out, and Liam had gone grocery shopping along with every English citizen, stocked up, and hunkered down for the promised three-week lockdown. No way he was leaving England, not before Saoirse could come with him. His birthday was a long way off yet. Flights would be back in the air come September, the quarantines would lift, and the visa agent had even hinted that their cohabitation through lockdown would look good for confirming his and Saoirse's relationship status on her visa application.

She was still typing. Liam hated English weather, but Saoirse made it easier to bear. She was his family, after all.

The cold was seeping in through the window behind him. He turned, and the darkness outside stared back at him before he drew the thick curtain closed. He checked his phone. 7:00 pm and the sun had already been set for a good half-hour. He checked the news, and the English Prime Minister's tousled head appeared below a headline that speculated whether or not lockdown would be forced to extend for another three weeks. Liam closed his eyes and chucked his phone across the couch. September seemed a lot closer than it had.

July 2020. Australia.
The memory of the message still ached inside her. The tirade she'd received, from family no-less, for posting something about masks, something about looking after the community. Something she'd hoped was warm and might bring some cheer to those who saw it. Instead, an angry message telling her to wake up.

It was so hard to wake up this winter. Not in the way that message had meant – to conspiracy and violence. It was just … in bed, she was warm. Warmth was everything. Blankets wrapped tightly around her, two pairs of socks and her old high school hoodie. Emma crawled further into her blanket now. So, so warm. As if comfort might melt away the ache. The message-ache *and* the older one – the ache she'd grown used to over the months. The one that hurt more quietly. The one that hurt the most.

Some days, the warmth felt like enough. Some days, it could only hold her as her eyes glazed, and hours slipped by, alone.

In bed, after a day spent waiting, that ultimate warmth, that moment just before the oblivion of sleep when her body felt truly at peace, could finally come. The darkness could hold the room, but she didn't need to see, only to slip away. Only sometimes were there tears needing to be released before she could sink away. Even then, that great warmth was a relief. And in bed, she could dream – and her dreams these days were full of arms, her own arms around others' bodies, and blessed, blessed arms of loved ones, strangers, men she'd watched on television that day, or old friends she'd not seen in years, their arms around her. And the ache, the one kept at bay all day with blankets, would seem to fade in each dreamt embrace. Finally: touch.

She longed for these dreams, though she knew she shouldn't. They never lasted. And mornings, waking from unreal companions, only felt lonelier.

In her dreams, the brightness of other people's smiles felt like balm. But the imprints they left upon her retinas when she opened her eyes only made the sight of her dim, empty room more painful.

July 2021. England.
Lockdown was lifted.

Lifted again, rather – but this time felt a little more certain, though Liam hedged certainty with caution these days; everyone did. Caution over whether Saoirse's visa would finally be granted in time. Caution over whether the tickets he'd booked (the second set, these ones) would really get him home or whether these, like the last ones, would become useless as Australia snapped shut its borders again. Or perhaps a new strain might pop up the next town over from him, and he'd be forced back into waiting.

Waiting. A part of him was empty, the part that kept reminding him his twenty-fourth birthday was only two months away. And he was still in Leeds. Still not home. Still waiting on restrictions to end.

A woman, not wearing a mask (it wasn't law anymore, but Liam still wore his), blew out her cheeks at him as they waited at a bus stop together. 'Warm one, isn't it?' she observed, unprompted. Liam nodded without conviction, as another cloud passed over the sun. Twenty-five degrees Celsius, he remembered. He was pretty sure that had been today's forecast. Warm for July in Leeds, certainly.

He ran a hand over his pale arm.

December 2021. Australia.
Emma's stomach gurgled a little, and she skulled more water. She was still getting used to freedom. The end of October had seen the end of Melbourne's sixth lockdown, and suddenly she was wearing real shoes again almost every day, suddenly her diary had events scheduled, suddenly the shops were just the shops, and a purchase of a single chocolate bar was not an 'unessential journey' but a delight.

And now this. Her friend's family had always thrown the best parties, and they had been sorely missed over the lockdowns. She adjusted the hem of the dress she'd bought online two months ago, and headed down the dark driveway towards the revelry and party lights, water bottle clutched in her hand.

She never left the house without it, these days. The water bottle. Her mouth was so un-used to conversation that sometimes it would dry up, and she'd quietly nod as her companions spoke on, unscrewing the lid as subtly as she could, trying not to gag before she could bring the water to her mouth. Her therapist said it was quite normal, these bursts of dryness. Still irritating.

She reached the veranda and the first cluster of people, silhouetted against the bright house lights. She gave the first cluster of hugs, and a flurry of 'hello, it's been so long!'. Her first party since lockdown. Since many lockdowns.

The cluster told her they liked her dress. She liked it too, and she liked this music, and she liked this house. She was so ready for this kind of company again. Her knuckles were white around the neck of her bottle.

She found herself whisked inside and around, talking to so many familiar faces. The music made it difficult to hear and to concentrate, but it was good music – it always was, at these parties. It was dance music, and soon she was dancing. Her ribs seemed to stretch out in joy as she remembered what it was to move and shake with others, chest and arms and neck reaching up and out and creaking back to life.

It was only a little, at first: when she stared up at the strings of fairy lights on the ceiling above for just a little too long, and tiny spots in front of her eyes made her shake her head a little to clear the feeling they left her with. But it grew, the dizziness, into more than a little. Fellow dancers were shouting lyrics around her, everyone jumping in time, her own feet bouncing heavily as she mouthed the words of the song. The woman in front of her wore a dress with sequins that shifted, glittering, as she jumped and danced. There was a holler, and a man swung his phone around the crowd, and the flash caught Emma right in the eye as the people beside her sung louder and waved their arms to the camera. Emma's heart jumped as someone's hand barely missed her face, their ring glinting an inch away from her as it soared past. Too dizzy. Too much.

The door gave way before her as she pushed outside, away from the house. It closed heavily behind her. The night outdoors beckoned with a new quietness, as she half-ran-half-stumbled into the empty garden, and the walls she left behind muffled out the dancing, and the shouting.

Emma let her heart pound. Slowly, it sank down to the rhythm of the shadowy garden, soft, and steady. She rubbed her eyes, rubbing away the imprint of bright lights on her retinas.

So still, out here. Still, and quiet … this is what she had grown used to.

She let her forehead rest in her palms.

Behind her, she heard the door open and shut. A torch beam illuminated the grass around her, and she turned to see someone walking over, torchlight bobbing with them.

'Emma?'

She felt her mouth tighten. She pursed her lips, and nodded, raising a hand. It was Alfie, the brother of the friend whose party this was. Emma squinted a little as he came near, and he quickly directed the torch beam away, the glare softening to a gentle light.

'Heading out for some fresh air?' Alfie said.

Emma nodded, smiling.

Alfie held something out to her. It reflected the torchlight, and her smile broadened as she took her water bottle from him, gratefully gulping down the cool water and feeling it loosen her throat.

'You left it in the kitchen, but no one bothered with it. Most are too drunk to get the lid off anyway,' Alfie reassured her.

Emma laughed, and sat down on the grass.

Alfie sat beside her.

The torch lay between them, lighting up the ground around them and the edges of each other's faces as they talked and laughed. The party continued on inside and barely caught their attention as it gently spilled out onto the lawn around them.

December 2021. The plane.

So close.

The ticket was his third. The first two had gone unused; the flights had never taken off. But this one, this one had got Liam into the seat he now sat in, had been sat in for hours, left leg bouncing a little under his pull-out tray. He adjusted his mask on his face. He'd done three tests – a PCR and two RATs – before the flight took off. And they'd all confirmed it: he could finally use that ticket.

The engine noise shifted, became a little higher pitched, a little whinier. So close, now.

He'd left Saoirse at Heathrow airport, with a promise to come pick her up when her own plane landed in Melbourne three months from now. She had a few more things to finish up before she could leave England. But Liam couldn't wait.

It had been grey, so grey outside that tiny window when he'd left England over twenty hours ago. For the last few hours it had been blue like he'd forgotten sky could really be; and now, now it was grey again as the bitumen runway rushed past beneath the plane, the blue still up above but hidden for a moment as the great wheels pulled to a stop. But he knew it was there. Could see it reflected in the wing.

The airport and his bags and finding the right way out, all of that was *now*, it was *here*. He had landed. He was home.

The chatter of Australian voices around him felt like tasting a childhood recipe. And there was his cousin, by the baggage carousel. Her eyes were watering above her mask as he stepped in for a hug, her arms around him were three years older than he remembered them, and his own eyes leaked into her hair. She had a metal bottle clutched in one hand; he could feel it digging into his back as she gripped him tight, but he didn't mind in the least.

They collected his luggage, Emma insisting on carrying the heaviest suitcase, and Liam letting her believe the one she held was indeed the heaviest.

'The car's not far off,' Emma said, retrieving her keys from her pocket. 'And traffic didn't look too bad on the way up. By the way, bit late, but – happy birthday.'

They walked through the airport together, and Emma, a few steps ahead, removed her mask as she left the building, stepping out into the carpark.

The frame of the automatic doors passed above Liam's head, and beyond them the full Australian sun beamed strong and hard over his upturned face. He felt it on his arms, felt his thick, English clothes already making him prickle with sweat, his white hand on the handle of his suitcase shining under the light.

Emma was waiting three steps ahead, her own hand shielding her eyes. 'Perfect day for it,' she said, gesturing. 'It's been a bit cold and cloudy, the sun faded a bit there the last week or so. But it's come back for you!'

Liam chuckled. He looked around, at the Australian licence plates, the eucalyptus tree a few hundred metres away. He raised his hand to look at it, sunlight bright behind it. His fingers brushed his forehead, already warm to the touch. How could a glare like this ever fade?

LAURA JAYNE is a second-year writing and literature student at Victoria University. She writes fairly constantly, whether it be poetry, stories, or the non-fiction for which she has a growing interest. She has previously written a sci-fi novella, is part-way through the draft of a fantasy tale, and recently won a sonnet writing competition as part of her poetry studies. Her short story 'Isolation' is semi-autobiographical and was written with the 'help' (read: interference) of her two cats, who like to sit on her keyboard.

COVID baby

ANNIE GREEN

My two-and-a-half year-old granddaughter is what we would now call a COVID baby. She was born in September 2019, just months before the discovery of COVID. She was reared in isolation, in a series of long lockdowns, all contained outside the 'ring of steel' which separated Melbourne from the regions where she lived.

We rarely saw each other in person. FaceTime on our phones became our primary mode of communication. As a grandmother, I was desperate to see her. She breathed life into my now-isolated existence.

We would be in touch every day. On the phone I would see her asleep in her mother's arms. I would see her splashing in muddy puddles in her red gumboots. We would sing 'Twinkle, Twinkle' together. I would see her dance in her long Elsa dress. I would watch her dip her hands into her yoghurt and spread it all over her face with guilty delight. And, when she learnt to speak, she would say, 'I love you, Gran,' and hug the phone.

As she became more adept at holding the phone, she would walk with me, on the screen, around the house. I would often end up on the floor looking at the ceiling whilst she played with Lego or

I would be left in her doll's pram. I would call out to be found. I was often abandoned.

Eventually she became more skilled with the phone. She learnt to hold the phone at a certain angle and distance to get the best framing. It became an appendage to her and I was rarely abandoned in a toy basket anymore.

Some months ago, her mother – my daughter – rang me from her local playground. We chatted about our domestic lives for some minutes before she handed the phone to my granddaughter. There was the inevitable 'I love you, Gran. I miss you, Gran,' and general chatter about not much. After a few moments she began to drift off the screen.

I started to hear the faint chatter of other children until a boy's voice boldly asked, 'Who are you talking to?'

'My gran,' my granddaughter replied.

'Hi, Gran,' the boy called, neither of us able to see each other. 'She's talking to her gran,' he seemed to call to others.

A series of cheery, loud 'hello, Gran's seemed to swoosh past the phone. I realised she was sitting next to the slide and I had become part of a game. Perhaps these little ones were also used to virtual grandmas. We were all very happy to accommodate each other in the game.

After some time, the slide game subsided. I was still balancing somewhere off the screen when I noticed we were walking under some kind of tree canopy. I could hear the deliberation of her stride across what sounded like a gravel path. We were getting faster by the moment, the tree canopy speeding up as though I was looking out of a moving train.

'Ida,' I called. 'Stop, darling. Let's find Mummy.'

She accelerated. I could sense her liberation.

'Ida! Ida!' I called desperately. 'Ida, stop!

Then another voice, a woman's voice, came. 'Hello, little girl. I'm Lily's grandma. Where's your mummy?'

The movement stopped.

'Hello,' I yelled, 'I'm on the phone here. I'm her grandma. I'm trying to stop her and find her mother.'

'Come on, let's find mummy.' The woman spoke warmly.

'I'm here. On the phone. I'm the grandma,' I yelled again, feeling trapped, not heard.

We started to move slowly again. Me, now looking at the gravel path, suspended, limp, useless. After what felt like ages, we stopped.

'Oh, thanks,' I hear my daughter say in a very relaxed tone to the other grandma.

Too relaxed, I think.

My daughter takes the phone and realigns the screen. I'm now upright again and looking at her. 'Why did you let her wander off like that?' I ask grumpily.

'She's fine.' My daughter replies curtly as she turns away from me to continue her conversation with a friend.

I am annoyed. I say 'goodbye' abruptly, wanting to get out of my entrapment in the phone.

My daughter replies with a lilting 'bye', the upward inflection being just a little annoying to my ears.

A quick, hard tap of the red button and I'm disengaged. Thank goodness.

I gather myself, and my grumpiness, and walk away from the phone. I take a few deep breaths and reassure myself, 'Yes, she's fine. She's just fine.'

ANNIE GREEN has had a long career as a teacher and artist in the creative arts, particularly in dance and visual arts. She has written as an adjunct to this work, focusing on the beauty, complexity and humour in the everyday. The pandemic has provided an endless source of material for her. She lives in inner Melbourne on Wurundjeri land.

Lorikeets

JESSICA KILKENNY

When I lie in bed I can see just about every inch of my apartment. It is small and old, butter-yellow paint peeling from concrete walls. The walls are thick, but the ceilings are thin and I can tell exactly when my upstairs neighbour has his kids for the weekend, although actually I don't mind the sound of other people. My bedroom has wide windows that open into a little lane, which is where I'm meant to park my car but it's too narrow to get into, so instead I associate the lane with loud, unhinged men and the quiet-but-firm police who tramp up and down there all night. When I lie here in the mornings, though, sunlight spreads into a warm glow through the gauzy curtains. A nectarine tree hangs a little over the fence into the lane, and lorikeets from the park across the road fill it every morning. Next door, where the nectarine tree grows, is a huge block. An old Italian couple live in a house there with vast curving windows and immaculate lawns.

Sometimes when I'm carrying my shopping in I see the old man, and he says to me, 'You good,' like it's a statement not a question. He shuffles back down his driveway and back into his house. Sometimes he's the only person I speak to properly, face to face, for days at a time.

* * *

After lockdown begins, I kill a lot of time on dating apps. I meet a man, Sam, who is publishing a zine and wears crew neck woollen jumpers with flannelette shirts underneath. We talk for days and days, messages and ideas and compliments rallying back and forth. He asks me to write something for his zine, so I write him a poem. He asks me on a date, so I download Skype. On Saturday, I go into my miniscule ensuite and shower. I dry and style my hair, I put on a little black skirt and a soft white jumper. I brush glittery purple across my eyelids. Before he calls, I pour myself a glass of wine and sit at my desk watching the little blue icon. I am unbelievably nervous, but when he finally calls it's fine, easy even. When he is in the middle of telling me a story about his housemates my internet drops out and for a while I'm just sitting there in my apartment on a Saturday night drinking wine and staring at the frozen image of a boy I don't know.

Later, we transfer the call to our phones and we each go for a walk through dark streets, illuminated only by golden streetlamps and the blue glow of the phone.

We talk for seven weeks and then it fizzles into nothing, which is nobody's fault.

About a month after lockdown is over, I get a package in the mail. Inside it I find Sam's zine, with his piece spread over one page and the poem I wrote opposite it. We never speak again.

* * *

My friend throws a party online. In my apartment, I have earphones in, my laptop volume pushed to its upper limits. I've dressed for the occasion, as though this party is real, but instead I go nowhere and see no one and I drink wine on my couch and message my friends on the server. Every now and then I close my eyes and imagine I'm on a dancefloor somewhere instead of at home drinking alone on a Saturday night. The music stops and I close the lid of my laptop. The room is lilting a little and the apartment block is silent, and I feel old, like my twenties were decades ago. Which is strange, I think to myself, seeing as I'm still years away from thirty.

* * *

On a Monday while I'm teaching to a blank screen full of black squares, I get a text. My friend has had a baby – her first. The baby is scrunched and red and my friend is in the ICU, alone. No one can visit either of them – her husband was barred at the door by a nurse of indiscriminate sex and age and personality, a person-shaped body underneath a wrapping of crinkly blue paper-fabric. I bet that when that person got home that night they cried in the shower while they washed the smell of disinfectant from their body.

* * *

My mornings look like this: I wake up, put on my most comfortable clothes and make myself a coffee. I unlock my phone and let the notifications roll in. The sick and the dead punctuate the start of my day. I feel fear and then I let it go.

In the evenings after work, I have my great outing for the day. I tie my shoelaces deftly, thread my house key on a chain around my neck, and step out into the cold street. There is a huge park right where I live; I am lucky. I walk nowhere with purpose, heavy headphones timing my footsteps with the drumbeat. I mostly listen to loud music, fast and reminiscent of being somewhere at four in the morning with a lot of other people. I imagine what it's going to feel like when I'm back in a sweaty room with giant speakers and my heart fills up until I can't breathe and then bursts.

Sometimes, though, when the sky is darkening and filled with bats and I can see the flickering lights of the city, I revisit a favourite album and feel the words becoming a part of my skin like a tattoo: *I will assume form / I'll leave the ether.*

* * *

One Saturday, I go into my miniscule ensuite and have a shower. I dry, and style my hair, put on a little black skirt and a soft white jumper. I brush glittery purple across my eyelids. I open the door, I leave the house. It is the first time in my life, I think, that I am actually dressed up for *myself.* I see myself moving through the park with imaginary eyes, and I am solid, sure, whole. When people walk towards me, I forget how I'm meant to act. Do I look them in the eye? Do I smile? People approach and my eyes act of their own accord, roving. These trees and that grass and that river and those rocks: this park, it saves me.

* * *

On weekends my brother sends me a photo of the Saturday crossword. I pull it up on my iPad and then video call him while my mother finds a pen and settles at the back of the garden. My mother and brother sit underneath an elderly elm tree, and in my muted apartment the screen is like a holy mosaic – shifting leaves and light and my mother's golden head bowed in concentration. Off-screen, my brother calls the clues to me even though he knows I can already see them. One very bright morning, my mother knocks her coffee and there is a general scramble – loud noises, a hand reaching for something behind the camera. The screen is caught in the crossfire, hit backwards. I am facing up, up directly towards the bright sky and branches of the elm, full of lorikeets bustling and fluttering right over my mother's head.

She says, 'I'll call you back, hang on,' but they don't call back. I don't mind, I just sit and read a book.

* * *

Late on a Sunday afternoon, I go for my walk. Only two hours is permitted, and I have to wear a mask, but that's okay because I can put a hand out and touch leaves, stroke a dog's soft head, brush a mosquito from my arm. At the curve in the path there is a small track which leads down to a viewing platform with a little bench seat on it. I sit there, looking with unfocused eyes at the seething clouds of leaves around me, the river snaking below me, the bruised full sky above me. I don't notice the boy approach until I feel the bench shift with his weight. My body is startled; I flinch away. He looks at me and I see him mouth an apology under his mask as he moves to another bench a little further away. Come back, I want to say. That's not what I meant. But the gravel path between us might as well be a ravine, a sinkhole, the river Styx.

Later, as I weave back through the park, my allotted time almost up, I feel the first drops of a storm. Almost everyone has gone home; the paths usually full of dog walkers and joggers and prams are empty. I stop on the edge of the embankment and look down into the valley below. I am above the river, the trees, everything. The sky cracks open and the rain hits like a wall and my face is up, my body is open, I am laughing, and it really feels like the first time I've felt something in months even though I'm actually okay; really, I am. I am good.

* * *

One night my mother calls me, and I know something is wrong. Our family dog is old, but not that old, surely? She tells me about seizures and weight loss and says she's taking him to the vet. I sit on my couch and try to read a book, but my eyes won't focus on anything and my brain can't think until she calls me back and says he's gone. I can't remember the last time I saw him, or what I said to him. Whatever it was, it certainly wasn't goodbye.

* * *

Finally, we are allowed out of our houses. After work on Friday, I pack my little white car and drive alone down highways and through impossibly-misty bent roads. The air changes; I can sense the cold dark ocean spreading out towards my right. My headlights illuminate crabbed trees and fat coastal saltbush. A deer springs up at the edge of the road and then is gone again. When I finally arrive at the cabin I sit in my car for a minute, silent, shocked into stillness by the incandescent figures of my friends in the window, passing drinks and laughing. After a while, I unpack my things, lock my car, and go in.

The next afternoon we go to the beach. We sit in a shape without form; we lean into each other and kiss each other and do handstands on the wet sand. We are cells dividing, merging. One of the girls brings down a saucepan of mulled wine and we pour it into keep cups. The longer we are there the sandier the pot of mulled wine gets, but we keep drinking it, hands wrapped around our cups to hold in the warmth. We huddle together like penguins in a documentary, watching people, birds, dogs, each other. A few of the girls strip naked and swim in the icy tributary, their sleek bodies lithe like seals. I take my wine down to the water and stand with my pants rolled to the knees. At my feet, tiny silver fish dart, visible just for a moment at a time between the pull of the waves and then gone again.

It gets dark, and we pack up our things and trudge back up to the cabin through the campsite. It is filled with families who have set up tents and caravans, and it's late but everywhere we hear different blends of music, and there are rainbow fairy lights and disco balls and eskies opening and closing and movement and laughter. We get back to the cabin and collect in a wide circle underneath a marquee, people sitting on top of each other, shifting in and out of chairs. Inexplicably, someone has brought a huge basket full of wigs and we all pretend to be someone else, slipping personalities and affectations and relationships on and off and on again.

In the morning we drag our chairs out onto the tiny deck out the back of the cabin. It looks directly into a wall of forest-y bush, the wet, dense foliage a kind of greenscreen. Six of us are sitting out there, hands wrapped around coffees, scarves around our necks. We are silent, but the world around us is loud and large – leaves drip, something moves in the bushes, fairy wrens flit from branch to branch. The birds chatter in the trees. I lean my head back on the soft fabric of the camping chair, and through my closed eyelids the thin winter sun is glowing like a dying campfire. I feel a murmur, a disturbance, I open my eyes. A lorikeet perches next to me on the chair and we sit there, together, close enough to touch until he stretches his rainbow wings and disappears into the canopy above.

JESSICA KILKENNY is an English teacher and aspiring writer living in Melbourne. When she is not writing, she can be found browsing bookstores and op shops, and going on long meandering walks with her dog.

Virtual competition

PRATEETI SABHLOK

The trolley I'm pushing rolls to a stop as I fumble with my phone in one hand. I'm scrolling through my notes app with fingers stretched, trying not to drop my phone. My mum told me about a recipe for fish curry over a recent facetime. I'd saved a list of spices that I needed to get – somewhere – but I can't remember where. My notes app seemed like a good place to start.

A few lists of movies I want to watch and books I want to read.

An outdated record of gas and energy bills I've paid.

And a note I'd typed as a matter-of-fact observation to categorise my emotions:

2020 Grief.

2021 Anger. Apathy.

I'm grieving.
I'm angry.
And I'm apathetic. I think.

I find the list of spices in a random Google doc, and drop the required cumin and turmeric into my trolley from the shelves. I safely put my phone away. I'm ready to go home.

Virtual competition

As I continue pushing my trolley, the rows and rows of different coloured products, highlighted by the fluorescent lights, loom on either side of me. A teenager stacks ramen noodles in the aisle as I walk past.

The supermarket is one of the few places I'm allowed to go, and everything feels almost like normal.

As soon as I get through self-checkout and walk into the carpark, I take my mask off and hang it from my wrist like a bracelet. A young couple struggling with bags from Myer and Glassons do the same. Their masks are off with one hand and quickly stuffed into a pocket. Shopping bags are carefully distributed between fingers and limbs during the entire process, so nothing touches the ground. We all have new habits these days.

My phone buzzes in my pocket. I'm struggling with my own bags, so I don't check it until I've fumbled my shopping bags into the car. I take a deep breath once I'm in the front seat. The hustle and bustle of the shopping centre can't affect me past locked car doors. I get my phone out.

> Ananya, how are you coping with the lockdown? With the snap lockdown and extension, do you think the virtual nationals filming day can go ahead? The girls missed so many trainings

I sigh. The text is from one of the parents at our synchronised swimming club. Their daughter has been doing the sport for four years, but for half of that time the doors to the pool have been closed. If I was her, I wonder what I'd say when someone asked how long I'd been doing the sport. Would I say two years, four years or four years with a long explanation?

We created a synchronised swimming club to swim, but the strong, vibrant community from two years ago has recently started to wear out like the shoulder straps of old bathers, getting so baggy you have to chuck the entire thing in the bin.

I don't know what to text back.

After the very first lockdown, for most of us, it was something a bit different to run an online session and peek into everyone's bedrooms and living rooms and meet their pets. The nosy part of us got to be satisfied. We thought, *this is just for now; sanity will return soon.* But the fear hasn't left, and our eyes hurt from staring at the screen.

I don't know what to text back, but I know I need to say something to show that I'm pushing through so they push through too. I'm the coach with high expectations of my swimmers. The one that yells and assigns the hardest warm-ups. I can't be the one to admit it's all a bit too much.

> Not the best outcome, we are already planning to ask if we can get an extension if we can't film due to the lockdown. We will do the best we can!

* * *

I enter the pool. Bright lights, humidity, and a constant background noise. The lights on the ceiling are so bright that the shadows from the diving blocks can't escape. It's 4:30 pm and school just recently ended. The space is filled with swimming lessons, kids playing with their friends, and adults pretending to watch but really checking work emails.

If I concentrate on these things, I can pretend it's 2019 and I haven't participated in one of Google's top searches for 2021: TikTok pasta.

I'm a bit late, so I walk briskly to the corner of the pool where we start the session. I nod at parents sitting on the benches nearby and approach the athletes already stretching. I'm thinking about what we are going to work on today. The laminated sheets of paper instructing people about which locker to use and where to sit fade into the periphery; COVID-19 social distancing signs are so common they have the same relevance as 'don't dive' signs.

First session after another lockdown (number four to be exact, with virtual Nationals postponed).

First session after more Zoom sessions in which the kids stared at the coach on the screen but didn't understand how to, or couldn't be bothered to, follow along. Cameras were all off by the end of the hour.

There are about five swimmers here on time. This is usually the part where I yell something like, 'arm swings and leg swings!' I'm not sure, though. Should I say something to acknowledge another post-lockdown first session back?

I exhale. When I was learning social cues growing up, I didn't get taught what to say when meeting members in a sports club again after an extended period of time apart due to government-imposed restrictions. So I dump my bag from my shoulders instead and pretend to look for something inside it.

At least the swimmers don't seem to care about me or my silence. They are excitedly talking to each other and sitting in a pose akin to a stretch but not actually stretching anything.

'Arm swings and leg swings!' I decide to say, as I usually do. One by one the athletes find a spot and get to work. I'm the high-expectations coach, but today I decide not to be strict about straight knees and pointed toes.

One of the side-effects of four lockdowns: the dreams of children. Professional sporting dreams disappearing just as fast as the amount of notice we get before another lockdown.

After the warm-up on land, I tell the swimmers to hop in. When I was swimming, I dreaded the moment the coach would say the words 'hop in'. For some reason, even though I had specifically chosen a water sport, getting wet wasn't something I looked forward to. Most of the time, I see the same expression on their faces just before they need to get in the water.

Today everyone gets ready quickly, diving in before I can even tell them what to do.

The session runs quickly. Swimming, skills, and routine. When I start playing the routine music, I catch myself peeling the skin on my thumb as I watch. There is heat in my chest as I see the impact of lost days of training. There's nothing we can do about it now.

By the end of the session, my body feels lethargic and I try to quickly pack up the underwater music speaker so I can go home.

My hands get wet as I untie the underwater speaker from the flagpole. The knot on the flagpole stops it from sinking all the way to the bottom of the pool. I pull it out of the water and start winding up all the cords and wires, trying my best to keep things neat. As I'm packing up, I see one of the parents approach me. It's Peter. He often helps at club fundraising BBQs. I think about how we haven't had many of those lately, so maybe he's been secretly enjoying all the additional free time.

'How's Jess doing?' Peter asks, as I roll up cords and unplug them from the outlet. Jess is one of our swimmers and Peter's daughter.

'She was doing well today, listening to all corrections and had a good attitude,' I reply. I've finished packing everything up, and I stack the different parts on top of each other, ready to roll it into the storeroom.

Peter glances around the area where we are standing. Probably trying to make sure the person in question doesn't make an unwanted appearance. His brows are furrowed, hands clasped together. 'Jess was very upset during this last lockdown, crying most days and wouldn't do any schoolwork.' He sighs. 'Good to hear she was fine at training. Let's hope none of this happens again.'

Jess is twelve years old and has just started high school. I imagine being twelve, missing my primary school friends and struggling to make new friends, doing every class online using the least engaging medium for anything ever (Zoom lectures). I would probably be crying most days too.

'At least we still have the virtual Nationals to look forward to,' I say. One of my reflexes in social situations that make me feel uncomfortable is to be as positive as possible.

Anyway, I mean it.

At least we still have virtual Nationals to look forward to.

* * *

What are the virtual Nationals? Well, 'Nationals' is a competition with clubs across Australia. At the start of the pandemic – in April 2020 – Nationals were cancelled. But we thought this year we would be able to have the competition as usual. Swimmers meeting their peers from across the country, parents in the stands, and chaos in the pool.

Lockdown after lockdown changed those plans.

Not wanting to completely cancel for the second year in a row, the format of sending through filmed routine videos that could be judged virtually was developed.

So that's the virtual Nationals.

* * *

It's mid-morning. My work laptop is open on my desk and I am supposed to be 'working from home', but I'm checking social media apps on my phone. There have been things in the news again. Leaks from the *Herald Sun* on Twitter.

As I scroll through the apps, I see an independent fact-checker has flagged a post as misinformation. *It must be true, then*, I think jokingly. I never thought my whole world changing would creep on me while I was on my phone.

I'm in our morning catch up meeting, headphones on. I can hear my co-workers talking but my attention can't be pulled from my phone and my feed as I scroll and refresh constantly. The press conference is soon. Our lives could all change by tomorrow, once again.

My co-worker is rambling on about a simple point. We understood what they meant after the first minute, but they are repeating the same point in unique, different ways. This repetition takes up additional time in the meeting, so we feel like we are doing work. I'm finally about to put my phone away when it pops up: 'Victoria to enter five-day snap lockdown as more COVID-19 cases recorded.'

A cold feeling settles just below my rib cage and starts spreading across my torso. Just last week I had said, 'At least we still have the virtual Nationals to look forward to.'

I had some hope that things would be different this time, but another lockdown is as predictable as the feeling of hunger after a long swim session. During this lockdown, I will only lose a bit of income and I don't have to worry about much. For people in a similar situation to me, lockdowns can be a good escape from everyday responsibilities. The problem is that those same people often don't care about the suffering they can't see.

I'm pulled from my thoughts by the familiar, 'bye, talk to you later,' that my co-workers say to end the call. I quickly unmute and add my own, 'bye,' and hang up. I managed to get through that entire meeting only saying one word.

I finish reading the article. I don't have time to digest any further as my phone starts buzzing.

> I'm leaving work early to pick up competition bathers, we can film tonight at the pool?
>
> Will we be doing virtual nationals filming tonight?
>
> Hey Ananya, did you see the news? Another lockdown…

Virtual competition

The desk I'm sitting at and the chair beneath me feel hard. We have scheduled training tonight and the lockdown won't begin until 11:59 pm. This gives us the chance to swim our routines and film so we don't miss the deadline that was already extended once. The parents of our club are ready to drop work, get kids from school early – do anything to give them this last chance. I have to support them.

I won't be able to do any more work today; I open up Skype, explain the situation and log off early. During the next few hours, I do everything with a nervous system that can't settle down. I can feel my lunch churning.

Contact all swimmers and parents. Find out who can come today. Tell them the time, where, and what to bring.

Pack make-up and hair stuff – everything needed to complete a last-minute competition transformation.

Look at the upcoming training timetable we had spent weeks organising and writing. Realise all that volunteer work will now go to waste.

Sit on the couch and look at the turned-off TV. Wait.

'Just another curveball,' as my old coach would say. 'We practice for curveballs because we never know when they're going to happen.'

I knew, somewhere within me, this might happen. And I still didn't prepare to catch this ball. I stood in one spot and let it hit me in the face.

* * *

Even though I was ready early and spent a good amount of time sitting on the couch counting the number of frayed threads, I'm late getting to the pool (as usual). I think I'm prepared for the absolute confusion that's about to be tonight, but I also feel I could be walking into a situation that will leave me scribbling in my diary for hours at night.

The first thing that goes wrong is I realise I've forgotten the gelatine at home. The gelatine is a crucial piece of competition equipment we melt and paint on our hair (ballet buns if it's long, slicked back if it's short) so it doesn't move in the water. I wasn't sure about doing the whole process on a rushed night like tonight, but it might not feel like a real 'competition' if we just swim in our usual training caps. I need to drive twenty minutes back *and* forth to get it.

The second thing that goes wrong is I realise I don't have an order for the routine filming tonight. On the pool deck, while coaching and giving corrections, I have to organise a routine order that gives enough of a break to the swimmers with multiple routines. I have to send screenshots from my phone to the parents running around helping to make sure everyone knows their turn.

The third thing that goes wrong is the dive pool space we asked for – promised to be made available to us at 8:00 pm with an hour to get through our routines and film – becomes available at 8:30 pm because of a misunderstanding with the dive club. So instead of one hour, we have thirty minutes to get through all our routines before the pool closes. I calculate the time. It will be tight.

The fourth thing that goes wrong is everyone's performances.

Routines choreographed online when we couldn't meet in person, routines repeated as we didn't have the time for something new and fun, constant interruptions, swimmers leaving due to anxieties developed during lockdowns and finally, finally, everything we worked towards coming down to this day.

At the moment, I am not a fun person to be around. The heat of the pool, people coming up to me to ask for guidance every five minutes, trying to juggle getting swimmers ready and coaching – I want to dive in the water and keep my head down until all I can hear are the splashes of my arms moving through the water.

At the end, we take pictures and celebrate.

Sometimes, I think humans are too adaptable. We will get used to anything, even if we shouldn't. Everyone did their best, but your best when you weren't allowed to train on and off for two years is a diluted best.

Maybe all of these things would have gone wrong even if every day was the same as before 2020. But, unfortunately, I'll only know if I get the chance to drop in to a parallel universe.

* * *

My arm is aching. The basket I'm holding is filled with milk, canned tomatoes and so much fruit it's weighing my shoulder down. I switch arms. I should have got a trolley.

I'm currently debating between two different brands of peanut butter. Should I go with the cheaper one, or should I get the more expensive one with less sugar? I decide on the cheaper one.

I'm currently in another lockdown for my health, but I've never felt weaker. I switch the basket between my arms again and continue walking through the aisles. I just browse, looking around for anything on sale.

Staying apart keeps us together: that's the Victorian Government slogan that we see in big print at every press conference. I'm stuck wondering how I'm supposed to do that for a community based on moving together. 'We can have a virtual event!' I suggested. Parents and swimmers sick of it shook their heads firmly no on my screen.

I stand in the supermarket with a basket full of groceries held in one straining hand. Will I be back here again one day? The supermarket feeling almost like normal?

How will I categorise my emotions in 2022?

PRATEETI SABHLOK is an eastern-Melbourne local with a passion for storytelling and sport. She keeps busy through volunteering for sport and was awarded the Maroondah City Council's Young Citizen of the Year award in 2019.

2020–2021

ZOE CLARK

29/3/2020
There hasn't been time. Only the promise of it, in the future, when this new world of mine, of ours, was supposed to open up, bigger and wider. Now sometimes the air feels stale, mainly in the afternoons, and I can't get rid of the dust no matter how much I wipe down surfaces. Tricky thing, that dust. It floats up, convincing you it has gone, only to settle back down again when you're not looking. Dust doesn't matter outside. It sinks into the ground because the earth is porous and kind, not like these artificial shiny things we've created to make ourselves feel like we're living the good life. This virus, they say, can survive on plastic and stainless steel for days. Turns out it has had a taste of the good life and it likes it too.

I just want dirt. I want dirt and mud and those small pebbles you can dig up with your toes from the riverbed. I want to take off my glasses and let my eyes rest on the blurry horizon, mixing tree trunks with leaves and the flocks of cockatoos sweeping the riverbank as the day rests its weary bones. I want to hear the snap of deadwood and the crackle of flames as the campfire is prepared for cooking dinner. I want to drink a grainy coffee in a tin mug, and when I'm finished, I want to flick the dregs out onto the dirt, recklessly. I want to hear the thump of a footy on a shin, and the laughter that endless play brings. I want a long, tight hug with my fast-growing nieces and nephews; the kind of hold that, in the moment, feels like it has no end. And believe me, when this is done, I will have that hold. I want to trip over a guy rope in the dark, or walk the tentative walk over sand after washing in the river, trying to keep my feet clean. It never works, by the way. The sand is soft and always finds your heels, makes its way up the sides of your feet and in between your toes. We know this, but we always try – that gentle, tightrope walk from river to tent. I want to wash my babies in a bucket and watch their eyes open with wonder at the sky above them, fuss over their rosy cheeks and wrestle leaves out of their hands. I want to hand them over to aunties and uncles and grandparents, for cuddles and play and walks and snoozes. I want to deliver them to Grandma and Papa's tent way too early, when Grandma is snoring and Papa is pottering around outside. I want to show them the moon and the stars, maybe some jet streams during the day, if we still have those. I want to hand my babies over to their cousins, to be showered with attention and play. I want to cool my wrists in the river, feel the rush of dunking my head under the water for the first time, rub the coarse sand into my calves and boast about the comfort of my camp chair by the fire.

Winter, 2020
It is a Friday afternoon and I sit in an armchair in the corner of my babies' bedroom. Soft instrumental music floats from the cheap CD player on the floor across the room. I have heard these songs so many times that I don't even recognise them as songs anymore. Sometimes I hear them when they're not there, just echoing around in my skull like a tired memory. The cot bars obscure the line of sight between me and the baby sleeping in the corner. The winter sun bleeds through the cracks between curtain and window frame,

and I can't tell if the stench of old poo is coming from the baby in my arms or the nappy bin on the other side of the room. I notice that its lid is propped accidentally open and there is nothing I can do about that without waking this baby who hasn't quite learned how to sleep independently yet.

My mouth is dry. My feet are cold despite two pairs of socks and my worn-out slippers. I realise it has been forty-eight hours since I last showered. I long to sit with a friend. Just sit, rest my eyes on them, maybe casually touch their arm, and pretend not to notice when a bit of saliva accidentally flies out of their mouth and lands on my face when they laugh. What I would give to have a friend's spit land on my face right now.

It is 2020 and I find myself living literally in a state of disaster, raising twin babies with my partner. I need to write this down very plain and simple because although it feels so huge right now that it would be impossible to forget, so too did the moments after giving birth, and my memory of that is foggy at best. I don't know who this is for. Any more than I ever know who I write for. But this needs to be documented and even though I am stuck in this house, in this room, in this chair, with this baby in my arms, I still have my phone. I still have my right hand. I still have these minutes.

To be clear, this is how we are living right now: it is currently illegal for us to travel further than five kilometres from our house unless for the stated exceptions. It is also against the law to be in public without wearing a face mask, unless you have a medical condition that prevents this. We are not permitted to leave the house for any other reason than to either exercise for one hour or go to the shop to buy essential items. A curfew is in place. We can't leave the house at all between the hours of 8:00 pm and 5:00 am unless there is an emergency.

We are not permitted to have any visitors to our house, nor are we permitted to visit anyone else. We are allowed to exercise with one other person who doesn't live with us as long as we maintain

1.5 metres distance from each other, wear face masks and do not travel further than five kilometres from our homes. This is the beautiful loophole that has meant I can see my friend and her baby, my parents, and my sister-in-law.

I would be breaking the law if I hopped in the car and drove to visit either of my sisters and their families. I would be breaking the law if I went to see any of my friends except for the one who lives within five kilometres of me. I would be breaking the law if my friend and her baby came around and sat on the grass with me and my babies.

I don't write this to complain or criticize. I write this to remember. If I put this here, I don't have to carry it in my head.

14/9/2020
I turned thirty-three when the world fell to its knees. It was sunny. We grabbed our hats, put our babies in the slow, hulking station wagon that my parents had kindly given us, and drove to Eastland so I could buy take-away coffees and sandwiches. We took them to Dandenong Creek and sat on one of those big tables with bench seats made out of heavy, grey, wooden sleepers sunk deep and fixed to the ground. We walked along and discussed whether our planned camping trip would be able to go ahead or not. S was worried about being able to buy enough food from the shops. People had started to panic buy. I told him not to worry, it all sounded a bit silly, and surely we'd be able to go.

15/9/2020
This morning, S is going to his Pops' funeral. Ten people are permitted, so he will be there with his sisters and his cousins. I'll go to Mum and Dad's so I can watch the service via video link while they look after the babies.

There is so much sadness and grief everywhere I look that it seems futile to try to wrap words around it on a screen. Fucking screens. Screenshots of Zoom 'meetings' of family members living just suburbs apart. Somewhere, there is a huge pile of data growing like a beast. It contains messages between friends saying things like 'thinking of you' and 'I hope you're coping OK in this second lockdown' and 'I wish there was more I could do'. It contains countless records of online orders of bunches of flowers and trays of donuts and cheese platters sent to friends on their birthdays. An endless list of take away dinner orders. Search histories asking the same questions again and again and again: 'Can I go for a walk with my friend and our babies?' or 'When can I see my grandchildren again?' I don't know where this pile is, but it has to exist.

3/11/2020
K visited us yesterday. She brought with her a lasagne and an enormous smile hiding behind her mask. She read *Pig the Pug* to E at the kitchen table. I watched as my daughter sat on K's knee and grabbed gently at her long hair. After we put the babies down for their afternoon nap, we sat in the backyard and talked about getting older and more conservative, admitting that, secretly, maybe we both wouldn't mind getting married and buying a house one day. We talked a little bit about work, a little bit about other people. It occurred to me that being with her is easy and calm. There is no rush. The pace of conversation is dynamic but not frenetic. There's room for me to move my eyes around and look at pieces of sky between the branches swaying above.

21/6/2021
On the winter solstice we rearrange the furniture and pack away some of the baby toys. There's plenty of space in the top of the cupboards, says S. Our eyes meet for a moment as we wonder who or what we're keeping them for. We can't have that conversation yet. It is sunny on the winter solstice, and this makes a tremendous difference to everyone's mood. There have been days during this

last month, when all we were allowed to do was go outside, when it felt like it might never stop raining. The rain made me sad. I felt defeated by the rain. I felt defeated by the blackout caused by the terrible storm. I felt defeated by being told by the government for the fourth time that I could not see my family, that I could not take my kids to the library, that I could not see my friends.

I don't know what I'm trying to write. I don't know how to write. The other day I was supposed to meet my friends at a Lebanese restaurant in Brunswick East for lunch, because we could. But instead, I drove to my parent's empty house and cleared up the storm damage in their backyard. When I arrived, I called my friend to tell her that I just couldn't do it. She was wonderful. She always is. I told her she always has a knack of making me feel better. I am, I think, slowly putting myself back together. Words are coming back. Maybe because I am reading more. Sleeping more. I have learned to exist without conversation and now find it sometimes unbearable in its pace and volume and demands. I find it hard to listen and respond, to keep track.

4/7/2021
I sit at a table in a large, modern café, the kind with bad jazz and no soft furnishings and too-eager-yet-inexperienced wait staff. I order a coffee and then the regret comes along with the jitters and that familiar feeling of not knowing where to rest my eyes or my hands. I am meeting with two friends I have known for years. I am feeling stressed listening to one of them talk about her recent ordeal of moving house and the difficulties she is having with getting her in-laws to take their shoes off when they visit. I say things in response, and my words clunk together. As they tumble out of my mouth, I want to gather them back up, put them in my bag and take them home. There are things we don't ignore but don't talk about. Pregnancy loss. Death of a parent. Cancer. I notice the human smell of a chain-smoker on a rainy day. On

my way to the toilet at the back of the café I walk past a group of women having their photo taken, smiling like primary school kids, assembled in rows up against the wall.

27/7/2021

It is the middle of winter, and I am sitting in my car in the Woolworths car park in Croydon listening to a podcast about the importance of microbiomes for babies' health and long-term immune systems. I can taste red onion in my mouth from the salad that S made us for lunch. It is mainly cloudy, but not raining like it has been for days, and this morning there was sunshine. I am thinking about going into the supermarket and looking at the products and maybe buying a chocolate bar to eat in the car. I am glad to not be at home listening to my kids kicking against sleep with all their cheerful glee. I am wondering how many people have taken to sitting for longer than they need to in cars in car parks.

I look up, and I can't be sure but I see a person walking past my car, lifting their hoodie up slightly, and tucking what looks like a naked Barbie doll into the top of their pants, the kind of pants you go running in. They catch my eye for a fraction of a moment before crossing the car park. Distracted trying to secure the doll in place, they nearly get hit by a slow moving car before making their way through the automatic doors of The Reject Shop.

18/8/2021

Two men walk side by side around a park in Croydon. Face masks tucked under chins. Take away coffee cups in their right hands. Cigarettes burned down nearly to the stubs in their left. The man closest to the cobblestone curb that separates the path from the grass does a peculiar dance with his feet and then I notice the stub between his forefinger and thumb has disappeared. Before, I picked up my bag of library books from the cart outside the library. It felt like Christmas. I almost cried. When I called the library earlier to arrange to pick up my reserved books, I asked if they could just pick a few books for my kids. I was expecting three or four, but the bag was packed with books picked by a stranger who was kind enough to ask me what kind of books my kids were interested in. I thought about knocking on the window and making some kind of exaggerated gesture of thanks to get through the tinted glass. Instead, I had a sip of water from my bottle, readjusted my mask, and walked to the supermarket.

This morning, getting the kids out of the house and into the car felt like dragging sandbags through rough surf. Or something else hard. I've never done that. So maybe it's clearer to say that getting the kids out of the house felt like trying to get shoes and socks and jumpers on two toddlers, whilst also organising snacks and finding both drink bottles, but also going to the toilet and changing a dirty nappy and remembering to put it in the bin and wash my hands, but then also letting the kids brush their teeth because they followed me into the bathroom, and then herding them out again but somehow the broom is in here and now one of them is sweeping the water on the floor of the shower base. Yeah. It felt like that.

31/8/2021
Dear pandemic,
    Something about being grateful for this moment
    It is 8:30 am on a Tuesday morning at the very end of the calendar's winter and I am getting dressed in the bathroom after a lovely, long shower
    I can hear gleeful laughter coming from the lounge room
    Our children with their dad
    My partner
    Our family
    All here on a weekday morning
    All here every weekday morning

A reminder that of all the things we've missed or lost or hold anger and sadness for
There is also this.
And the smell of sunscreen.

ZOE CLARK holds a BA in International Studies and a Graduate Certificate in Visual Arts. Using drawing, photography, collage and writing, Zoe makes artwork about everyday moments that often go unnoticed. She has a particular interest in the different uses of public and private spaces, the tensions between privacy and freedom, surveillance and convenience. During the pandemic, she has spent most of her time caring for her children but writing when possible. This piece is an edit of writing entries made over the last three years.

Crossing the border

BRUCE CLARK

I remember being about six years old and waking in the back seat of the car. Without asking and annoying Mum and Dad, I looked outside to see why we had stopped.

Was it a flat tyre? A common enough occurrence on such long road trips, especially in the days of rubber tubes and before any steel bands under the treads. No, it wouldn't be that. We would have been alerted and all roused out to stand like refugees by the roadside while Dad jacked up the car and dealt with the spare. Spare? Do cars still have spares? Buggered if I know where mine is if they do. As for knowing how to fit and work a jack …

No, everyone was still inside the car, dutifully upright in our assigned places – even Dad – but something was happening. A band of bright lights arched over the roadway some distance up ahead.

'What is it?'

'It's okay, mate. Nothing to worry about.'

'Is it an accident?'

'No, mate. It's all good. They just need to do a bit of a search. We'll be on our way soon.'

I couldn't see how. We were caught in quite a queue, and nobody seemed to be moving. They? Who were *they*?

In the queue, nobody was being allowed from their cars, even to stretch. Up where the queue ran into the lights, the only figures I could see moving about wore khaki uniforms and big hats, even now, at night, and they seemed to be searching the cars with torches. Did they have guns? Would we be turned away? Banished? Do we have the right papers?

A red-and-white striped barricade was raised in front of the front car. It started up and ambled through. The barrier dropped again to halt the next, and *they* started searching again.

'Will we be sent back?'

'No, mate. If there's anything wrong, they'll make us wait a while and sort it out. That's all.'

When I remember all this now, I think of how poor Dad must have been knackered. He'd been at work all day in the city, but we were heading down to Grandma's dairy farm over the State border for her birthday tomorrow. In order not to waste most of the day travelling, and because he was thinking of how easily our poor old Morris Oxford overheated, he decided to drive at night and we'd stay a couple of nights at the farm before he drove us all the way back again, on a two-lane highway, at sedate pace. Do we ever truly appreciate the sacrifices of our parents?

I remember, of course, the assurance in his voice, the calm, the strength. At the time I remember thinking, this is how he must have been during the war.

I could never imagine him being in a war, carrying a gun, shooting people. But already at that age I knew that it had happened. There were books about it in our house, pictures of all our adult relations in uniforms. Dad even had a greatcoat he'd dyed black, but we all knew the story of its original colour. He'd been a soldier before he was Dad. Was that why he was so calm? Was that why *they* didn't frighten him? Were *they* like the enemy he had to fight ... and shoot at?

The men had finished with another car. Apparently they had done nothing wrong either. They moved on. The barrier fell. The old Morrie churned into action. We rolled forward. Up ahead, *they* started on another car.

'Who are they, Dad? Who are they looking for?'

'None of us, mate. Just take it easy.'

Another voice rolled round our silent car then, and this one didn't seem to be heeding Dad's advice.

'Where's the cat?' Mum asked sharply, as if it had been a sudden thought.

My sister was awake by then. 'He's on my lap,' she replied grumpily, grudgingly, sleepily.

'Is he on the blanket?'

'Yes ... of course ...'

'Put him under your legs and put the blanket across your knees.'

'Why ...?'

'They might take him off us otherwise.'

What? *They* were going to take Silver?

'He'll probably be okay,' Dad assured, before adding, 'But just in case ...'

Silver was set under the blanket that was across my sister's knees, and tented in. There was no complaint. He had been asleep, anyway, and would sleep on. That was good. But it seemed we were smugglers now. Mum never travelled anywhere without her cat. What did *they* want with a cat? Was it some disease? Germ warfare? One of those awful viruses they lectured us about and lined us up at school to give us needles for? Tommy Marshall had once had polio. He was okay now, but he wore these calliper things on his legs. I hated them as much as I pitied him. He didn't ask for pity. I just gave.

The Morrie had started up again. It was our turn. We rolled forward till the red-and-white barrier glowed directly in front of our headlights.

'Turn the engine and lights off please, sir.'

Sir? No 'mates' here, then. This is how people talked in the army, or how police talked to people they arrested. What had we done wrong?

Suddenly I was blinded.

Through the glass of the side window, a wide-beamed torch swept in like a searchlight. It first lingered on my face while I tried to fight off the beam with my hands across my eyes. Then it traversed down to the floor at my feet, back up and across the seat, into my sister's face, down to the covered floor at her feet. Don't move, Silver. Please, don't move. They might have guns.

The searchlight ceased its search without asking for any uncovering. My sister was getting old. Maybe he felt too embarrassed to ask to see her legs.

At the same time as we were being seared by the intense torchlight, another source was doing the same to my parents in the front.

'Could you open the boot please, sir?'

Back then, that meant getting out of the car, going round the back, and manually unlocking the lid. Not like these days, where you are asked to 'please stay inside the vehicle' and "pop" the boot. Stay inside the vehicle. With your germs and your refugee cat.

'That will be all for tonight, sir. Going far?'

Dad told him about Grandma's farm.

'Good luck with it all …'

Dad returned to the driver's seat, the barrier arced upwards through the air, the Morrie gave a grunt of frustration at being urged back into service, we rolled past the barricades, and started to lumber up to a decent cruising speed. With the Morrie, that always took a while.

'I never even thought about whether we packed any fruit,' Mum said, the smile of relief that must have been on her face flowing back to us in her voice in the darkness.

'Were they looking for food, Dad?'

I seem to remember some chuckles.

'It's just the Tick Gates, mate. They were looking for ticks.'

On Silver? In our fruit? I suddenly felt an itch on my right leg. I was still scratching it when we reached the farm and drove in past the glowing eyes of the cattle.

A journalist in the paper the other day had written that 'the Australian States have never erected barriers between them and never will ...'

Is that what *they* call propaganda? Or maybe revisionism?

I tried to imagine telling this story to my own children and convincing them that we once had to line up for a military search to prove our innocence and credentials and pass through a military barricade to go from Queensland into New South Wales.

I could tell them, but they'd never believe me.

BRUCE CLARK was a high school English teacher for over forty years in his home state of Queensland. As well as teaching literature, he has practised the craft of writing across a wide range of genres, including musical theatre, plays, and poetry, and has self-published two political thrillers (available on Amazon). His ambition is to be a proper writer when he grows up.

Against all odds

OLWYN BACKHOUSE

What are the odds that I cannot just survive a pandemic, but thrive in the process? If given the scenario two years ago of being locked down with only Hubby for company, I would have opted for slitting my throat! Ours is a complex relationship of Yin and Yang. We have been together for fifty years. The First Born describes it as two-and-a-half life sentences. The incongruity of two such different people cohabiting for half a century is perplexing. Hubby is conservatively right-wing in his politics, and I am passionately left-wing. He is an 'old-fashioned' man, and I am a progressive woman. I am a big-picture person, whereas he sees the world in detail. Even physically we are opposites. He is a towering, lean, bean of a man. Me? Well, I am a five-foot-nothing dumpling on legs. In saying that, I have shed twenty kilos over the course of the pandemic. Heaven knows how, because I have been living off the fat of the land. I may have scant toilet paper supplies, but my fridge resembles a fromagerie!

Best I introduce myself so you can feel at home as you catch a glimpse into our Lockdown 2020 experience. I live on an acre of land in the hills with Hubby, who is also known as Riley (i.e., The Life of Riley), The Head Gardener, Pierre, and various other chummy names depending on the mood I am in. I believe myself to be the most 'normal' of people, but Hubby is another matter altogether! In the most loving terms, I would describe him as obliviously and unashamedly eccentric. He hums along like an old bumble-bee. I am more akin to a blowfly in a bottle. The 'pandemic' has been but a word to him. Unlike me – a woman of passion and impulsivity – Hubby exists in a time warp of focused routines that cannot be interrupted by a mere pandemic. Breakfast utensils and ingredients are set out the night before on a wooden tray we were given as a wedding present. It sits in the same familiar place on the bench. Sometimes an irresistible urge takes over and I swap the teaspoon for a tablespoon or hide the mug. I stop at gluing the tea-stained mug to the old tray, because the consequences would outweigh the hilarity.

The secret of a long marriage is not to see too much of each other. Lockdown put paid to that strategy. To add insult to injury, Melbourne's claim to fame is 'the world's most locked down city'. Our Premier and Chief Health Officer are both now celebrities in their own right, with daily press conferences that last for two hours. They tell us how important it is to 'stick to the rules'. On 16 March 2020 the Premier declares Victoria to be in a state of emergency, thus invoking emergency measures to curb the spread of COVID-19. Hubby and I cannot travel in a car together; we cannot travel more than a five-kilometre radius from our home; we are only allowed out of the property once a day for a walk; an 8:00 pm curfew has curtailed our nightlife; and our orgies have been put on hold due to social distancing!

In moments of paranoia while being stranded with Hubby in our mountain hideaway, I wonder if we are the centre of a bizarre experiment. Are we the only people isolating? Is everyone around us a mere actor in a plot to see if two old people with only each other for company will thrive or kill each other in the process? My biggest fear is that I will end up talking in the same peculiar manner as Hubby.

Each morning of lockdown, I emerge from my morning haze, stretch and yawn in the Heavenly Bed that has cocooned my old body throughout the night. Slowly, after a long contemplation about what exciting things that another day in lockdown holds, I trundle downstairs. I am numb to Hubby's cheerful chatter that puts a screeching flock of early-morning cockatoos to shame. Meaningful morning interactions never commence before 10:00 am for me. A quad-shot espresso burbles on the stove and fills the kitchen with its aroma. Hubby continues with his monologue as I quietly retreat to bed to wake up gently with my coffee and the less-than-cheerful news of the pandemic that invades every home on the planet. Deaths, mass graves, overrun hospitals, panic buying, and there's no hope of relief in sight.

Several times, I stir in the night with panicked anxiety about apocalyptic dystopian futures, then I grab my phone in the dark to check Johns Hopkins University COVID-19 statistics, wishing the numbers to decrease. As the cases grow, I am consumed with dread. The media shows sick people collapsed on the streets and once bustling tourist attractions devoid of life. Cities are deserted and supermarket shelves are stripped bare.

I long for my old life, but once the caffeine has kicked in and the sun is shining I am determined that a pandemic will not defeat me. Hubby can be heard eating the same breakfast of cornflakes and sliced banana he has had for the last fifty years. No matter what shortages the pandemic brings, I will break into my nest-egg stashed away under my mattress to buy the black-market bananas, only because there is not the room to set up a small banana plantation in my bathroom. The clatter of a metal spoon constantly impacting the ceramic bowl is akin to a troop of monkeys' maraca practice. More than once I have suggested to Hubby that perhaps he consider a rubber spoon, to which he responds with a chuckle.

Once Hubby has finished his breakfast, he transforms into the Francophile 'Pierre' as he watches the French News and writes his diary in French. Every year, he has filled an A4 page-a-day journal to full capacity with details of his day. The Second Born laughingly says that every page is the same, so a 'copy and paste' would do the trick. We cart these tomes around with us from house to house wherever we go. They now help to anchor our house with their weight, which is a boon since climate change is wreaking more ferocious winds that rip off roofs and uproot trees. Languages, including English, have never been Pierre's forte. Twenty years ago, I was puzzled when he announced he was going to learn French. 'Best you learn English first!' I laughed. Then the penny dropped. My glib comment of wanting a French lover, after a New Year's Eve kiss from a young Frenchmen, had been taken literally!

It's 8:39 am and Pierre is perched on his adjustable 'electric' (powered) chair in readiness for the French News. Meanwhile, I eat breakfast in bed and watch an episode of *Why Women Kill*. At exactly 9:21 am Hubby turns up at my bedside as regular as a cuckoo in a Swiss clock. I pause on a blood-thirsty scene of my program while Hubby bursts forth with a summary of what 'The French' are doing about the virus. I listen with glazed eyes and a smile on my face, knowing that it won't last for more than five minutes because the next episode of his morning routine starts soon.

It's now 9:30 am and Hubby is off for his walk. Most locals are walking every day. We are all like deprived animals seeking out whatever morsels of human contact we can. Some brave and desperate souls slip through the five-kilometre radius net and find their way up the mountain, but once here they are instantly spotted as intruders and are received with accusing looks of disdain. We are starting to become hyper-vigilant, insular and protective. We are discovering things about ourselves that we would rather not recognise.

Hubby is well-known in the area because he is such a friendly soul who stands out in a crowd. He dresses in the most spectacularly eccentric clothing combinations. Vibrant green and red Christmas shirts emblazoned with Santas on surfboards are worn from December to December again! His ragged pants are pulled up as close to his armpits as the crotch will allow. His jumpers all display holes where the compulsive weeding with a hoe has worn through every layer in the exact same spot. The ensemble is finished off with a support belt, a hand-me-down hat replete with chin-strap, huge plastic sunglasses, and the ever-present mask made from a sock diligently worn under his nose. My dress code is much less flamboyant, but a pandemic is not a time to lower one's standards, so each afternoon I 'play ladies' and change into 'proper' clothes. I have a new hobby – online shopping! It not only keeps the economy going, but I get an extra outing each day to the local post office, where masked locals throng to chat about their recently acquired hobbies during lockdown – online shopping and baking making the top spots.

It's 9:35 am and I am determined to finish the episode of *Why Women Kill* before calling upon all my willpower to leave the Heavenly Bed, but not before imitating a *maneki-neko* as Hubby waves delightedly outside my window. I am also in possession of a *Yes, Dear* button given to me by The Third Born. It has far more polite responses than the profanities that increasingly enter my vocabulary. Hubby has become more religious in contrast to my growing irreverence as the pandemic stretches on.

The TV watching is over, and I am up and running. I take a long hot shower. No one is allowed to have visitors, so there's no need to do housework. A once house-proud woman, I have slipped into senile squalor. I chuckle as I walk past once shiny black electronics that are now coated in velvety grey dust and bear the words 'Dust Me' flamboyantly written with my forefinger! Hubby's walks take a long time because he speaks to everyone he sees. I hurry myself to don old clothes and gardening boots, and beam as the crisp mountain air welcomes me outdoors. With a sense of purpose, I gather my weapons of choice to sculpt the garden into a place of beauty before The Head Gardener returns full of protestations. Our garden is beautiful. It has a sense of Yin and Yang. Somehow, with our differing relationships with it, the garden has asserted its own will to achieve a harmonious Feng Shui. My nemesis is the best weeder ever. No longer can he bend down to pull those pesky weeds out, but he has a Dutch hoe that is in constant use. Sometimes I have seen weeds withhold their growth until he and his hoe have passed by! Plant growth is another matter altogether. I trim and prune, The Head Gardener rescues cuttings and plants them randomly all over the garden, and then I 'harvest' them to hide them deep in the green bin before he discovers my bounty. He is truly distressed by my garden 'sculpting' because he perceives it as destruction. I see the garden as a whole and am equally disturbed when it's not aesthetically pleasing from all angles.

The Head Gardener eventually returns from his walk, rhythmically banging his hiking pole down the driveway. He surveys the garden for damage before asking if I would like a cup of tea, as he has done for the last fifty years. I roll my eyes and mutter under my breath because the last cup of the dreaded brew that passed my lips was forty-nine years ago! Hubby does not register my annoyance. Regardless of the discombobulated messages passing between us, we each make our own hot drinks and sit sipping them contentedly outside in the winter sun – two old people on matching old cane chairs. Ours is an imperfect tapestry – a conundrum of discordant patterns, clashing colours and higgledy-piggledy stitches – that somehow manages an unusual harmony.

Hubby goes inside and updates his diary with the morning's events, then we are onto our next task. The hills are busy with only one form of transport: trucks, chugging up dirt roads, delivering soil and mulch to occupy the residents in their isolation. Since we moved into our home eleven years ago our property's elevation has increased by 15cm with all the mulch. Copious loads have been spread over the garden by The Head Gardener, who takes delight in counting the number of barrow-loads he does. Since joining the mulching brigade, I have been instructed on the protocols. I'm not much for discipline, even less so when I am told I must! When I am asked for the count, I deftly pull some random numbers out of my head. Most rubbish said convincingly with aplomb and authority is believed as truth. All this work in the garden has turned me into a muscle-bound Amazon. My new party trick is to pop the sealed lids of jars with my bare hands! The sound of pressure releasing on metal under the force of my sinewy old hands is a joy beyond words in my ever-narrowing world!

It's time to change into better clothes to have our daily catch-up with our neighbours. None of us will be beaten by restrictions, so we devise to meet socially-distanced on our own properties with hot drinks in hand. They live on the higher side and have erected a makeshift bench, which has subsequently been relegated to the junk heap because it ended in tears one day. We sit on our chairs two metres below them in whatever sunshine there is, whilst finding a spot to see the neighbours' faces through the thickly foliaged camellias sporting masses of blooms. I announce that I have put my lipstick on for the occasion, only to hear Hubby say that he should, too! I see the look on their faces, and I wonder once again if Hubby and I are the subject of an elaborate experiment.

It's 2:00 pm and Hubby's battery is running low, whereas mine is just kicking in. We eat lunch together as we catch up on the daily press conferences, then switch over to the US news to see if their president has any more helpful hints to solve the pandemic, other than injecting people with disinfectant. Hubby has dropped off to sleep in his chair with his mouth open. I take a photo and send it to The Offspring who ask if he is dead.

No time to waste. The winter's day is closing in and I have things to do. Somehow, I manage to cram in a visit to the post office, pick up some coffee, do my online grocery shopping, prepare sumptuous meals, wash clothes, and chat with friends. Amazing how much time a person has when housework is not high on the agenda. The dirt coating the windows is providing an extra layer of insulation, too. I leave The Old Man to have his nap and I frolic upstairs to my paints, where an easel proudly displays the fruits of my newly discovered passion. It was but a month ago that I announced excitedly that I was going to paint! The next day, Hubby and I were resurrecting an easel, searching out the grandchildren's old paints and raiding paintbrushes and a putty knife from the shed. I don't care if we ever get out of lockdown as long as I can paint!

It's 4:00 pm and I am rugged up and ready for my daily walk with a friend. We have fallen into a familiar pattern. We discuss our lockdown social calendars which take all of three minutes, our ailments take another two minutes, then we talk about our childhoods and warm, familiar things that people of the same vintage have in common. Blissfully unaware of time, we trek the mountains until the sun sets behind the trees. My friend goes back to an empty house, but when I enter our home I am greeted by Riley as if I have been away for months. The house radiates warmth and welcomes me with a comforting familiarity. Riley is sitting at the kitchen bench that he has gradually taken over with his drawing. Within no time, the aromas of delicious food permeate the kitchen. Riley is in his happy place when eating my meals that he has never once complained about in our entire married life. We watch the increasingly miserable news over dinner, then The Old Man nods off in his chair. I resist the urge to send a second photo to The Offspring because they will worry about our welfare!

I slip into the next room, turn on YouTube bouzouki music and dance frenziedly in case there is an opening for a Greek wedding dancer post-pandemic! The noise emanating from our house will have the neighbours thinking we are partying. Alas, not so. The Old Man's slumber is interrupted. He prepares to escape into a *James Bond* movie. Each one is catalogued with a tick to indicate how many times it has been watched. Hubby settles in for the night with *James Bond* turned up to maximum volume. In the kitchen I turn the old mug upside down and swap the teaspoon for a ladle, before padding upstairs to bed. I fall into a deep slumber, the incongruent sounds of loud explosions and laughter in the background.

It's morning again. I have no idea what day it is because a pandemic does that to you, but it's a new day. My book sits on the floor where it fell last night. My latest painting looks like a masterpiece without my specs on. From downstairs I hear the same annoying yet comforting sounds of Hubby's morning routine, and I feel a warm glow of affection towards this man I have shared my life with for so long. I smile and ask myself, what were the odds of me saying this pre-pandemic?

OLWYN BACKHOUSE is known to most of her friends and family as 'Olly'. Since retiring from social work, she has spent her time socialising, walking, renovating, gardening, reading, writing and painting. Her long-suffering family, including the ever-present 'Hubby', her three 'Offspring' and her four 'Conspiratorial' grandchildren, are her constant support and inspiration. Life is a tale, after all!

The tides of life

SHEILA KNAGGS

I sense you're not yourself right now. My precious world. I don't know how. You've changed. And yet. It's all a blur – My life was here. And now it's there! I open up my morning eyes. I hold my breath – there's no surprise. I close them once again. And then. Nope – the same! Again. Again.

I turn towards the dawn's new light. Were mornings always this darn bright? 'Get up. Get limber. Face the day – of course they were!' I hear you say. 'You failed to notice them before – too busy rushing out the door. Now here's a chance to change your ways. To learn to love these brand-new days.'

Don't lecture me, dear world of mine. It's all so strange – just give me time! My days were full of busy stuff. And now they're filled with hours of fluff. An excursion to the fridge is BIG! Bottles calling: 'Take a swig! Go on … I dare you! Glug me down.' I eye the shelves – I brood and frown. I feel as if I'm going mad. Unused lettuce looking sad. I close the door and walk away. But last night's pizza calls out: 'Hey! – come and get me. Stick me in that gob of yours. You're way too thin!' I know it's such a wicked lie. I cannot even zip my fly. But in it goes. And what the heck – no one sees below my neck. These days of Zoom-ing in and out of people's lives. What's that about? Is this the way it's going to be, from now … through all eternity?

I pace my loungeroom. Sit back down. Stand back up. My dressing gown! It's pulling where it used to fit. It must have shrunk – I'm such a twit! I must have washed it way too hot. But never mind, it's all I've got. Slippers on. No socks required. Now … What to do? I'm fully fired!

Online shopping – that's the go. Twelve sets of sheets, I'll have you know. Purchased at a bargain price. All in white … but very nice. I feel a buzz. I'm all afloat. My mind is on a magic boat. I'm shopping from my comfy chair – I haven't even brushed my hair. Excitement builds. The days go by. I cannot sleep. I'm on a high! – but all that changes very soon. Like a rabid wolf beneath the moon. I howl. I pace. I check the deck – where's my parcel? What the heck!

But moping round and feeling glum doesn't get me off my bum. I haven't seen my mum or dad. I'm missing them. I'm very sad. My dad is sitting all alone. My mother's in a nursing home. My sister's gone to hospital – her head's not feeling very well. What a mixed-up mess we're in – I begin to think it's going to win!

I watch the TV day and night. I check the news. There's no delight. The world I love has gone to war. An enemy lurks behind my door. It waits for me to leave the house. I fear its trap. I'm like a mouse. This enemy cannot be seen. It's sneaky. Deadly. Very mean! It aims its gun, it doesn't care. It shoots its poison in the air. It doesn't matter who you are. How good – how bad – how near – how far – if it turns its head … and you're in its sight … prepare for it to steal your light.

But as time drifts by … fear starts to numb – I leave the house to brave some fun. An excursion to the coffee shop. Sounds exciting. In I hop. Husband drives and goes and gets. Whilst in the car I wait. And next. Down to the beach we park our car. Watch the people from afar. It's like we're on a movie set. We see our children. Out we get. But we dare not walk too close in case we cop a fine.

We slow our pace. We've come in twos. Not threes or fours, even though we share the same indoors. We've left the house in different cars. We've donned our masks – it's quite bizarre! Our destination is the same. And though our children share our name, they dare not come too close in case they break the law for cramping space.

Oh, dare I cough?! My throat's a-tickle. But if I cough, I'm in a pickle. I stifle it beneath my mask. It's the strangest thing – a laborious task. What will these people think of me, coughing here so publicly? What can I do? I must act fast. Don't let me cough, that's all I ask. I hide behind a coastal bush and take my mask off in a rush. And out it spurts for all to hear – there is no coming back from here. Sheepishly, I leave the shrubs and glance around, but all is good.

No one seems to notice me. I lurk beneath a flowering tree. Hubby smiles and takes my hand. We wander down towards the sand. The kids have left us in their wake. My cough was all that they could take. I watch the sea; I hear her rage. My eyes are drawn to her great stage. And all at once I understand that time is precious – life is grand!

And so, begins a love affair – the beach and me, and the fresh sea-air. Every day, I venture down, grab a coffee – lose my frown. Some days, I walk along the shore, lost in thought, as I explore. Other days, I sit and stare, as time moves on, without a care. This gentle life is like a drug – it has me hooked … like a big, warm hug. I never thought I'd feel this way. About the quiet of a day. The ocean looks so beautiful. I gaze on her. My heart is full. She's become my balm for these strange days – I've come to crave her soothing ways. Day in, day out, I walk her shores. I no longer hide behind closed doors.

I take a chance and lower my mask; the sea air gives my face a blast. People smile and wave hello, as dogs all scamper, to and fro – these are my COVID Five-K crew – companions in my world askew. I come to know them, day by day. I come to hope that they're okay. I wonder if they see me, too. Can this be real? Is this all true?

I hear the caw of one lone gull. And beneath my smile, my heart is full.

I never noticed birds before. But now they leave me wanting more. I sit and stare. They dip and glide. All alone or side by side. I'm mesmerized by what I see. These lovely birds. So wild. So free! How blind I've been. Too blind to see. What's always been in front of me. And now I have the chance to change. To flip my world. To rearrange. I watch the pelicans overhead. Watch seagulls swoop and dive for bread. The black swans float across the bay. This is my time. This is my day. There is no place I'd rather be. These COVID rules have set me free. They've slowed me down. They've sat me still – I've worked from home, against my will.

But like these birds who've caught my gaze. Who've entertained me these strange days. Who've shown me how to glide and soar. Who've mesmerized me at the shore. I feel the air beneath my wings. I hear the beat my own heart sings. I shall not waste a second more, regretting like I did before. I'll take the time that I've been given. I'll steer my path – I won't be driven. Stranger days I have not seen. Stranger things I could not dream – pandemic, earthquake, storm and fire. The stakes – they could not get much higher. Global warming. One last shot. Our precious earth is all we've got. Mother Nature bows her head – if we don't act soon, we'll all be dead.

That now said – let's not be dead!

Let's do the things we need to do. Let's find some way to make it through. Let's listen more and talk much less. Let's work to live and not repress. Let's learn to love with open hearts. Let's give our world a brand-new start. Allow some time to heal and grow. To learn from those who really know.

The tides of life wash in. Wash out. A moment's what it's all about. The here and now. The sun. The rain. Each bird. Each shell.

Each tiny grain. My thoughts and dreams. A sandy beach. And floating by. Just out of reach. One strange tale. From one strange time – and how I lived it – all in rhyme.

SHEILA KNAGGS lives on the Mornington Peninsula with her grown family. She has always loved writing, especially poetry, but working for many years as an integration aide in a local primary school has drawn her more towards writing for children. She is delighted to say that her first picture book, *Fairy Beach*, (also inspired during lockdown) will be published in 2023 with Affirm Press.

Finger lime

ASHLEIGH MOUNSER

I began 2020 knowing that it was going to be the worst year of my life. But in March it began to seem as if my bad year was infectious. All around me, the rumblings of coronavirus grew louder and louder until the din seemed to drown out everything else. I was twenty-five years old, not a cent to my name. I had spent the last eight years travelling with my boyfriend, Brian, and friends. I had lived in twelve different houses since I left home at eighteen, I was especially proud of the fact that everything I owned in the world could be bundled into my scratched-up Toyota Yaris.

I built those first months around visits with my grandfather – my pop. After surgery, a bout of radiotherapy, several appointments with specialists, and what felt like an inhumane number of false hopes, there was nothing left to do but wait.

In every childhood photograph of dance recitals, netball games and school awards nights, the silhouette of Pop can be seen in the background. Now I steadied myself to watch that silhouette fade.

The storm of coronavirus raged. At their house on the lake, I brought Nana and Pop blueberry scones and coffee and I sat on the rug in the furthest corner of the room. We waved hello and goodbye. With anxiety, I watched the numbers of attendees allowed for funerals dwindle.

Finger lime

I spent my twenty-sixth birthday locked up in our townhouse, faking a bar crawl from room to room – espresso martinis in the office, margaritas in the bathroom, a wine tasting in the garage, sick to my stomach in the bathroom.

I had always been happy with the choices I made. I didn't have much – more holes in my shirt than shirt, nothing much in my bank account. But I had seen the Okavango Delta at dusk, the hippos opening up their behemoth toothy mouths; I'd eaten puri chaat at streetside stalls in Dhaka, and skinny-dipped in the ocean in Zanzibar. But in 2020, for the first time, I began to think that I had wasted time. Pop would never see me publish a book, or buy a house, or marry Brian.

Brian had been trying to settle down for eight years. Brian with dark hair like sheep's wool, who loves to dance, who watched me wander around the planet for years, without ever asking me to sit still. When I mentioned in passing that we might get married, he thought I was joking. He said he couldn't afford a ring, I said I didn't want one. He bought one anyway. As soon as we could, we'd get married in the lake house I grew up in, and Pop would be there.

On 8 May, Pop woke feverish and confused. It was my sister's birthday, and we ate takeaway aloo gobi on the floor of his bedroom while he drifted in and out. I felt the shape of my ring in my pocket, and kept my mouth shut.

I waited until we were alone, and I showed Pop the ring. He frowned, trying to make out the shape of things.

'You haven't slept at all, have you?' He tutted.

'I'm alright,' I whispered.

So that was it. I should have called him last week to tell him. Why did I take for granted that there would be another day, another week?

Brian arrived, and we slept on the floor of the office, my whole family crowded into the lake house.

On 10 May, just like that, he was lucid again. I wasn't going to waste time again. In the end, Brian made the announcement.

That night, I made an enormous bowl of spaghetti, sprinkled with herbs from the garden. We opened a bottle of Moët, and even though he couldn't taste a thing since the radiotherapy, Pop took a glass.

'We're happy for you,' my mum said, smiling.

But Pop corrected her, 'We're happy for us.'

Pop died that night. I heard his raspy breathing cease from the office, and I lay in the leaden silence.

We could only have twenty people at the funeral, so Brian waited in the car. *Sorry for your loss* was mixed with *Congratulations*. We sat in the funeral home divided by households. I watched my uncle cry from across the room. If it was any other time in history, I would have bought a one-way ticket to Puerto Rico.

Three months later, Brian and I bought our first home with the money we saved by staying put. A solid brick 1970s-era building on a quarter acre, near a lake.

In November, Nana sold their house. It was too big now that she was alone. The floorboards creaked. She took down Pop's collection of tools from where they hung on the pegboard in the garage. In plastic containers of rusty nails, we found pictures of Nana in Myanmar, draped in a red-and-yellow sarong, half a lifetime ago. We dug up a finger lime tree from the garden and drove it back to Wollongong. Nana lives in a neat little flat in a retirement village now. In her new living room, there's a stack of photographs of Pop on the cream-coloured carpet, waiting to be hung.

A second wave of COVID-19 cancelled our New Year's plans. I feel as if I have been murmuring *It is what it is* in ceaseless litany for months. We sit in the garden and watch the fireworks from the safety of our wonky tile patio. We open a bottle of Moët and toast to our new, gentler lives. We're happy for us.

In 2019, Brian and I spent most weekends dancing at clubs until 2 am, sleeping in on Sundays until midday. Now, I wake up at dawn (partly because we still don't have blinds), and I walk down by the lake. I drink my coffee in the still-partly-furnished living room. Then I get to work – weeding, demolishing decades-old slabs of concrete, beautifying the garden for a wedding. I cut garden stakes with my pop's rickety old table saw. The room under my house is filled with Pop's old things: spanners, hammers and screwdrivers, lengths of fraying rope and the odd thing I haven't worked out yet. Too many times to count in a day, I get the overwhelming urge to call him and ask how to get a straight angle with a hack saw, or what the long metal thing with the blunt end is possibly used for.

The time had come and gone to put away childish things, but sometimes it feels too fast. Like one of these mornings when I wake up early, before I've got my bearings, like I might go stand on the driveway of a house Pop will never see, waiting for him to pick me up and take me to school.

My fiancé harvests zucchini and pumpkin in his new gumboots, in the hat my nana made him which reads *Farmer Brian*. At the back of the garden, the finger lime tree faltered at first, but now new roots are clinging to unfamiliar soil, as if it had always been here.

ASHLEIGH MOUNSER is an Australian writer who has been published across print and media. In 2016, Mounser graduated as a Deans Scholar with a Bachelor of Creative Writing from the University of Wollongong, and later completed a Graduate Certificate in Screenwriting at the Australian Film Television and Radio School. She was *Sydney Morning Herald*'s Young Writer of the Year in 2012, the overall winner of the Future Leaders Writing Prize, winner of the 'Time to Write' contest conducted by the University of Melbourne, and recipient of three arts grants from the Bouddi Foundation for the Arts, presented by John Bell. Her debut feature film *Questions and Comments* premiered at festivals across Europe, America and South Africa and has received numerous laurels. Her children's novel, *How to be Cooler Than the Moon*, is currently represented by Australian Literary Management and is seeking publication.

Sweet tooth

MARIA B. JOSEPH

Cinnamon froth. She pulled her surgical mask down to below her chin and slurped. The waitress's footsteps echoed in the cafe now that half its tables were removed. Sitting the requisite distance away on the long, red, vinyl bench, a man was tapping away on his laptop. He had found the darkest spot, away from the late-morning sun spilling through the windows. He had replaced his mask, empty mug to the side of him. She was used to seeing half a face now, hidden behind masks, behind screens, eyes grazing left to right.

The hot coffee found the hole in her tooth that had been steadily growing throughout the lockdown. The proximity of a dentist to a patient's bared mouth was unthinkable for the germs and the transition of them. She had this image of her dentist, Dr. Tagliabue, underemployed, sprawled forlornly on his own dentist chair using the mirror tool to check his nasal hair. Maybe, now that the people were allowed out again, she would make an appointment to get her tooth sorted. Then again, maybe not: pain upon pain was more pain, surely?

Since Pamela had last been to the café, they had branched out into scented candles and novelty items. Displays were dotted hopefully between the tables. Beside her table was a stand of men's gifts, including a 'retro' shaving set and a toilet brush in the form of the American president. Three clocks, in varying sizes and colours, hung on the feature brick wall behind the man. None of them actually gave the correct time, so she checked her phone – not that the time particularly mattered. She rocked her foot, waiting for her almond croissant to arrive. Suddenly she jumped; someone had abruptly turned on the cafe's background music. Silence was stirred and mixed.

The man. Bald. She didn't mind that. He wore a striped business shirt. Too conservative? She couldn't see if he was wearing a ring or not. Since the lockdown, she had taken down her dating profile because what was the point if you couldn't meet in person and go out on a date? Video calls, her friend Sandra had pointed out. Yet she wasn't comfortable with that; she had yet to find an angle where she didn't have a giant snoz and triple chins. Camera mirrors were never kind. Surely in person she was better.

She'd had a date in this café before the lockdown. She wore lipstick; those were the days when you could see the lower half of a face. It didn't go well. When they started talking about tennis and she defended the equal pay for the female players – equivalent skill, talent, hours of training, the commercial pull of famous players proven – he countered with the 'fact' that the women's game was boring, so that was that. Not important in the overall scheme of the planet burning and people with lungs calcifying, but important, nonetheless.

Then she was startled out of this stewing in the past, silence skipping once again, a sip of her cappuccino almost going down the wrong way.

'Hello, how are you gorgeous?'

Was the man addressing her? She couldn't tell if he was actually looking at her.

'Hi, sweetie!' He waved.

How lovely, he's calling me sweetie? Oh … he was talking into his laptop camera. His eyes smiled.

'Don't worry, Daddy will be able to fly back soon to see you.'

Pamela heard an audible clap and 'yeah!' from a young voice on the other end. She smiled at the kid's joy and was rewarded with the arrival of her croissant.

She had a terrible sweet tooth which had been well-fed throughout lockdown. Chocolate had always been a weakness, and the new time on her hands allowed her to experiment more, especially when a trip to the supermarket was a rare and luxurious outing. She studied each and every item in the aisles. She had not known, for instance, that Spam, the World War II staple, was still for sale. Starting at one end of the lolly aisle, she worked her way down, reliving a childhood of Jaffas and Bounty bars, enjoying herself continentally with Lindt and Baci, then making the extraordinary discovery of Terry's Chocolate Orange and wondering why she had never heard anyone speak of this deliciousness before. Chocolate filled a stomach she couldn't be bothered to cook for.

At the beginning of lockdown, she found herself jobless. Teaching the English language to international students was no longer possible, as the language school closed and a lot of the international students went home. More than a slight inconvenience for all concerned.

At first, she was elated by the long stint of free time. She painted the fence, weeded and pruned, washed windows, doing her spring cleaning in the autumn. Gardens around the neighbourhood were suddenly at their best. Dogs were deliriously happy, never having been walked so often by so many members of the family, all home at once.

Pamela's favourite walk was down to the wetlands created by the council, complete with a boardwalk, swamphens, and ducks. They had preserved some of the old river gums and she did a loop around, enjoying the brisk wind, though feeling a bit deficient because she didn't have a dog. Neighbours nodded at each other from behind their masks and crossed to the other footpath if impending contact looked like it would be too close.

Old school, she re-watched her many comedy DVDs. Unfortunately, some jokes are hard to laugh at more than once. She decided to teach herself knitting via YouTube but kept getting the left hand confused with the right in the mirror image.

'What are you knitting?' Sandra asked her over the phone.

'It's supposed to be a jumper. The sleeves look a bit too hard so it might end up being a vest.'

'Why'd you start with something so hard, you duffer!'

Sandra was a colleague from a previous school, who encouraged her students to use Australian idioms such as 'duffer', 'derro' and 'drongo'. Somewhere in China there was a former student calling a co-worker a 'dipstick' in a strong Australian accent.

'Well, I don't know. The jumper in the magazine looks really nice, winter coming and all that.'

'Ever heard of knitting a scarf?'

'I've still got the ten-or-so Nanna knitted and sent me from England for Christmas when I was a kid, snowflakes and reindeer on them!'

Pamela also started baking, thinking she would try flourless chocolate cakes and brownies. Still, when you live by yourself there is a limit to how much you can consume. She made up small parcels of brownies and placed them anonymously in her neighbours' mailboxes. She wondered if they ate them or warned their kids off by saying they could be poisoned or that the packaging could be contaminated with the dreaded germ. To make her neighbours laugh, she taped a poster to her rubbish bin which read: '2020: the year my bin went out more than me.'

Kids around the neighbourhood had stuck drawings of crooked rainbows in their windows, like prisoners asking to be freed. The local playground, immensely popular because it had a flying fox, was roped off and closed. Instead, kids pedalled by on their miniature bikes, trying to keep up with their panting and slobbering hounds. The kids were allowed to go unmasked, laughing joyously, especially those who had been set free from school.

In trying to pull out a dead lavender bush, Pamela twisted her ankle. She dragged a kitchen chair out onto the porch and contented herself with knitting some part of the jumper and watched the street. She wrapped herself in a rug against the bitter wind and wore a beanie over her uncut and undyed hair. Life scrolled by in front of her: the occasional car, a dog being dragged by the lead on its backside because it didn't want to go for another damned walk. There was rain and more rain, all good for the gardens. People now waved at her as they went by, expecting her there, the marker at Number 15 – a third of the way through their walk.

After lunch every day, an elderly Sikh gentleman in a lime-green turban went by on his postprandial stroll. He always nodded hello at her but went determinedly on. A mother from Number 22 tumbled out onto the street at unpredictable hours with a toddler in a pusher, a boisterous Labrador pup tied to the pusher handle, and a girl and a boy on scooters shooting away in front as she half-jogged trying to keep up and keep the puppy from getting tangled in the wheels.

'Mum, are we going to the playground?' the young girl stopped her scooting and turned back to ask.

'No, I told you already. It's still closed!'

'But it's there, I can see it!' The girl pointed furiously.

'I know, I know, but it's not allowed.'

'But Muuuumm!'

These adults with their weird rules.

Eventually, as evening came on, Pamela would return inside to see that dust and lint and grime had reinstated themselves, but she was over cleaning. She warmed another can of soup, having given up on cooking anything more complicated. She put in another DVD and sucked on wedges of chocolate orange. She chewed on the left side of her mouth to avoid the hole deepening in the back molar on the right.

Then she started to sit outside at night. Sleep didn't come easily when she had done nothing in the day to wear herself out. She wrapped herself in one of her grandmother's red scarves, her bulky, grey, woollen coat over cotton PJs, her black beanie, a black, cloth mask and plush aqua-blue slippers. Pamela noticed that her waving at this time of the night didn't have quite the same effect as it did during the day; people were a tad disconcerted when she waved at them from the darkness of her porch.

The few cars crept away to their dens, and televisions were switched off. The flickering blue lights of phones were invisible behind dense blinds. Night creatures rustled through the bark in the front garden. A ginger tom slunk across the road. Looking up, she was disappointed the streetlights were still in use, as they diminished the mighty efforts of the Milky Way to impress. One night, she heard an approaching *thump, thump, thump* – a giant kangaroo bounding his way down the empty street, his tail smacking the pavement. 'Huh,' Pamela thought; nothing more. Knitting in the yellow glow of the streetlight, the jumper – a soothing lilac – was now cascading over her knees. She had held the slab up to her burgeoning girth and decided it still needed more length.

She dropped a stitch one night, when she realised a man was standing beside her mailbox staring at her from behind his mask.

'Hi!' He gave a tentative wave.

'Hi.' She was frozen with her knitting needles poised.

'I liked the sign on your rubbish bin. Made me laugh.'

She supposed he was smiling. 'Glad you liked it.'

'You can't sleep either?'

'No, not really.'

'Yeah, that's how it is.' He shrugged his shoulders and moved off towards the park.

The next day, the two scooter kids from Number 22 stopped on the footpath in front of her. They were wearing only T-shirts; much too-little for the cool weather. Her lilac jumper-in-progress was pooled at her feet, keeping them extra warm.

'Hello,' ventured the boy, his tousled mouse-brown hair falling untidily over one eye.

'Hello.' Pamela smiled with her eyes.

'Are you the person who made the brownies?'

'Oh, yeah, that was me. Did you like them?'

The girl nodded briskly.

'Yup,' the boy confirmed. They hung there for a moment in silence.

'Would you like me to bake you some more?'

There were vigorous nods from both this time.

'OK, I'll see what I can do.'

'Look, I have a tooth about to come out!' The boy opened his mouth wide and used his finger to wriggle one of his front teeth. 'I got two out already!'

'Has the Tooth Fairy been?' Pamela enquired, using a serious tone.

'Yes, I got $2 for each tooth!'

'He keeps trying to pull his tooth out so he can get more money,' his envious younger sister accused.

Pamela shook her head. 'Oh, no, the Tooth Fairy doesn't pay up if it doesn't happen naturally.'

'Really?' The boy quickly stopped wriggling the tooth with his finger.

'Hey, Charlie, Josie!' A call came from up the street. 'Come back here! What are you doing out?' Their mum, wearing a dressing gown and hanging on to her toddler, was about to set off after them.

'You better go home,' Pamela whispered in pretend urgency.

Without a goodbye, they turned their scooters and pushed off mightily towards their despairing mother.

Later in the week, Pamela mixed another batch of brownies and for an added touch bought lolly dentures to set in the icing on top. She wrapped them in paper with a label saying they were from the

Tooth Fairy, then left them in Number 22's mailbox that night. Here's to some more teeth falling out, my fellow sweet tooth. She smiled wryly.

Daffodils that she had planted at the beginning of lockdown were starting to raise their heads and as the days went by a gang of magpies moved in, scalping the fresh yolky buds, biting off bits of juicy succulents, and sharpening their beaks on her newly painted fence.

Bloody hooligans, she thought, *I've waited almost a whole year for those to bloom.*

Still, it was hard to be petulant about spring and birds doing what birds did, *their* lives having changed none.

She didn't have to wear her bulky coat anymore, though masks were still a necessity. Her lilac jumper was now on its way to becoming a blanket and that was warmth enough against the ambivalent spring weather. She had been able to walk properly on her ankle for several weeks but had lost all interest in going out for walks seeing as the neighbourhood came by anyway.

One night when it was particularly balmy and everything was asleep, she felt reckless. Stripping down to the nude, keeping on her mask, and holding her blanket behind her, needles and all, she ran down the middle of the street, thinking *wooo-hoo*! She did a U-turn at the top of the rise and ran as fast as she could all the way back. She could hardly stop laughing as she gulped for breath back on her porch.

Later that week, she decided to try the flying fox in the playground with only her mask and 'cape' on. It was amazing how addictively fun it was. She must have tried it at least eight times before her arms began to ache as she flung herself down the suspended wire.

A few nights later, the same man, sulphurous under the streetlamp, was standing beside her mailbox. He wore torn jeans, sneakers, his black mask, and a black T-shirt with 'Aloha' printed on it.

He waved. 'Hi.'

'Hi.' She didn't know which house this guy belonged to and had never seen him during the day.

'Still keeping night hours, I see.'

'Um, yeah. You too, I see.'

'Yeah. It's even nicer to walk out late now it's warmer.'

She nodded.

He paused and looked down at his toes. 'Not going on the flying fox tonight then?'

'Ha!' she guffawed. 'Oh, no, you didn't see that?!'

'Well, yeah. Nothing creepy or anything, I didn't follow you. I like to sit on the bench near the river gum and well then you just sort of appeared with your long blanket. It looked fun!' He laughed, then reiterated, 'Nothing creepy, I swear.'

'Oh my god. I'm so sorry.'

'Don't apologise! I was thinking I might try it myself tonight. Though I might keep my clothes on. I don't have one of those, er, long blankets to keep me covered.'

She laughed. 'Well, I highly recommend it; it's fun.'

He still didn't move off and she realised he was about to ask her to come too.

'I'm just about to head in. Have fun!' She rose from her seat and waved.

Weeks passed, Christmas was approaching, and the lockdown was lifted, though still not the rule requiring adults to wear masks. Back at the cafe with the pointless clocks, Pamela took a bite of her croissant and recalled the previous Sunday in the park. She had bought a chocolate raspberry muffin and gone to sit on the bench beneath the river gum. The reopened playground was in uproar with delighted kids swarming and masked parents circling with worry.

Then she was suddenly accosted by Charlie the toothless. 'The Tooth Fairy! The Tooth Fairy!' He jumped up onto the bench beside her and tried hard to see what she was eating.

'Charlie!' a male voice called. A young man in torn jeans and a black 'Aloha' T-shirt rushed up. 'I'm sorry if he's bothering you.'

'No, not at all.' Did he recognise her, sans-knitting and in daylight?

'She's the Tooth Fairy, Dad.'

'Don't be silly.' The young dad shook his head and raised his eyebrows. He took his son by the hand. 'How bout we see if we can get on the flying fox. You remember how much fun it is? You can pretend to be a superhero.'

Back in the cafe, Pamela had finished her almond croissant and was smiling at the memory, her mask still removed.

'Was it that good?'

The man on the red banquette looked directly at her.

'Um, yes, delicious in fact.'

'I might order one myself, then. My daughter's with her mother in Sydney.' He sighed. 'I feel like something sweet.'

She grinned. 'Nothing wrong with something sweet every now and then.'

'Another coffee?' he asked.

MARIA B. JOSEPH is an emerging poet and writer. She was awarded third place in the national section of the Alan Marshall Short Story Award in 2011, as well as being commended in the local section in 2005. Two historical fiction novels – *My Island Solitary* and *Queen Victoria's Gold* – were long-listed for the Michael Gifkins Prize NZ, and in 2022 her manuscript *Rabaul* was short-listed. Maria was born in Auckland and grew up in Adelaide. After living in Kenya, Japan and Singapore for many years, she now calls Melbourne home.

IngramSpark

IngramSpark is an award-winning publishing platform, offering print and ebook distribution services through a single source. Focus on what you do best—create innovative content—while we do the rest: **print**, **ship**, and **distribute**.

Multiple Formats

Do it all with IngramSpark! Print your book in colour or black and white, as a hardcover, a paperback, an ebook, or all three!

Zero Inventory

Print what you need when you need it with print-on-demand technology. With printing facilities across the world, IngramSpark gets your books where they need to go with speed and reliability.

Global Distribution

Self-publishing with IngramSpark connects your book to over 40,000 independent bookstores, ebook retailers, libraries, chain stores, and more!

Share Your Story with the World

      www.ingramspark.com

www.ingramcontent.com/pod-product-compliance
Lightning Source LLC
Chambersburg PA
CBHW030252010526
44107CB00053B/1673